Our Foundational Leadership Proposition

In a world captivated by the notion of emotional intelligence (EQ) as the crucial determinant of success, it's essential to recognize that the dichotomy between EQ and IQ oversimplifies the multifaceted nature of leadership intelligence. While emotional intelligence undoubtedly plays a pivotal role, it would be a grievous oversight to discount the profound impact of analytical and practical intelligence.

Consider, for instance, the towering figures in various industries who have shaped our world. Take Elon Musk, an epitome of audacious vision and technological prowess. His relentless pursuit of innovation and unyielding commitment to advancing humanity are emblematic of the indispensable role that practical intelligence plays in realizing monumental feats.

Similarly, let's reflect on the unparalleled analytical acumen of visionaries like Steve Jobs. His ability to distill complex ideas into elegant, user-friendly solutions transformed entire industries. This exemplifies how analytical intelligence, far from being overshadowed by EQ, synergizes to drive innovation and progress.

Moreover, Bill Gates, renowned for his strategic foresight and astute business acumen, epitomizes the pivotal role that practical intelligence plays in navigating the intricate landscape of leadership. His capacity to envision the future and strategically steer his endeavors towards success stands as a testament to the indispensable nature of holistic leadership intelligence.

These luminaries, among a myriad of others, underscore a fundamental truth: effective leadership is not confined to a simplistic dichotomy—this either-or scenario. Instead, it thrives within the dynamic interplay of resilience, alongside an array of other critical intelligences. Practical and analytical intelligence, while undeniably significant, are but two facets of a multidimensional tapestry. The constellation of essential intelligences for triumphant leadership also encompasses ethical discernment, cultural acumen, creative ingenuity, and relational adeptness. It is within the symphony of these intelligences that the crucible of true leadership excellence is forged, transcending boundaries and propelling organizations towards unparalleled success. This holistic fusion, a testament to the boundless potential of human intellect, breathes life into visionary endeavors, shaping the course of industries and inspiring generations to come.

In our journey to reimagine leadership, we must transcend the limiting paradigm of EQ versus IQ. Instead, let us embrace a holistic framework that recognizes and celebrates the manifold facets of leadership intelligence. Through this lens, we equip ourselves to tackle the complexities of modern leadership with nuance, wisdom, and unwavering determination.

Reimagining Leadership Beyond the EQ VS IQ Paradigm

The Resilient Leader

Embracing Resilience for Success

Actionable Leadership Principles - Straightforward and Effective

The New Leadership Landscape and Why the Future of Business Hangs in the Balance

Professional and Collegiate Reference Edition

William Stanek's Empowered Leadership©
& Inspirational Journeys© Mastery Series

William R. Stanek
Author & Series Creator

Reimagining Leadership Beyond the EQ VS IQ Paradigm

The New Leadership Landscape and Why
the Future of Business Hangs in the Balance

The Resilient Leader

Embracing Resilience for Success

Published by Stanek & Associates
in conjunction with
Big Blue Sky Press for Business
www.williamrstanek.com.

Copyright © 2024 William R. Stanek. Seattle, Washington.
All rights reserved. Photographs of the author are © HC Stanek. Fine-art photographs and illustrations are © William R. Stanek and were created by the author.

No part of this book may be reproduced, stored in a retrieval system or transmitted in any form or by any means, electronic, mechanical, photocopying, recording, scanning or otherwise, except as permitted by Sections 107 or 108 of the 1976 United States Copyright Act, without the prior written permission of the publisher Requests to the publisher for permission should be sent to the address listed previously.

Stanek & Associates is a trademark of Stanek & Associates and/or its affiliates. All other marks are the property of their respective owners. No association with any real company, organization, person or other named element is intended or should be inferred through use of company names, web site addresses or screens.

This book expresses the views and opinions of the author. The information contained in this book is provided without any express, statutory or implied warranties.

LIMIT OF LIABILITY/DISCLAIMER OF WARRANTY: THE PUBLISHER AND THE AUTHOR MAKE NO REPRESENTATIONS OR WARRANTIES WITH RESPECT TO THE ACCURACY OR COMPLETENESS OF THE CONTENTS OF THIS WORK AND SPECIFICALLY DISCLAIM ALL WARRANTIES, INCLUDING WITHOUT LIMITATION WARRANTIES OF FITNESS FOR A PARTICULAR PURPOSE. NO WARRANTY MAY BE CREATED OR EXTENDD BY SALES OR PROMOTIONAL MATERIALS. THE ADVICE AND DISCUSSION IN THIS BOOK MAY NOT BE SUITABLE FOR EVERY SITUATION. THIS WORK IS SOLD WITH THE UNDERSTANDING THTAT THE PUBLISHER IS NOT ENGAGED IN RENDERING PROFESSIONAL SERVICES AND THAT SHOULD PROFESSIONAL ASSISTANCE BE REQUIRED THE SERVICES OF A COMPETENT PROFESSIONAL SHOULD BE SOUGHT. NEITHER THE PUBLISHERS, AUTHORS, RESELLERS NOR DISTRIBUTORS SHALL BE HELD LIABLE FOR ANY DAMAGES CAUSED OR ALLEGED TO BE CAUSE EITHER DIRECTLY OR INDIRECTLY HEREFROM. THE REFERENCE OF AN ORGANIZATION OR WEBSITE AS A SOURCE OF FURTHER INFORMATION DOES NOT MEAN THAT THE PUBLISHER OR THE AUTHOR ENDORSES THE INFORMATION THE ORGANIZATION OR WEBSITE MAY PROVIDE OR THE RECOMMENDATIONS IT MAY MAKE. FURTHER, READERS SHOULD BE AWARE THAT WEBSITES LISTED IN THIS BOOK MAY NOT BE AVAILABLE OR MAY HAVE CHANGED SINCE THIS WORK WAS WRITTEN.

Stanek & Associates publishes in a variety of formats, including print, electronic and by print-on-demand. Some materials included with standard print editions may not be included in electronic or print-on-demand editions or vice versa.

Country of First Publication: United States of America.

Cover Design: Creative Designs Ltd.
Editorial Development: Andover Publishing Solutions
Content & Technical Review: L & L Technical Content Services

You can provide feedback related to this book by emailing the author at williamstanek @ aol.com. Please use the <u>name of the book</u> as the subject line.

1st Edition. Version: 1.0.1.0b

Library of Congress Cataloging-in-Publication Data

Stanek, William.

   Reimagining Leadership Beyond the EQ vs IQ Paradigm: The Resilient Leader : The New Leadership Landscape and Why the Future of Business Hangs in the Balance : Professional and Collegiate Reference Edition / William Stanek. — 1st Stanek & Associates ed.

> **Note** I may periodically update this text and the edition and version number shown previously will let you know which version you are working with. If there's a specific feature you'd like me to write about in an update, message me on Facebook (http://facebook.com/williamstanekauthor). Please keep in mind readership of this book determines how much time I can dedicate to it.

> **Special Notice for Groups and Teams** Are you part of a group or team seeking comprehensive Empowered Leadership© and Inspirational Journeys© training? We offer tailored programs for groups of 12 or more, designed to equip you with the tools and strategies needed to thrive in today's dynamic landscape. Discover the power of collective growth and resilience! For inquiries and customized solutions, please reach out to Jeannie Kim jeannie.kim @ reagentpress.com.

> **Bulk Orders Available** Looking to equip your team or organization with the transformative power of "The Resilient Leader, Embracing Resilience for Success"? We offer special pricing and customized packages for bulk orders. For more information and to place your order, please contact Jeannie Kim jeannie.kim @ reagentpress.com.

Table of Contents

- Our Foundational Leadership Proposition i
- Table of Contents vii
- Foreword 15
- **Part 1. Let's Get Started!** 17
- **Welcome. Ready to Reimagine Leadership?** 21
  - Getting the Most out of this Book 21
  - More on How to Use This Book 23
  - Share & Stay in Touch 25
- **Part 2. Your Leadership Journey Begins** 27
- **The Dynamic Nature of Intelligence** 29
- **The 8 Pillars of Leadership** 31
  - Emotional Resilience 101 33
  - Creative Intelligence 101 33
  - Practical Intelligence 101 34
  - Cultural Intelligence 101 34
  - Intrapersonal Intelligence 101 35
  - Interpersonal Intelligence 101 35
  - Ethical Intelligence 101 36
  - Analytical intelligence 101 36
- **Unlocking Full Potential** 38
- **The Changing Landscape of Leadership** 39
- **The Historical Roots of Leadership Theories** 40
  - Leadership From Ancient Greece to the Industrial Revolution 40
  - Leadership in the 20th century 41
- **Emerging Trends in Modern Leadership** 43
  - From Servant Leadership to Adaptive Leadership 43
  - The Broken Paradigm of EQ VS IQ 44
- **From IQ Dominance to the Emergence of EQ Dominance** 46
  - The Shift from IQ to EQ 46

The Historical Progression of Leadership Theories 47
Critiques and Realities of the EQ vs IQ Paradigm 50
The Limited Focus of the EQ VS IQ Paradigm 50
Understanding Multiple Intelligences 50
The fallacy of an Either-Or Paradigm 52
The Relevance of Emotional Resilience 53
Understanding Emotional Resilience 53
Harnessing Emotional Resilience for Effective Decision-Making 56
The Limitations of Intellectual Intelligence (IQ) 59
Practical Scenarios and Complex Challenges 59
Real-World Application of Intelligence 61
The Interplay of Multiple Intelligences 62
The Relevance of Analytical Intelligence Beyond IQ 65
AQ Empowers and Can be Refined 65
AQ in an Ever-Changing Landscape 66
AQ Improves Teams and Organizations 67
Intrapersonal Intelligence Transcends EQ 69
Self-Improvement, Purpose and Determination 69
Intrapersonal Intelligence in Leadership and Beyond 70
Interpersonal Intelligence Beyond EQ 72
Dynamic Communication and Building Relationships 72
Leadership Beyond the Norms 73
Navigating Complex Challenges Beyond IQ and EQ 76
Rethinking Leadership in the 21st Century 78
The Call for a Comprehensive Approach 78
Embracing a Multi-Intelligence Framework 80
Setting the Stage for a Holistic Approach 83
Cultivating a Balanced Leadership Intelligence Profile 86
Holistic Intelligence—A Comprehensive Model of Intelligence 89
Transformative Potential: How Holistic Intelligence Can Reshape Lives 91
A New Era of Leadership 93

Part 3. Embracing Resilience for Success 95
Cultivating Emotional Resilience 97
The Resilient Soul: A Guiding Affirmation 97
Affirmation Instructions 97
Defining Emotional Resilience in Leadership 99
Emotional Resilience: A Dynamic Trait 99
The Role of Emotional Resilience in Authentic Leadership 100
Key Components of Emotional Resilience 101
From Self-awareness to Empathy 102
From Adaptability to Coping Mechanisms 103
From Problem-solving to Growth Mindset 103
Differentiating Emotional Resilience from Emotional Intelligence 105
ER vs. EQ: Understanding the Distinction 105
Scope of Application 106
Adaptability in Adversity 106
Cognitive Processes and Understanding 107
Interaction with Other Intelligences 107
Thriving in the Face of Adversity 107
Comprehensiveness of Response 107
Proactive Growth Orientation 108
A More Comprehensive Look at Resilience 108
Synergy between Emotional Resilience and Emotional Intelligence 110
Lessons from Resilient Leaders 112
Cultivating a Culture of Resilience 113
Being Authentic in Leadership 114
Navigating Setbacks and Adversities 115
Emotions as Catalysts: How Emotional Resilience Drives Effective Leadership 117
Honest Expression of Emotions 117
Being a Driving Force Behind Effective Leadership 118
Building Blocks of Emotional Resilience 120

Self-Awareness: The Foundation of Emotional Resilience 120
Emotional Regulation: Manage Response in High-Stress Environments .. 122
Empathy and Compassion: Connecting Through Empathetic Leadership 124

Mindfulness and Emotional Regulation Techniques 127
Mindfulness: Gaining a Deeper Understanding of Self 127
Emotional Regulation: Responding Skillfully to Challenging Situations 128

Developing Adaptive Coping Mechanisms 131
From Reframing Perception to Accepting Emotions 131
From Gaining Perspective to Setting Realistic Expectations 133
From Time Management to Self-Compassion 134

Building a Supportive Network: The Power of Emotional Resilience in Teams 137
From Open Communication to Growth Mindset 137
From Skill Development to Meaningful Contribution 138
From Healthy Team Dynamics to Mental Health 139

Practical Exercises for Strengthening Emotional Resilience 141
Individual Reflection and Journaling: A Journey into Self-Awareness 141
Embarking on a Journey of Reflection 141
Making Progress on the Journey 142
Why Use Reflection Journaling? 143
Deepening the Journey 144

Group Sharing & Support: Foster a Culture of Emotional Resilience ... 145
Icebreaker Activities 145
Sharing and Support 146

Scenario Analysis: Enhancing Response Strategies 149
Real-World Scenario 1: Crisis Management in the Financial Sector 150
Real-World Scenario 2: Leading Through a Global Pandemic 153
Real-World Scenario 3: Navigating a Complex Merger 157
Real-World Scenario 4: Crisis Response in the Public Sector 161
Real-World Scenario 5: Innovating in the Technology Sector 165
Real-World Scenario 6: Resilience in Educational Leadership 169

Measuring and Monitoring Emotional Resilience 173
Defining Metrics for Emotional Resilience 173
Cultivating a Resilient Organizational Climate: Tools for Assessment........ 175
Sustaining Emotional Resilience Over Time 178
Continuous Learning and Adaptation: A Resilience-Building Journey 178
Foster a Resilient Culture: Leadership Practices for Long-Term Success... 181
Case Studies: Applying Resilience in Leadership 185
Case Study Instructions 185
Case Study Analysis 1: Mary Barra - General Motors 187
Background 187
Problem/Objective Statement 187
Reflective Questions 187
Analysis and Discussion 187
Conclusion with Key Findings, Decisions, or Outcomes 189
Case Study Analysis 2: Elon Musk - Tesla and SpaceX (USA) 190
Background 190
Problem/Objective Statement 190
Reflective Questions 190
Analysis and Discussion 190
Conclusion with Key Findings, Decisions, or Outcomes 192
Case Study Analysis 3: Christine Lagarde - European Central Bank 194
Background 194
Problem/Objective Statement 194
Reflective Questions 194
Analysis and Discussion 195
Conclusion with Key Findings, Decisions, or Outcomes 196
Case Study Analysis 4: Jack Ma - Alibaba Group 198
Background 198
Problem/Objective Statement 198
Reflective Questions 198
Analysis and Discussion 198

    Conclusion with Key Findings, Decisions, or Outcomes 200
  Case Study Analysis 5: Marillyn Hewson - Lockheed Martin 202
    Background 202
    Problem/Objective Statement 202
    Reflective Questions 202
    Analysis and Discussion 203
    Conclusion with Key Findings, Decisions, or Outcomes 204
  Case Study Analysis 6: Carlos Ghosn - Nissan-Renault-Mitsubishi 206
    Background 206
    Problem/Objective Statement 206
    Reflective Questions 206
    Analysis and Discussion 207
    Conclusion with Key Findings, Decisions, or Outcomes 208

Part 4. Emotional Resilience Self-Assessment 211

The Power of Self-Assessment: Unveiling Paths to Growth 213

Self-Assessment 1-2-3! 215
  Instructions for the Self-Assessment: 216
  Scoring the Self-Assessment 217

Making the Most of Your Self-Assessment Score 219
  Interpretation of Scores: 219
  Very Low Emotional Resilience: Embarking on the Resilience Journey 220
  Low Emotional Resilience: Cultivating Foundational Resilience 222
  Moderate Emotional Resilience: Building a Stronger Foundation 225
  Average Emotional Resilience: Elevating Your Resilience Quotient 227
  Above Average Emotional Resilience: Getting to Resilience Excellence 230
  High Emotional Resilience: Optimizing Peak Resilience Potential 232
  Exceptional Emotional Resilience: Masterful Mastery of Resilience 235

Reassessing Your Emotional Resilience: A Path to Growth 238
  When to Consider Reassessment 238
  Achieving a New, Higher Level of Emotional Resilience 239
  Responding to a Decline in Emotional Resilience 241

Afterword for the Self-Assessment	244
Closing Reflection	247
Index	249
About the Author: William R. Stanek	267
The 8 Pillars of Leadership	271

Foreword

In 2016, I teetered on the precipice of mortality, spending eight harrowing days in the hospital as medical professionals navigated the delicate dance of uncertainty. Each heartbeat felt like a victory, a testament to human tenacity. Amidst the recovery, I grappled with a condition whose name now eludes my thoughts, but its impact on my world was indelible. To them, it might have seemed a minor concern amidst a constellation of afflictions, but to me, it held the weight of worlds.

For an artist and writer, losing the ability to conjure images in the mind's eye is akin to a maestro losing their baton, a navigator without a compass. It was an agonizing farewell to oil-painted canvases, delicate watercolors, and the dance of ink on paper. Yet, within this storm, the ember of my writing endured, refusing to be extinguished. It was a relentless companion, coaxing coherence from chaos.

The road back to artistic expression was a grueling odyssey, a symphony of triumphs and setbacks. With each step, I was stitching the tapestry of resilience, weaving determination and creativity into every fiber of my being. Through dogged persistence, I have emerged on the other side, having mostly reclaimed what was lost.

Venturing into the realm of leadership intelligence has been a profound odyssey, a journey shaped by the hands of mentors and the chorus of supporters. Their guidance has been the beacon that illuminated my path through uncharted territories. First and foremost, I extend my deepest gratitude to the Chief Officers of Fortune 100, 500, and 1000 companies. Your trust in me to tackle the most intricate challenges, often in seemingly insurmountable circumstances, has been both a humbling honor and a source of immense empowerment.

I am indebted to the multitude of leaders who have graced my path throughout my career. Each shared interaction, every challenge met together, has contributed to the insights and principles encapsulated within these pages. Your unwavering dedication to excellence, your steadfast commitment to your teams, and your embrace of innovation have served as an unwavering wellspring of inspiration.

To my esteemed colleagues and mentors, both past and present, I offer my heartfelt thanks. Your collective wisdom and diverse perspectives have enriched my comprehension of leadership intelligence. It is through our collaborations that many of the concepts presented here have taken root.

A special appreciation goes out to those who provided invaluable feedback and insights during the development of this book. Your thoughtful contributions were instrumental in refining the ideas and ensuring their accessibility to a wide audience. Your willingness to engage in spirited discussions, to challenge assumptions, and to share your own experiences has been truly invaluable.

This book stands as a testament to the collective wisdom of leaders, from eras past to the present, who have indelibly shaped the world. It is a tribute to the countless individuals who have shown that leadership is not confined to titles, but is defined by actions, by the impact we have on those we serve. It is a celebration of the boundless potential within each of us to lead with purpose, with compassion, and with an unwavering commitment to positive change.

Finally, to my family, whose unwavering support has been a bedrock of strength, I extend my deepest thanks. Your unwavering belief in me and in the significance of this work has been an ever-present driving force. This book is as much a reflection of your encouragement as it is of my own journey.

With deepest gratitude, *William R. Stanek.*

Part 1. Let's Get Started!

You're reading 'The Resilient Leader, Embracing Resilience for Success,' a vital addition to the Reimagining Leadership Beyond the EQ vs IQ Paradigm library. This comprehensive collection encompasses core volumes, dedicated to each of the essential 8 Pillars of Intelligence. Additionally, you'll find action plan volumes dedicated to providing complimentary hands-on materials that enrich your learning experience. The library also includes workbooks and other valuable resources. Together, they equip you with a holistic understanding of the multifaceted aspects of leadership intelligence crucial for success in today's dynamic business landscape.

Regardless of which book(s) you chose to explore, you'll find a consistent foundation of knowledge. Every volume starts with essential context. However, 'The Resilient Leader, Embracing Resilience for Success,' stands out as the cornerstone of your leadership journey. This volume will be frequently referenced in other books within the series, emphasizing its critical role in your learning path.

Within the Reimagining Leadership Beyond the EQ vs IQ Paradigm library, you'll find a constellation of knowledge, including:

- The Resilient Leader—Embracing Resilience for Success
- Emotional Resilience Now—A Resilience Action Plan for Leaders
- The Innovative Leader—Leading with Creativity and Innovation
- Creative Intelligence Now—An Innovation Action Plan for Leaders

Each of these volumes contributes to your journey of enhancing leadership intelligence. They offer a wealth of insights and strategies to empower your leadership endeavors.

Before you continue, take a moment to center yourself with the photograph on the next page.

As you gaze upon this Hawaiian horizon, where the sun meets the sea, envision your leadership journey stretching out before you. Like the rhythmic crash of waves against the rocky shoreline, your path may be marked by challenges, yet it is also adorned with moments of beauty and triumph.

Just as the sun dips below the horizon, signaling the close of one day and the promise of another, your journey in leadership is a series of endings and beginnings. Embrace them all, for they are the threads that weave the tapestry of your growth and resilience.

The interplay of light and shadow in this Hawaiian sky mirrors the dynamic nature of leadership. Each experience, each decision, shapes your narrative. With each step, you etch your unique story into the sands of time.

In this moment, on this shore, you stand at the threshold of a transformative journey. Let the spirit of the islands infuse your path with vitality and inspiration. Embrace it fully, for the leadership narrative you craft is a testament to your potential, your purpose, and your impact.

And if ever the winds of uncertainty threaten to steer you off course, return to this photograph. Let the timeless beauty of this moment serve as a beacon, guiding you back to the essence of your leadership journey. Remember, every challenge met, every triumph celebrated, is a testament to your strength and resilience. Embrace the path, for it is uniquely yours to shape.

When faced with crossroads, remember this mountain road. It symbolizes the choices, the uncharted territories, and the possibilities that await. As you stand at the precipice of decisions, know that each step, even the uncertain ones, contributes to your leadership odyssey. Embrace the journey, for every turn leads to growth, to wisdom, to your unique legacy. Keep forging ahead, for the road not taken is the one that defines your extraordinary story.

"The greatest glory in living lies not in never falling, but in rising every time we fall." - Nelson Mandela

Welcome. Ready to Reimagine Leadership?

The Emotional Intelligence (EQ) VS Intellectual Intelligence (IQ) Paradigm is a flawed construct that oversimplifies the complexities of human intelligence and its role in leadership. Critiques of this paradigm highlight the need for a more nuanced and comprehensive approach to assessing and developing leadership intelligence. By embracing a multi-intelligence framework that encompasses emotional, practical, ethical, cultural, relational and analytical dimensions, leaders can unlock their full potential and navigate the intricate challenges of the 21st-century business landscape. This paradigm shift is essential for fostering authentic, adaptable, and impactful leadership in today's dynamic organizational environments.

Getting the Most out of this Book

As you embark on this journey, it's important to recognize that the value you derive from this book lies in your approach to it. Think of it as a finely curated toolbox, meticulously designed to assist you in redefining and reimagining leadership. The potential is immense, but it requires a mindful and considered engagement.

Much like savoring a fine wine, it's in taking the time to appreciate the nuances of each concept, story, and idea that you'll glean the deepest insights. Rushing through, attempting to wield every tool simultaneously, is akin to upending the toolbox in haste—it might create a cacophony, but it won't lead to a harmonious outcome. Instead, consider employing these tools one or so at a time, allowing their impact to resonate and integrate into your leadership approach.

This book is designed for the thoughtful leader, one who recognizes that leadership is not a one-size-fits-all endeavor. It's an intricate dance, a balance of principles, and practicality, a continuous evolution. By delving into these pages with a spirit of inquiry and an open mind, you're not only equipping yourself with the knowledge but also with the wisdom to navigate the complexities of leadership.

Consider this book a guide, a companion in your leadership journey. It's not prescriptive, but rather, it offers a tapestry of perspectives, strategies, and case studies from which you can draw inspiration and adapt to your unique circumstances. Just as a seasoned navigator reads the stars and the currents to chart their course, you'll find within these pages the insights and tools to steer your leadership towards excellence.

Approach this book with a spirit of curiosity. Allow yourself to question, to reflect, and to challenge conventional notions of leadership. Embrace the discomfort of growth, for it is in this crucible that true transformation occurs. The stories shared here are not only testimonies of triumphs and challenges but also invitations for you to introspect and apply these learnings to your own leadership narrative.

Remember, leadership is not a solitary endeavor. It is a collective, ever-evolving journey. As you engage with this book, consider how the concepts and practices discussed resonate with your team and organization. Encourage open dialogues, seek diverse perspectives, and foster an environment where you and your organization can flourish. By doing so, you're not only enriching your own leadership but also cultivating a culture of excellence within your sphere of influence.

Each section in this book is meticulously crafted to offer a multifaceted exploration of leadership beyond the EQ VS IQ Paradigm. Whether you're delving into the theoretical underpinnings, engaging with real-world case studies, or immersing yourself in practical exercises, approach each section as a unique facet of a larger whole. Together, they form a comprehensive guide that empowers you to navigate the complexities of leadership with confidence and integrity.

Consider this book as a compass, not a map. It provides direction, but it's up to you to navigate the terrain. Your leadership journey is distinct, shaped by your experiences, values, and aspirations. Use this book as a resource to refine your leadership compass, to calibrate your decisions, and to illuminate your path forward.

In the end, the true measure of this book's impact lies in the actions you take, the conversations you initiate, and the changes you inspire. Apply the insights gained here with intentionality and authenticity. Let them permeate your leadership style, infusing it with the 8 Pillars of Leadership explored in this book. As you embark on this transformative odyssey, remember that leadership is not a destination but a continuous voyage, and this book is but a guiding star along the way.

More on How to Use This Book

William Stanek is an esteemed author, renowned worldwide bestseller, and trusted consultant with over three decades of experience. He has been a guiding force for Fortune 100, 500, and 1000 companies, navigating them through some of the most transformative periods in modern history.

"The 8 Pillars of Leadership" is the first volume in William Stanek's Empowered Leadership© & Inspirational Journeys© Mastery Series. This comprehensive professional and collegiate reference edition reimagines leadership beyond the traditional EQ vs. IQ paradigm.

The Empowered Leadership© & Inspirational Journeys© Mastery Series is a collection of volumes dedicated to empowering leaders with practical wisdom and actionable insights. Each volume delves into a specific aspect of leadership, providing a holistic approach that encompasses emotional resilience, practical intelligence, and ethical intelligence, among other intelligences.

This book is designed to be a comprehensive resource for leaders at every level and in every industry. Whether you're a seasoned executive or a budding entrepreneur, you'll find valuable insights to enhance your leadership journey. Here's how you can make the most of this book:

1. Thorough Reading   Begin by reading the book cover to cover. This will provide you with a foundational understanding of the principles and concepts explored in each section of this book.

2. Case Studies, Reflective Exercises & More   Throughout the book, you'll encounter case studies, reflective exercises and more that encourage introspection and self-assessment. Take the time to engage with these activities and exercises, as they will help you apply the concepts to your own leadership style.

3. Application to Real-World Scenarios   Consider how the lessons learned can be applied to your specific professional context. The book provides practical application, allowing you to see the real-world implications of the concepts.

4. Discussion and Collaboration   Engage in discussions with peers, colleagues, or fellow students. The discussion prompts provided at the end of the book can serve as a starting point for meaningful conversations about leadership.

5. Further Exploration   Explore additional resources recommended in the book for a deeper dive into specific topics. This will enhance your understanding and provide you with a broader perspective on leadership intelligence.

6. Continuous Learning   Leadership is an evolving field, and staying updated with the latest insights is crucial. Use this book as a springboard for your ongoing leadership development journey.

By following these steps, you'll be able to extract the maximum value from "The 8 Pillars of Leadership" and apply its principles to your own leadership endeavors. Remember, effective leadership is a continuous journey of growth and self-improvement, and this book is here to support you every step of the way.

> **Note**   While every effort has been dedicated to crafting this book to the highest standard, we acknowledge that despite our best endeavors, occasional typos, errors, or oversights may arise. Your keen eye and feedback are invaluable to us. If you come across anything, please don't hesitate to inform us. We are committed to promptly rectifying any identified issues, making updates accessible online and incorporating them in the forthcoming editions of the book. Your contribution is instrumental in perfecting this work.

Share & Stay in Touch

The marketplace for business and leadership books has changed substantially over the years. In addition to becoming increasingly specialized and segmented, the market has been shrinking rapidly, making it extremely difficult for books to find success. If you want William to be able to continue writing and write the books you need for your career, raise your voice and support his work.

Without support from you, the reader, future books by William will not be possible. Your voice matters. If you found the book to be useful, informative or otherwise helpful, please take the time to let others know by sharing about the book online.

To stay in touch with William, visit him on Facebook, LinkedIn or follow him on Twitter. William welcomes messages and comments about the book, especially suggestions for improvements and additions. If there is a topic you think should be covered in the book, let William know.

William R. Stanek (http://www.williamrstanek.com)

LinkedIn at https://www.linkedin.com/in/williamstanek/

Twitter at http://www.twitter.com/WilliamStanek

Facebook at http://www.facebook.com/William.Stanek.Author.

The Day Ends at the Seashore Limited Rare Print - The Sunset Collection in Canvas Print with Floating Frame

Beyond his contributions to the world of business and leadership, William is also an avid artist and photographer. His creative pursuits provide a unique perspective that enriches his writing. To explore William's artistic endeavors and discover the world through his lens, visit his online art and photography portfolio at

https://360studios.pictorem.com

Part 2. Your Leadership Journey Begins

As you step into this transformative phase, remember that every milestone, every challenge, and every triumph is a thread woven into the tapestry of your leadership journey. Embrace each moment with curiosity and purpose, for it is through this journey that you will discover the true depth of your leadership potential.

Let your gaze linger on the boardwalk that stretches ahead, disappearing into the horizon. Much like this path, your leadership journey unfurls before you, an odyssey filled with boundless opportunities and unforeseen turns. The distant pagoda-like structure beckons, a symbol of your destination, a testament to your aspirations.

Embrace the ebb and flow, for just as the tides shape the estuary, experiences shape leadership. The interplay of shadows and light in the sky above mirrors the dynamic nature of challenges and triumphs you'll encounter. Each step is a stitch in the fabric of your leadership narrative, weaving together resilience, wisdom, and growth.

With every footfall, you write your own story of leadership. As you traverse this boardwalk, know that you carry with you the potential to create profound impact. The journey itself is your canvas, waiting for the brush strokes of your unique vision. Embrace it with an open heart and a steadfast spirit, for the path you walk is yours to shape and yours to own.

The Dynamic Nature of Intelligence

My journey through the intricacies of leadership has unfolded amidst some of the most crucial moments in modern history. From the tense era of the Cold War to the turbulent times of the Iraq War, I found myself navigating through significant conflicts that tested our nation's resilience. What distinguishes me is my exceptional ability not only to adapt but to thrive in these high-pressure environments. Time and again, I was thrust into senior leadership positions, defying my relatively junior rank. This speaks volumes about my knack for evaluating critical situations and skillfully guiding those around me, often individuals significantly senior to me, toward resounding success.

My experiences, shaped in the crucible of the military and other arenas, have granted me a profound insight: genuine leadership surpasses mere titles or years of service. It revolves around the ability to inspire and influence, to steer a team through even the most daunting challenges. In my role as a technology consultant, I often assumed the mantle of the "fixer" - the one summoned when situations seemed dire and hope was fading. Surprisingly, I discovered that more often than not, the root cause of many seemingly insurmountable problems was not a technological failure, but rather a breakdown in leadership and intelligence dynamics.

Recognizing this recurring pattern, my consulting focus naturally evolved towards uncovering people-centric solutions. It became evident that the success of any endeavor, particularly in the fast-paced and constantly evolving landscape of technology, hinges on the human element. This revelation forms the foundation of the principles expounded in our book. It underscores the vital role of emotional resilience and other intelligences in the realms of leadership and decision-making.

By delving into the human dynamics that underpin every facet of professional life, our book aims to provide a comprehensive guide for individuals looking to not only excel in their roles but also to lead with authenticity, empathy, and strategic acumen. It explores the intricate interplay between various intelligences, illustrating how they converge to shape effective leadership, decision-making, and problem-solving. Through a series of exercises, case studies, reflective practices, and more, readers will gain invaluable insights into honing their own intelligences, fostering a deeper understanding of themselves and those they lead.

Ultimately, this book is a testament to the idea that true leadership is a holistic endeavor, one that demands a keen awareness of oneself, an astute understanding of others, and an unyielding commitment to ethical and principled decision-making. It's a call to action for leaders at every level and in every industry to embrace the complexities of human dynamics and to harness them as a force for positive change and lasting success. Together, let us embark on this journey of reimagining leadership intelligence, shaping a future where leadership transcends convention and inspires profound transformation.

The 8 Pillars of Leadership

Books on intelligence often suggest that our cognitive abilities and emotional tendencies are set in stone, unchangeable throughout our lives. They paint a picture of intelligence as static, unyielding to growth or development. However, we hold a different perspective. While the core capacity for processing information may have a baseline, the methods and depths of this processing can be refined and expanded upon. Picture your mind not as a fixed vessel, but a dynamic ship capable of adopting new strategies and approaches to learning.

In our comprehensive exploration of leadership intelligence, we challenge the notion that one's intellectual faculties and personal traits are immovable. We believe that individuals harbor a remarkable capacity to nurture and enhance their proficiencies across various dimensions, ranging from emotional resilience to practical discernment, ethical decision-making, and beyond. It's within these realms that true leadership prowess is forged, transcending data processing to encompass profound understanding, application, and integration of information.

Intelligence, as we envisage it, transcends the mere capacity to assimilate data. It encapsulates the ability to glean insights, connect disparate pieces of information, and synthesize them into meaningful, actionable knowledge. This skill, far from being a fixed attribute, is a dynamic ability that can be honed and refined over time. Through structured exercises, critical reflection, and practical application, our book serves as a compass for those seeking to embark on a continuous journey of intellectual growth and development that encompasses the 8 Pillars of Leadership, shown in Figure 1.

The 8 Pillars of Leadership

Analytical Intelligence
Ethical Intelligence
Interpersonal Intelligence
Intrapersonal Intelligence
Cultural Intelligence
Practical Intelligence
Creative Intelligence
Emotional Resilience

EQ VS IQ Paradigm

Emotional Intelligence (EQ)	Cognitive Intelligence (IQ)

Figure 1. Beyond the EQ vs IQ Paradigm: The Spectrum of Multi-Intelligences.

> **Note** Throughout this book and others in the series, we will explore the spectrum of multi-intelligences, interchangeably referred to as either 'multi-intelligences' or 'The 8 Pillars of Leadership'. The 'Q' in EQ and IQ represents Quotient, which essentially means intelligence.

The traditional discourse on intelligence has long been dominated by the dichotomy of Intellectual Intelligence (IQ) and Emotional Intelligence (EQ). While IQ measures cognitive abilities and EQ assesses emotional awareness, these metrics offer only a partial understanding of human capabilities. The landscape of intelligence is far more diverse and intricate, encompassing a spectrum of distinct dimensions. Visualizing this paradigm shift, the diagram illustrates how these multiple intelligences extend beyond the conventional EQ vs IQ framework, revealing a more comprehensive model of human intelligence.

> **Note** In this book, you may observe that certain terms are capitalized in specific contexts but not in others. This distinction is made to emphasize their defined usages versus their more general application. Trust in the proofreaders to handle this, much like the wizard behind the curtain, and pay it no further concern.

Emotional Resilience 101

Central to our discourse is the concept of emotional resilience, a quality often considered an inherent disposition. However, we firmly assert that Emotional Resilience (ER) is not a stagnant trait, but a dynamic skill that can be fortified through dedicated effort. By engaging in exercises designed to foster emotional strength and endurance, individuals can enhance their capacity to navigate through challenging situations with grace and proficiency.

Emotional Resilience stands as a testament to the resilience and adaptability of the human spirit. It transcends the realm of understanding emotions, delving into the capacity to rebound from setbacks, manage stress, and uphold a positive outlook even in the face of adversity. This vital intelligence equips individuals with the strength to weather storms, ultimately leading to greater personal growth and professional achievement.

> **Note** One way of viewing emotional resilience is an intelligence that encompasses EQ and transcends it. It's important to understand that while emotional resilience is highly influenced by emotional intelligence (EQ), it also involves cognitive processes related to understanding and managing emotions, and interacts with and leverages other intelligences. See "Differentiating Emotional Resilience from Emotional Intelligence" in "Cultivating Emotional Resilience" to truly understand what this means. Explore further in our book 'Emotional Resilience Now—A Resilience Action Plan for Leaders,' where we delve deeply into the 35 critical characteristics of emotional resilience. This comprehensive guide not only elucidates these traits but also offers a practical roadmap for understanding and fortifying them.

Creative Intelligence 101

Creative Intelligence (CrQ) is an essential component of our exploration as well. In a world characterized by constant innovation and change, leaders must be adept at generating, combining, and transforming ideas into innovative solutions. Our book offers a roadmap for nurturing creative thinking, providing readers with actionable steps to foster a culture of innovation within their organizations.

Creative Intelligence illuminates the path to innovation and ingenuity. It encompasses the ability to not only conceive novel ideas but also to meld and transform them into practical solutions. Creative thinking is the heartbeat of problem-solving, driving product development, and ensuring adaptability in dynamic environments. A leader armed with CrQ possesses the means to navigate the ever-evolving landscape of challenges with finesse and originality.

> **Note** In the spirit of clear communication, we believe in using language that is accessible and easily understood. While acronyms have their place, we recognize that an overabundance can hinder rather than aid comprehension. In this book, we've taken care to use acronyms sparingly, reserving them for instances where they truly enhance understanding. Our aim is to ensure that every concept is presented in a way that is straightforward and approachable, allowing you to engage with the material without unnecessary linguistic hurdles.

Practical Intelligence 101

Practical Intelligence (PQ), often referred to as "street smarts," is an indispensable compass in navigating the complex terrain of the corporate world. It encompasses skills like adaptability, common sense, and the ability to apply knowledge in practical contexts. This form of intelligence is not static, but a learned behavior that can be honed through experience, reflection, and intentional practice.

More specifically, Practical Intelligence encapsulates the wisdom derived from hands-on experience. It embodies the ability to effectively navigate the complexities of real-world scenarios, showcasing adaptability, common sense, and the judicious application of knowledge. PQ, the foundation of practical problem-solving, equips individuals with the ability to translate theory into impactful action.

Cultural Intelligence 101

Cultural Intelligence (CuQ) is vital in our globalized world. Understanding and effectively interacting with people from diverse cultural backgrounds is crucial. We impart invaluable lessons on building cultural awareness, knowledge, and adaptability, empowering leaders to navigate the complexities of an interconnected world.

Cultural Intelligence emerges as a linchpin in our interconnected world. It transcends geographical and cultural boundaries, requiring an acute awareness, knowledge, and adaptability in interacting with people from diverse backgrounds. In an era of globalized interactions, leaders who excel in CuQ forge connections that transcend language and tradition, thus paving the way for collaborative successes on a worldwide scale.

Intrapersonal Intelligence 101

Intrapersonal Intelligence (IntraQ), a profound understanding of one's own emotions, strengths, weaknesses, and motivations, is another dimension we explore. Those with high Intrapersonal Intelligence possess a deep self-awareness that enables them to navigate their professional and personal lives with clarity and purpose.

Intrapersonal Intelligence delves deep into the individual's inner landscape, fostering self-awareness and self-regulation. It empowers individuals with a profound understanding of self. Armed with this intelligence, individuals navigate life's twists and turns with a clarity of purpose and a steady compass guiding them towards lifelong growth and personal fulfillment.

Interpersonal Intelligence 101

Interpersonal Intelligence (InnerQ) extends beyond emotional intelligence and encompasses the ability to understand and navigate social dynamics. It involves building and nurturing relationships, effective communication, negotiation, and conflict resolution. This form of intelligence is dynamic and can be developed through intentional practice and reflection.

Interpersonal Intelligence encompasses a profound comprehension of social dynamics. It embraces the ability to influence positively, build trust, and navigate complex social interactions. Leaders equipped with this intelligence serve as catalysts for team cohesion, fostering collaboration, and resolving disagreements constructively.

> **Note** Interpersonal intelligence and intrapersonal intelligence are distinct pillars because they represent two fundamentally different aspects of human cognition and behavior. Interpersonal intelligence

> focuses on one's ability to understand and navigate social dynamics, including communication, empathy, and conflict resolution. Intrapersonal intelligence, on the other hand, centers on self-awareness, emotional regulation, and the capacity for introspection and self-reflection. While both involve relationships, they pertain to different dimensions—one external (interpersonal) and the other internal (intrapersonal) —and contribute unique skills essential for effective functioning in various contexts.

> **More Info** It's important to point out that in this and other volumes of the Empowered Leadership© & Inspirational Journeys© Mastery Series Intrapersonal Intelligence and Interpersonal Intelligence may occasionally be collectively referred to as Relational Intelligence (ReQ). Primarily, this is for ease of reference for those limited and very specific times where we want to refer to both the intrapersonal and interpersonal pillars of intelligence.

Ethical Intelligence 101

Ethical Intelligence (EthQ), the ability to make moral and principled decisions, is not a fixed trait but a learned behavior cultivated through experiences, values, and self-reflection. By engaging in practice and exercises that challenge moral judgment and ethical reasoning, individuals can elevate their ethical intelligence, contributing to a culture of integrity and accountability.

Ethical Intelligence underscores the moral compass that guides decision-making. It entails not only the ability to discern right from wrong, but also a commitment to principles such as integrity, honesty, and accountability to both individuals and the environment. Leaders anchored in EthQ inspire trust and model ethical behavior, establishing a foundation of integrity within their teams and organizations.

Analytical intelligence 101

Analytical intelligence (AQ), which includes critical thinking, logical reasoning, and problem-solving abilities, is a dynamic skill set that can be honed and refined over time. Through structured exercises and practical application, individuals can enhance their capacity to assess information, identify patterns, and make sound decisions based on evidence.

Analytical Intelligence constitutes the bedrock of informed decision-making. It encompasses the capacity for cultivating an analytical mindset, leverage technology, and transforming data into actionable knowledge. Leaders enriched with AQ are equipped to navigate complexity, ultimately driving their organizations towards strategic excellence.

Unlocking Full Potential

Our book stands as a testament to the belief that intelligence, in all its diverse manifestations, is not a rigid trait but a pliable skill set, ripe for development and refinement. Through a holistic approach encompassing emotional, practical, ethical, creative, cultural, intrapersonal, interpersonal, and analytical intelligence, individuals can shatter perceived boundaries and unlock their full potential. By immersing themselves in the content, practices and exercises presented, readers embark on a transformative odyssey toward heightened self-awareness, enhanced decision-making, and more effective leadership. This, we assert, is the true essence of intelligence—an ever-evolving capacity with the potential to shape not only individuals, but entire organizations and communities.

While emotional intelligence undoubtedly plays a critical role in a well-rounded person, it is imperative to acknowledge the existence and significance of various other intelligences. A truly holistic individual or leader possesses a diverse range of these intelligences, enabling them to excel in personal, professional, social, and societal realms. Solely fixating on EQ risks overlooking the myriad of capabilities that contribute to a person's overall success and fulfillment.

By transcending the confines of conventional intelligence paradigms, we forge a path towards a new era of leadership, one where potential knows no bounds, and success is defined by the rich tapestry of capabilities that contribute to individual and collective fulfillment. A leader who not only recognizes but actively cultivates and leverages these diverse intelligences becomes a beacon of inspiration, propelling their team and organization toward unprecedented heights of innovation, adaptability, and sustained success. They create environments where individuals flourish, harnessing the collective strength of their team's varied capabilities.

The Changing Landscape of Leadership

The landscape of leadership is continuously evolving in response to dynamic global challenges and technological advancements. In this section, we embark on a journey to explore the shifting paradigms of leadership and delve into the core competencies required to thrive in this ever-changing environment.

> **Author's Note** Our book is meticulously crafted to facilitate your growth, learning, and transformation into a resilient and dynamic leader. Any overlap and repetition you encounter have been deliberately woven throughout the content to reinforce key lessons and deepen your understanding. We encourage you not only to read, but to immerse yourself in this learning and personal growth journey.
>
> To derive the utmost benefit from this book, we recommend proceeding with thoughtful deliberation and a methodical approach. It's important to remember that there are no quick fixes or one-size-fits-all solutions. Mastery of the 8 Pillars of Leadership is an ongoing process, one that you will accomplish gradually and thoroughly by diligently following the step-by-step guidance provided in these pages.

The Historical Roots of Leadership Theories

Leadership has been a subject of intrigue and investigation for centuries, with scholars, philosophers, and practitioners seeking to understand the essence of effective leadership. The roots of leadership theories can be traced back to ancient civilizations, where leaders were often perceived as appointed by the gods, possessing innate qualities that set them apart from the masses. In these early societies, leadership was often intertwined with divine authority and hereditary succession.

Leadership From Ancient Greece to the Industrial Revolution

As societies evolved, so did conceptions of leadership. In ancient Greece, philosophers like Plato and Aristotle pondered the attributes and virtues of an ideal leader. Plato's "Philosopher-King" concept and Aristotle's exploration of virtues in his "Nicomachean Ethics" laid the groundwork for early philosophical discussions on leadership. These ancient thinkers emphasized qualities like wisdom, justice, and moral character as essential components of effective leadership.

It was the Roman Empire that introduced the concept of military leadership, where commanders held significant sway over armies and territories. Roman leaders like Julius Caesar and Cicero demonstrated the fusion of strategic thinking, communication skills, and decisiveness in their leadership styles. The Roman model of leadership exerted a profound influence on subsequent military and political leadership theories.

With the advent of organized religions, leadership became intertwined with spiritual authority. Religious figures like Moses, Buddha, and Confucius were revered as moral and spiritual guides, shaping the ethical dimensions of leadership. Their teachings emphasized principles of compassion, wisdom, and ethical conduct, which continue to resonate in contemporary leadership philosophy.

During the Renaissance period, the emergence of nation-states and the rise of monarchies spurred new reflections on what leadership means. Machiavelli's "The Prince" marked a significant shift, introducing the pragmatic concept of political leadership. Machiavelli's writings delved into the art of statecraft, advocating for strategic pragmatism and a focus on maintaining stability and power.

The Industrial Revolution brought about great transformative changes in society, giving rise to a burgeoning need for organizational leadership. The shift from agrarian economies to industrialized urban centers necessitated leaders who could manage complex enterprises. It was in this era that we saw the emergence of early management theories, such as Frederick Taylor's Scientific Management, which emphasized efficiency and task specialization.

Leadership in the 20th century

The early 20th century witnessed the rise of trait theories, which posited that effective leaders possessed inherent, unchangeable traits that set them apart. Scholars like Thomas Carlyle and Ralph Stogdill focused on identifying specific characteristics, such as charisma, decisiveness, and intelligence, associated with leadership effectiveness. While trait theories provided valuable insights, they fell short in explaining the complexity of leadership dynamics.

As the field of psychology advanced, so did theories of leadership. Behavioral theories, championed by psychologists like B.F. Skinner and Kurt Lewin, shifted the focus from inherent traits to observable behaviors. This new perspective highlighted that effective leadership was not solely dependent on personality traits, but also on behaviors that could be learned and refined.

The mid-20th century brought forth contingency theories, which acknowledged that effective leadership is contingent upon various situational factors. Scholars like Fred Fiedler and Hersey-Blanchard proposed that the most effective leadership style depended on the interplay between leader characteristics, follower characteristics, and situational context. This marked a significant departure from earlier theories, recognizing the contextual nature of leadership effectiveness.

The latter half of the 20th century witnessed the emergence of transformational and transactional leadership theories. James MacGregor Burns introduced the concept of transformational leadership, emphasizing the leader's ability to inspire and elevate followers to achieve their full potential. Concurrently, Bernard Bass expanded on transactional leadership, focusing on the exchange of rewards and punishments between leaders and followers.

In the 1980s, Daniel Goleman's groundbreaking work on Emotional Intelligence (EQ) revolutionized the understanding of leadership effectiveness. Goleman proposed that emotional intelligence, comprising self-awareness, self-regulation, empathy, and social skills, played a crucial role in leadership success. This major paradigm shift placed a newfound emphasis on the interpersonal and intrapersonal dimensions of leadership.

However, the EQ vs IQ paradigm, while illuminating, is not without its limitations. The dichotomy oversimplifies the intricate interplay of intelligences required for effective leadership. It implies that individuals are either emotionally intelligent or intellectually intelligent, neglecting the reality that leaders often draw on a diverse array of intelligences to navigate complex challenges.

The historical roots of leadership theories offer a rich tapestry of perspectives, from divine authority in ancient civilizations to pragmatic political leadership in the Renaissance. The evolution of leadership theories reflects the dynamic nature of societies and the diverse contexts in which leadership manifests. The emergence of EQ as a pivotal component of leadership underscores the importance of emotional intelligence in modern leadership paradigms. Yet, as we shall explore further, a more comprehensive framework that embraces a spectrum of intelligences is not only essential to navigate the complexities of 21st-century leadership, but crucial.

Emerging Trends in Modern Leadership

In the ever-evolving landscape of the 21st century, leadership paradigms are undergoing a profound transformation. Traditional hierarchical structures are giving way to more agile, collaborative, and inclusive models. One of the most notable trends is the shift from command-and-control leadership to a more participatory and empowering approach. Modern leaders are recognizing the value of engaging their teams in decision-making processes, fostering a sense of ownership and accountability.

From Servant Leadership to Adaptive Leadership

The concept of servant leadership is gaining prominence. This approach emphasizes the leader's role as a facilitator, mentor, and supporter of their team members' growth and development. Servant leaders prioritize the well-being and success of their followers, placing their needs above their own. This trend reflects a deeper understanding of leadership as a service to others, rather than a position of authority.

Another significant trend is the increasing emphasis on ethical leadership. In a rapidly changing global landscape, leaders are expected to navigate complex ethical dilemmas with integrity and transparency. Ethical leaders prioritize moral values, social responsibility, and sustainability in their decision-making. They understand that ethical conduct is not just a matter of compliance, but a foundational aspect of organizational culture and reputation.

The rise of digitalization and technology is reshaping the way leaders operate. The digital age demands leaders who are technologically literate, adaptable to new tools and platforms, and capable of leveraging data-driven insights. Effective leaders today harness the power of technology to enhance productivity, innovation, and communication within their organizations.

A key shift in modern leadership is the recognition of diversity and inclusion as imperative components of organizational success. Leaders are tasked with creating environments that celebrate diversity of thought, background, and experience. Inclusive leaders value diverse perspectives, cultivate a sense of belonging, and actively dismantle barriers to participation. They understand that diverse teams foster creativity, innovation, and adaptability.

Collaborative leadership is also emerging as a crucial trend in modern organizations. Leaders are no longer expected to be solitary decision-makers, but rather facilitators of collective intelligence. They foster a culture of collaboration, encourage cross-functional teamwork, and promote knowledge-sharing. Collaborative leaders understand that the collective wisdom of the team often surpasses the insights of any single individual.

Additionally, the concept of adaptive leadership is gaining traction. In an era of rapid change and uncertainty, leaders must be agile and responsive to shifting circumstances. Adaptive leaders are adept at navigating ambiguity, embracing change, and leading their organizations through transitions. They recognize that flexibility and resilience are essential qualities in today's dynamic business environment.

The Broken Paradigm of EQ VS IQ

The broken EQ vs IQ paradigm becomes evident in these emerging trends. It oversimplifies the multifaceted nature of modern leadership by reducing it to a binary choice between emotional intelligence (EQ) and intellectual intelligence (IQ). In reality, effective leadership requires a nuanced integration of various intelligences, including practical intelligence, cultural intelligence, ethical intelligence, and analytical intelligence, among others.

For instance, practical intelligence, often referred to as "street smarts," is essential in navigating real-world situations and making informed decisions in complex environments. Leaders with high practical intelligence excel at adapting to changing circumstances, demonstrating common sense, and applying knowledge in practical contexts.

Cultural intelligence (CuQ) is equally vital in today's globalized world. Leaders must possess the ability to understand and navigate diverse cultural norms, perspectives, and practices. This intelligence enables them to build inclusive and harmonious teams, forge connections with stakeholders from different backgrounds, and navigate the complexities of international business.

Ethical intelligence is a non-negotiable aspect of modern leadership. Leaders are entrusted with making principled decisions that uphold the values and integrity of their organizations. Ethical intelligence involves not only understanding ethical principles, but also consistently applying them in decision-making, even in the face of challenging situations.

Analytical intelligence, encompassing critical thinking, logical reasoning, and problem-solving abilities, is indispensable in today's data-driven business environment. Leaders must be skilled at analyzing information, identifying patterns, and making sound decisions based on evidence. This intelligence complements emotional intelligence by providing a structured approach to problem-solving.

Emerging trends in modern leadership underscore the need for a multi-dimensional approach that transcends the limitations of the EQ vs IQ paradigm. Effective leaders in the 21st century must possess a diverse range of intelligences, each contributing to their ability to navigate complex challenges, inspire their teams, and drive organizational success. A holistic view of leadership intelligence is essential to thrive in today's dynamic and interconnected world.

From IQ Dominance to the Emergence of EQ Dominance

Throughout history, the perception of intelligence in leadership has undergone a profound evolution. In earlier eras, leadership was predominantly associated with cognitive prowess and analytical thinking, encapsulated by the concept of intellectual intelligence (IQ). Leaders were often evaluated based on their problem-solving abilities, strategic acumen, and proficiency in making rational decisions. This paradigm of IQ dominance prevailed for much of the 20th century, shaping how leadership was understood and assessed.

The Shift from IQ to EQ

As organizations became increasingly complex and interdependent, a growing recognition emerged that effective leadership extended beyond cognitive abilities alone. The rigid focus on IQ failed to capture the nuanced dynamics of human interaction, emotional resonance, and interpersonal effectiveness that are integral to leadership success. This realization gave rise to the emergence of emotional intelligence (EQ) as a pivotal dimension of leadership acumen.

Emotional intelligence represents a seismic shift in how leadership aptitude is conceptualized. It introduces the recognition that emotions play a central role in decision-making, team dynamics, and organizational culture. Leaders with high EQ are adept at understanding their own emotions, as well as the emotions of others. They possess the capacity to empathize, communicate effectively, and navigate complex interpersonal situations with finesse.

The emergence of EQ challenged the conventional wisdom that intellectual prowess was the sole determinant of leadership effectiveness. It introduced a more holistic view of intelligence, one that acknowledges the significance of self-awareness, empathy, and relationship-building in leadership. EQ became a critical factor in evaluating leaders, with organizations recognizing that leaders who were emotionally attuned were better equipped to inspire and mobilize their teams.

This shift in focus from IQ dominance to the prominence of EQ marked a pivotal juncture in the evolution of leadership theories. It signaled a departure from the notion that leadership was solely the domain of individuals with high cognitive abilities, and highlighted the importance of emotional and social competencies. Leaders were no longer assessed solely on their analytical prowess, but also on their capacity to connect with and motivate their teams.

However, it is imperative to clarify that the emergence of Emotional Intelligence (EQ) was not intended to undermine the significance of intellectual intelligence (IQ). Rather, it was meant to emphasize the complementary nature of these two dimensions of intelligence. Effective leaders were meant to recognize the value of both cognitive acuity and emotional acumen in navigating the complexities of modern organizations. They were meant to understand that a balanced integration of IQ and EQ is essential for driving organizational success, rather than favoring one over the other. Despite this intention, the sentiment 'EQ trumps IQ' has been echoed, as stated by Microsoft CEO Satya Nadella (Inc.com, Oct 11, 2023), who expressed, What distinguishes successful people from everyone else ultimately boils down to two words: emotional intelligence.

The Historical Progression of Leadership Theories

The broken EQ vs IQ paradigm is evident in the historical progression of leadership theories. It reflects a tendency to oscillate between extremes, viewing intelligence in a binary framework—the search for a magic bullet. This oversimplification neglects the multifaceted nature of leadership and the interplay between different dimensions of intelligence. Leaders who excel in the 21st century are those who embrace a holistic view of intelligence, recognizing that it encompasses a diverse range of capacities, including practical intelligence, cultural intelligence, ethical intelligence, and analytical intelligence, among others.

Practical intelligence (PQ), for instance, is indispensable in translating knowledge into effective action. It involves the ability to navigate real-world situations, demonstrate adaptability, and apply knowledge in practical contexts. Leaders with high practical intelligence excel in making sound judgments in dynamic environments, demonstrating resourcefulness, and responding adeptly to unforeseen challenges.

Cultural intelligence (CuQ) is equally crucial in our interconnected global landscape. Leaders must possess the capability to understand and navigate diverse cultural norms, values, and practices. This intelligence enables them to build inclusive and collaborative teams, forge meaningful connections with stakeholders from different backgrounds, and navigate the complexities of operating in international markets.

Ethical intelligence (EthQ), encompassing principled decision-making and integrity, is non-negotiable for leaders in the 21st century. It involves consistently applying ethical principles in decision-making, even in the face of challenging situations. Leaders with high ethical intelligence prioritize moral values, social responsibility, and accountability, contributing to a culture of trust and integrity within their organizations.

Analytical intelligence (AQ), which encompasses critical thinking, logical reasoning, and problem-solving abilities, is foundational in today's data-driven business environment. Leaders must possess the capacity to analyze information, identify patterns, and make evidence-based decisions. This intelligence complements emotional intelligence by providing a structured approach to problem-solving, enabling leaders to make informed choices based on empirical evidence.

The evolution of intelligence in leadership reflects a transition from the dominance of IQ to the recognition of the pivotal role of EQ to the preference for EQ over IQ as a magic bullet and the only skill necessary for successful leadership. However, effective leadership in the 21st century requires a nuanced understanding of intelligence that transcends the confines of the EQ vs IQ paradigm.

Leaders who thrive in today's dynamic and interconnected world possess a diverse range of intelligences, each contributing to their ability to inspire their teams, navigate complex challenges, and drive organizational success. It is through this holistic view of intelligence that leaders can truly excel in the complex and ever-changing landscape of modern organizations.

Critiques and Realities of the EQ vs IQ Paradigm

The EQ vs IQ paradigm tends to reduce the multidimensional nature of human intelligence to a binary framework. It oversimplifies the complexities of human cognition, emotions, and social dynamics, failing to capture the full spectrum of intelligences that contribute to effective leadership.

The Limited Focus of the EQ VS IQ Paradigm

One of the primary critiques of the EQ vs IQ paradigm is its limited focus on practical intelligence, also known as "street smarts." This form of intelligence, crucial for navigating real-world situations, making pragmatic decisions, and adapting to dynamic environments, is often overshadowed by the emphasis on emotional and cognitive dimensions.

Traditional assessments of intelligence, particularly those focused on IQ, may not capture the full range of capabilities required for effective leadership. These assessments often prioritize cognitive tasks and logical reasoning, potentially overlooking critical dimensions such as emotional resilience, cultural intelligence, and ethical decision-making.

Contrary to a common misconception, intelligences are not static entities; they are dynamic and malleable. The EQ vs IQ paradigm mistakenly assumes that these capacities remain fixed throughout an individual's life. In truth, individuals have the potential to nurture and enhance various facets of intelligence through intentional practice and experiential learning.

Understanding Multiple Intelligences

Contemporary research in psychology and leadership studies supports the idea of multiple intelligences. The works of Howard Gardner, for instance, propose a model that encompasses various forms of intelligence, including linguistic, mathematical, interpersonal, and intrapersonal intelligences. This framework acknowledges the diverse ways in which individuals excel and contribute to leadership effectiveness.

Different leadership contexts may require varying combinations of intelligences. For instance, a leader navigating a cross-cultural team may heavily rely on cultural intelligence, while a leader in a data-driven industry may place greater emphasis on analytical intelligence. The EQ vs IQ paradigm fails to account for this contextual variability.

While emotional intelligence is rightly acknowledged as a crucial facet of effective leadership, it should not be juxtaposed with intellectual intelligence, nor should we overlook other facets of intelligence. Rather than substituting one another, these facets work in harmony. For instance, leaders with elevated emotional resilience are not only adept at understanding and managing emotions, but they also demonstrate strong cognitive abilities, illustrating the synergy between emotional and intellectual intelligence in successful leadership.

Practical intelligence, often downplayed in the EQ vs IQ paradigm, plays a pivotal role in leadership decision-making. Leaders with high practical intelligence excel in making judicious choices in real-world scenarios, demonstrating adaptability, and leveraging their "street smarts" to drive organizational success.

Ethical intelligence, encompassing principled decision-making and integrity, is indispensable in modern leadership. This dimension of intelligence ensures that leaders make decisions aligned with ethical principles and values, fostering a culture of trust and accountability within their organizations.

In today's data-driven business landscape, analytical intelligence is of utmost importance. Leaders must possess the capacity to analyze information, discern patterns, and make data-informed decisions. This form of intelligence complements emotional intelligence by providing a structured approach to problem-solving.

Effective leadership in the 21st century demands a holistic approach that integrates various dimensions of intelligence. Leaders who excel recognize the synergies between emotional, practical, ethical, and analytical intelligences, leveraging them to inspire their teams and drive organizational success.

The fallacy of an Either-Or Paradigm

The fallacy of an Either-Or paradigm is a failed one. The EQ vs IQ paradigm erroneously implies that individuals must prioritize one form of intelligence over another. In reality, leaders can cultivate a diverse range of intelligences, allowing them to excel in various dimensions of leadership effectiveness.

Leadership challenges are multifaceted and constantly evolving. They demand leaders who can adapt, innovate, and navigate complex scenarios. This necessitates a comprehensive approach that integrates various intelligences rather than relying on a singular dimension.

Leaders bring unique intelligence profiles to their roles. Some may naturally excel in emotional resilience, while others may possess a strong analytical acumen. Recognizing and leveraging these individual differences can lead to more effective and balanced leadership teams.

The imperative for lifelong learning and development cannot be overstated. Embracing a multi-intelligence framework underscores the vital significance of continuous growth. Leaders must be committed to honing various dimensions of intelligence throughout their careers, recognizing that growth in one area can significantly amplify overall leadership effectiveness.

The Relevance of Emotional Resilience

In today's dynamic and often turbulent business environment, leaders must possess the capacity to navigate challenges with fortitude and grace. Emotional Resilience, an often overlooked aspect of leadership, goes beyond understanding emotions. It involves the capacity to bounce back from setbacks, handle stress, maintain a positive outlook in challenging situations, and more.

Understanding Emotional Resilience

Understanding emotional resilience necessitates a deep exploration of the complexities of human emotions. It involves recognizing and processing a wide range of feelings, from joy and enthusiasm to frustration and disappointment. Leaders with high emotional resilience exhibit a level of self-awareness that allows them to manage their emotions constructively.

In an era characterized by rapid technological advancements and shifting market landscapes, change is an inevitable force. Emotional resilience empowers leaders to not only embrace change but also to thrive amidst it. It enables them to lead their teams through periods of transition with confidence and stability, fostering a culture of adaptability and growth.

Adaptability is a critical leadership trait, and it is intrinsically linked to emotional resilience. Leaders who possess a high degree of emotional resilience are better equipped to adjust their strategies, perspectives, and approaches in response to evolving circumstances. They view change as an opportunity for growth rather than a threat.

Emotional resilience profoundly influences a leader's decision-making process. When faced with challenging situations or complex choices, emotionally resilient leaders maintain a clear and focused mindset. They are less likely to be swayed by impulsive reactions and instead approach decisions with thoughtful consideration.

Leaders with high emotional resilience have the capacity to create a positive and empowering organizational culture. Their ability to maintain composure in stressful situations sets a tone of stability and confidence for their teams. This, in turn, fosters an environment where individuals feel supported and motivated.

Leaders serve as role models for their teams, and their behavior sets a precedent for how challenges are approached. When leaders demonstrate emotional resilience, they inspire their teams to cultivate similar qualities. This creates a culture of resilience that permeates throughout the organization.

Emotional resilience plays a crucial role in managing conflicts and navigating complex interpersonal relationships. Leaders who are emotionally resilient are better equipped to address conflicts objectively, mediate disputes, and guide their teams towards constructive resolutions.

In the midst of adversity or setbacks, emotionally resilient leaders maintain a long-term perspective. They understand that short-term challenges are part of a larger journey towards organizational success. This clear perspective allows them to stay focused on strategic goals rather than becoming mired in immediate obstacles.

Every leader encounters failures and setbacks along their journey. Emotional resilience empowers leaders to view these experiences as learning opportunities rather than shortcomings or insurmountable obstacles. They bounce back from failures with a renewed sense of determination and insight.

Effective leadership requires the capacity to manage stress and prioritize well being. Emotionally resilient leaders have developed strategies for self-care and stress reduction. They understand the importance of maintaining their own well-being in order to lead effectively.

Emotional resilience fosters empathy and understanding towards others. Leaders who have experienced their own challenges and emotions are better able to connect with the experiences and perspectives of their team members. This empathy builds trust and rapport within the team.

Emotional resilience is not solely an inherent trait; it can be cultivated and strengthened through intentional practice. Leaders can engage in activities such as mindfulness, self-reflection, and stress management techniques to enhance their emotional resilience, and we'll discuss this in depth in Part 3, 'Embracing Resilience for Success.'

Emotionally resilient leaders view adversity as a powerful teacher. They extract valuable lessons from challenging experiences, gaining insights that inform their future decision-making and leadership approaches. This continuous cycle of learning and growth is fueled by their emotional resilience.

Emotional resilience involves the ability to manage internal dialogue and self-talk. Leaders with high emotional resilience practice positive self-talk, which enables them to maintain a constructive mindset even in the face of adversity. This inner dialogue reinforces their belief in their ability to overcome challenges.

Emotionally resilient leaders recognize the importance of a strong support network. They surround themselves with trusted advisors, mentors, and peers who offer guidance and perspective. This network serves as a source of encouragement and empowerment during challenging times.

Emotional resilience allows leaders to strike a balance between vulnerability and strength. They are open about their challenges and emotions, creating an environment where authenticity is valued. This transparency fosters trust and cultivates a culture of openness within the organization.

In times of crisis, emotionally resilient leaders excel in adaptive leadership. They remain composed under pressure, make informed decisions, and provide a sense of stability for their teams. Their ability to lead effectively in crisis situations is a testament to their emotional resilience.

Emotionally resilient leaders also play a pivotal role in cultivating resilience within their teams and throughout their organization. They provide support, guidance, and resources to help team members navigate challenges. This collective resilience strengthens the overall capacity of the organization to face adversity.

Emotional resilience sustains a leader's motivation and drive over the long term. It provides the inner fortitude needed to persevere through challenges and maintain a sense of purpose. Leaders with high emotional resilience are driven by a deep commitment to their vision and mission.

Understanding and cultivating emotional resilience is crucial for leaders in the 21st century. It empowers leaders to navigate complexity, make informed decisions, and inspire their teams and their organizations through challenges. Emotional resilience is not a static trait, but a dynamic capacity that can be honed and developed over time. By recognizing its significance and implementing strategies to enhance it, leaders can unlock their full potential and lead with authenticity, empathy, and effectiveness. In the sections that follow, we'll embark on subsequent exploration of the diverse dimensions of leadership intelligence, and will further highlight emotional resilience as a fundamental component of effective leadership in the modern era.

Harnessing Emotional Resilience for Effective Decision-Making

The significance of emotional resilience in leadership becomes even more pronounced when we consider its direct impact on decision-making. In the fast-paced, high-stakes environment of leadership, the ability to make sound, rational decisions is essential. Emotional resilience equips leaders with the mental fortitude and clarity needed to navigate complex choices.

One of the primary ways in which emotional resilience enhances decision-making is by mitigating the influence of impulsive reactions. In emotionally charged situations, leaders with low emotional resilience may be more prone to knee-jerk responses driven by heightened emotions. This can lead to hasty decisions that are not necessarily in the best interest of the organization or team.

Conversely, leaders with high emotional resilience have cultivated the capacity to step back and objectively assess situations, even in the midst of strong emotions. They recognize the importance of maintaining a clear and focused mindset when making decisions. This ability to detach from immediate emotional reactions allows them to consider a broader range of perspectives and potential outcomes.

Emotional resilience enables leaders to effectively manage uncertainty and ambiguity in decision-making. In a rapidly changing business environment, leaders are often faced with incomplete information and unpredictable variables. The ability to navigate this uncertainty with composure and confidence is a hallmark of emotionally resilient leadership.

Leaders with high emotional resilience are also adept at managing the inherent risks associated with decision-making. They understand that every decision carries a degree of risk, and they approach this reality with a balanced perspective. Rather than becoming paralyzed by the fear of making the wrong choice, they assess risks thoughtfully and take calculated, informed steps.

The capacity to learn from mistakes is another critical aspect of effective decision-making facilitated by emotional resilience. Leaders who possess this quality view setbacks and failures as opportunities for growth and learning. They do not dwell on past missteps, but instead, extract valuable lessons that inform their future decision-making processes.

In addition, emotional resilience fosters adaptability in decision-making. Leaders with this quality are more flexible and open-minded when faced with changing circumstances or unexpected developments. They are less likely to become entrenched in a specific course of action and more willing to pivot when necessary.

Emotionally resilient leaders also excel in managing decision fatigue, a common challenge in leadership roles. The mental and emotional strain of continuous decision-making can lead to fatigue, which, in turn, can impair judgment. Leaders with high emotional resilience implement strategies to mitigate decision fatigue, such as prioritization, delegation, and self-care.

Emotional resilience empowers leaders to communicate decisions effectively. They possess the ability to convey their choices with clarity, transparency, and empathy. This is particularly crucial in situations where decisions may be met with resistance or dissent. Emotionally resilient leaders navigate such scenarios with tact and professionalism, ensuring that their rationale is understood and respected.

The impact of emotionally resilient decision-making extends beyond individual choices; it shapes the organizational culture as well. Leaders who consistently make decisions from a place of emotional resilience set a tone of stability and confidence. This resonates throughout the organization, creating an environment where individuals feel assured in the direction set by their leaders.

Emotional resilience also plays a pivotal role in crisis management and decision-making. In high-pressure situations, leaders must make critical choices under intense scrutiny and time constraints. Emotionally resilient leaders are better equipped to maintain composure and clarity in these scenarios, guiding their teams towards effective responses.

As we venture deeper into the dimensions of leadership intelligence, we'll continue to unravel the dynamic interplay between emotional resilience and other critical intelligences that collectively sculpt the landscape of leadership in the 21st century. Above all, it's crucial to understand that harnessing emotional resilience is central to making effective decisions in leadership. It empowers leaders to approach choices with clarity, objectivity, and adaptability. Far from being a static trait, emotional resilience is a dynamic capacity that can be actively nurtured and honed over time. By acknowledging its significance and integrating practices to enhance it, leaders can enhance their decision-making prowess and lead with authenticity, empathy, and effectiveness.

The Limitations of Intellectual Intelligence (IQ)

The concept of intellectual intelligence, commonly referred to as IQ, has long been revered as a hallmark of cognitive prowess. It encompasses an individual's capacity for logical reasoning, problem-solving, abstract thinking, and pattern recognition. While undeniably valuable, it is essential to recognize that IQ, as a standalone metric, possesses inherent limitations.

Practical Scenarios and Complex Challenges

In practical scenarios, leaders are often confronted with complex challenges that necessitate a blend of analytical thinking and a broader, more holistic perspective. The standardized nature of IQ assessments tends to overlook certain forms of intelligence that are equally vital in leadership contexts. For instance, creativity, adaptability, and emotional resilience—each a critical component of effective leadership—are not comprehensively assessed by traditional IQ measures. Thus, while IQ provides valuable insights into an individual's intellectual capabilities, it does not offer a complete picture of their leadership potential.

Another limitation of IQ is its static nature. Traditionally, IQ scores were considered stable indicators of an individual's cognitive capacity, implying that intellectual abilities remained relatively constant throughout one's life. However, contemporary research has challenged this notion, highlighting the dynamic nature of cognitive development. It is now widely recognized that individuals can actively engage in practices and activities to enhance their intellectual capacities.

Furthermore, IQ assessments often focus on discrete cognitive tasks and fail to capture the integrative thinking required in real-world leadership scenarios. Leadership decisions seldom involve isolated cognitive functions; instead, they demand the synthesis of diverse information, consideration of multiple perspectives, and the ability to balance competing priorities. This integrative thinking requires a level of cognitive agility that extends beyond the scope of traditional IQ measures.

IQ also tends to underemphasize the role of practical wisdom, or the ability to apply knowledge effectively in real-world situations. This form of intelligence, often referred to as practical intelligence or "street smarts," is a critical asset in leadership. It encompasses skills such as adaptability, problem-solving in unstructured environments, and navigating complex social dynamics—capabilities that are not adequately captured by standardized IQ tests.

Moreover, IQ assessments tend to overlook the importance of context in evaluating cognitive abilities. What may constitute effective problem-solving in one domain or industry may not necessarily translate seamlessly to another. Leadership demands the capacity to adapt one's intellectual toolkit to the specific challenges and nuances of a given context. This contextual intelligence is a dynamic and adaptive form of intellectual capacity that extends beyond the scope of traditional IQ assessments.

It is also worth noting that IQ does not directly measure an individual's capacity for learning and growth. While it provides a snapshot of current cognitive abilities, it does not offer insights into an individual's potential for development. This is a critical consideration in leadership, as effective leaders are often characterized by their commitment to continuous learning and improvement.

The reliance on IQ as a primary indicator of intelligence may inadvertently reinforce a narrow definition of what constitutes valuable cognitive abilities. It may undervalue other forms of intelligence, such as creative thinking, emotional resilience, and practical intelligence, which are equally crucial in leadership contexts. This can lead to a skewed understanding of leadership potential and hinder the identification of individuals with diverse yet valuable intellectual strengths.

While IQ undoubtedly represents an important facet of cognitive capacity, it is imperative to recognize its limitations, particularly in the context of leadership. The dynamic and multifaceted nature of leadership demands a broader and more holistic approach to assessing intelligence. By acknowledging the boundaries of logical reasoning inherent in IQ, leaders can cultivate a more inclusive and comprehensive understanding of intelligence—one that encompasses a diverse range of cognitive, emotional, and practical capacities.

Real-World Application of Intelligence

As we've discussed in the previous section, the concept of intellectual intelligence, commonly referred to as IQ, has long been revered as a hallmark of cognitive prowess. However, IQ is insufficient and various intelligences beyond IQ, such as Analytical Intelligence (AQ), Ethical Intelligence (EthQ), Practical Intelligence (PQ), and Creative Intelligence (CrQ), are crucial for holistic cognitive development.

Analytical Intelligence involves the ability to analyze information, think critically, and make data-driven decisions. This type of intelligence is crucial in today's data-driven world where leaders need to process large volumes of information to make informed choices. AQ complements IQ by emphasizing the importance of systematic analysis and rational thinking.

Ethical Intelligence encompasses an individual's ability to make morally sound decisions. It involves understanding the ethical implications of actions and considering the broader impact on stakeholders and society. EthQ goes beyond IQ and emotional intelligence (EQ) by emphasizing the need for principled and value-based decision-making.

Practical Intelligence focuses on the ability to apply knowledge and skills in real-world contexts. This includes adaptability, common sense, and the capacity to navigate complex, dynamic environments. While IQ measures theoretical knowledge, PQ assesses a person's ability to effectively use that knowledge in practical situations.

Creative Intelligence involves the capacity to generate novel and innovative ideas, solutions, and approaches. It encompasses imagination, originality, and the ability to think "outside the box." CrQ transcends IQ by valuing unconventional thinking and encouraging exploration of multiple perspectives.

The Interplay of Multiple Intelligences

In the context of leadership, challenges rarely conform to neat categories of either intellectual (IQ-related) or emotional (EQ-related) nature. Instead, leaders often grapple with intricately layered issues that demand a multidimensional approach. It is precisely in this terrain that multi-intelligences and our conceptualization of the 8 Pillars of Intelligence prove invaluable, offering a comprehensive toolkit to navigate complexity.

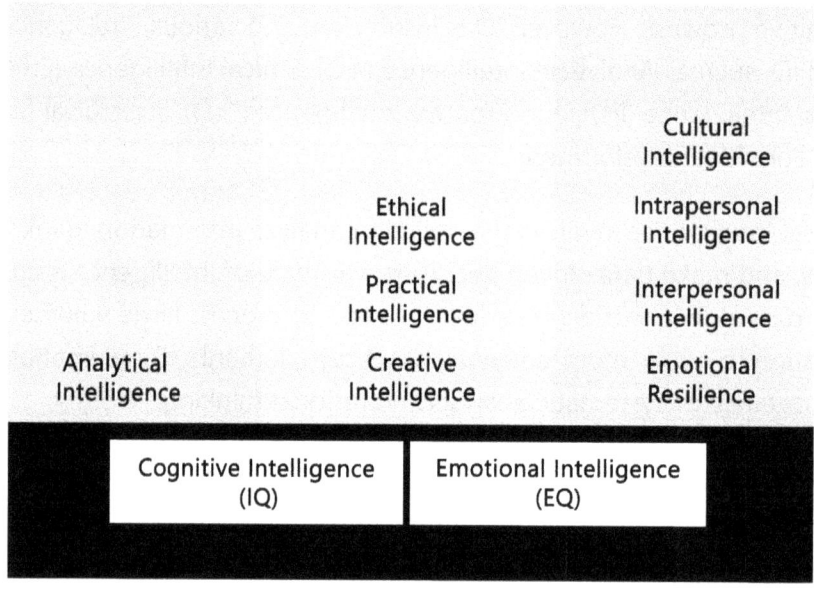

Figure 2. The interplay of multi-intelligences.

In today's globalized and swiftly evolving business environment, leaders must be adaptable and multifaceted. They are called upon to skillfully traverse diverse cultures, address ethical dilemmas, make judicious use of data, and foster a culture of innovation. Relying exclusively on IQ and EQ would be insufficient in equipping leaders for this multifaceted role.

In Figure 2, we illustrate the interplay between our multi-intelligences and the more conventional understanding of intelligence, shedding light on the specific domains where each of our multi-intelligences takes prominence. We show that our multi-intelligences extend beyond both IQ and EQ, while we simultaneously:

- Emphasize that analytical intelligence relies more heavily on cognitive processing, while also utilizing EQ.

- Emphasize that while emotional resilience is highly influenced by emotional intelligence (EQ), it also involves cognitive processes related to understanding and managing emotions.

- Cultural, Intrapersonal, and Interpersonal Intelligence are strongly influenced by emotional intelligence (EQ), but also involve cognitive aspects. Understanding different cultures and managing relationships requires both emotional and cognitive skills.

- Creativity, Practical, and Ethical Intelligence are not confined to either IQ or EQ but involve a combination of skills beyond both cognitive and emotional capacities.

The multi-intelligences we define, our 8 Pillars of Intelligence, foster adaptability and resilience, qualities that are crucial in a world characterized by uncertainty and change. Leaders with these intelligences are better equipped to pivot, learn from experiences, and thrive in dynamic environments.

In a competitive landscape, organizations require leaders who can drive innovation. CrQ, for example, plays a pivotal role in generating novel ideas and solutions, leading to breakthroughs and a competitive edge. Ethical lapses can have severe consequences for organizations. Leaders with a strong EthQ are better positioned to navigate ethical challenges, ensuring that decisions align with organizational values and societal norms. PQ is essential in ensuring that theoretical knowledge is translated into actionable strategies. Leaders who excel in PQ can streamline processes, optimize resource allocation, and enhance operational efficiency.

Effective leadership demands a harmonious integration of cognitive intelligence (IQ), emotional intelligence (EQ), and emotional resilience (ER). IQ pertains to problem-solving abilities, strategic acumen, and proficiency in making rational decisions, while EQ centers on recognizing, comprehending, and influencing emotions in oneself and others. On the other hand, emotional resilience involves the ability to bounce back from challenges, setbacks, and adversity, enabling leaders to maintain composure and adapt in demanding situations. This dynamic blend of IQ, EQ, and ER is essential in fostering a constructive and high-performing work environment.

Some additional strengths of the 8 Pillars of Leadership:

- Ethical Intelligence helps leaders recognize and mitigate unconscious biases, promoting fairness and inclusivity in decision-making processes.

- Practical Intelligence equips leaders with the ability to adapt to new technologies, market trends, and global challenges. This adaptability is essential for ensuring organizational relevance and sustainability.

- Cultural Intelligence is crucial in understanding and respecting different cultural norms, ensuring effective communication and collaboration.

- EQ and PQ play a significant role in assessing the long-term consequences of decisions. Leaders with these intelligences consider not only short-term gains but also the broader organizational impact over time.

The world presents leaders with multifaceted problems that often require a synthesis of different types of intelligence. Whether it's making ethically sound decisions in a data-driven context or finding innovative solutions to practical problems, a holistic approach is necessary to prepare leaders for success in today's dynamic and challenging world.

The Relevance of Analytical Intelligence Beyond IQ

Analytical Intelligence (AQ) transcends the boundaries of traditional Intellectual Intelligence (IQ) by incorporating a multifaceted approach to problem-solving. While IQ primarily measures cognitive abilities, AQ delves deeper into the realm of critical thinking, logical reasoning, and data interpretation. It goes beyond innate cognitive capacities and emphasizes the acquisition of skills that are invaluable in today's data-driven world.

AQ Empowers and Can be Refined

In a rapidly evolving global landscape, where data inundation is the norm, possessing high AQ is essential. It empowers individuals to sift through vast amounts of information, discern relevant patterns, and extract meaningful insights. This ability is critical for leaders who must make timely, well-informed decisions amidst a sea of data.

AQ is akin to a mental toolkit that equips individuals to dissect complex problems, identify underlying factors, and devise effective solutions. This skill set enables leaders to address challenges with a strategic perspective, considering not only immediate implications but also long-term consequences. It provides a structured framework for decision-making that IQ alone may not encompass.

AQ is a trainable attribute. Unlike IQ, which is relatively static, AQ can be honed and refined through deliberate practice and exposure to diverse problem-solving scenarios. Through activities, exercises and learning that mirror real-world challenges, individuals can sharpen their analytical prowess, enhancing their ability to tackle complex issues in their professional roles.

Leaders with high AQ possess the capacity to leverage technology to their advantage. In an era of advanced analytics and artificial intelligence, being adept at interpreting data and utilizing technological tools is crucial. AQ enables leaders to harness the power of data-driven insights, facilitating more accurate and efficient decision-making.

AQ is not confined to the realm of business and leadership. It extends its influence into various domains, including academia, research, policy-making, and even personal life. The ability to approach problems with a systematic, analytical mindset is a valuable asset across diverse fields, enhancing one's capacity to innovate and drive positive change.

In essence, AQ complements IQ by providing a practical, applicable dimension to intelligence. While IQ may provide a foundation of cognitive abilities, AQ equips individuals with the skills necessary to transform knowledge into action. It empowers leaders to navigate the complexities of the modern world, enabling them to make well-informed decisions that drive organizational success.

AQ in an Ever-Changing Landscape

AQ fosters adaptability and resilience. In an ever-changing landscape, leaders must be agile in their thinking and decision-making. They must be capable of assessing new information, adjusting strategies, and pivoting when necessary. AQ instills this flexibility, ensuring that leaders can navigate uncertainty with confidence and competence.

AQ promotes a culture of continuous learning and improvement. Leaders with high AQ are inclined towards seeking out new information, exploring different perspectives, and refining their problem-solving skills. This attitude of perpetual growth not only benefits the individual but also sets a precedent for a learning-oriented organizational culture.

Leaders with strong AQ are adept at transforming data into actionable knowledge. They possess the ability to discern relevant information from a sea of data, distilling it into insights that guide decision-making. This capacity is particularly vital in industries where data-driven strategies are crucial, such as finance, marketing, and technology.

AQ also plays a pivotal role in risk management. Leaders must be able to assess potential risks, evaluate their likelihood and impact, and formulate strategies to mitigate them. This requires a structured, analytical approach that goes beyond mere intuition. Leaders with high AQ are well-equipped to navigate risk scenarios, ensuring the sustainability and resilience of their organizations.

AQ Improves Teams and Organizations

At a team and organizational level, AQ fosters a culture of evidence-based decision-making. It encourages leaders to rely on empirical data and objective analysis rather than intuition or gut feelings. This approach not only leads to more accurate decisions but also enhances accountability and transparency within an organization.

In a rapidly evolving global economy, where innovation is key to gaining a competitive edge, AQ is indispensable. It enables leaders to identify emerging trends, evaluate disruptive technologies, and capitalize on new opportunities. This proactive stance towards innovation is essential for organizations seeking to stay ahead in their respective industries.

Additionally, AQ promotes effective communication. Leaders with high AQ are adept at distilling complex information into clear, concise messages that can be easily understood by diverse stakeholders. This skill is invaluable in ensuring that organizational objectives are effectively communicated and understood at all levels.

AQ also plays a crucial role in fostering a culture of continuous improvement. Leaders with high AQ are inclined towards seeking out new information, exploring different perspectives, and refining their problem-solving skills. This attitude of perpetual growth not only benefits the individual but also sets a precedent for a learning-oriented organizational culture.

This makes Analytical Intelligence (AQ) a pivotal dimension of intelligence that extends beyond the confines of traditional IQ. It equips leaders with the skills necessary to navigate complex, data-driven environments, fostering strategic excellence. Through a combination of critical thinking, logical reasoning, and data interpretation, AQ empowers individuals to make well-informed decisions that drive organizational success. It is a trainable attribute, allowing leaders to continuously enhance their analytical prowess. High AQ is not just advantageous – it is imperative for leadership excellence.

Intrapersonal Intelligence Transcends EQ

Intrapersonal intelligence transcends Emotional Intelligence (EQ) by encompassing a deeper understanding of oneself. While EQ primarily focuses on recognizing and managing emotions, intrapersonal intelligence offers a profound exploration of self-awareness and self-regulation, and an in-depth comprehension of one's values, strengths, and weaknesses. It allows individuals to navigate their inner landscapes, understand their motivations, and align their actions with their core principles.

Self-Improvement, Purpose and Determination

Intrapersonal intelligence empowers individuals to set meaningful goals and work towards them with purpose and determination. It involves self-reflection, introspection, and a profound awareness of personal aspirations. This level of self-knowledge and clarity enables individuals to make decisions and take actions that are in alignment with their long-term objectives.

Intrapersonal intelligence enables individuals to manage their internal dialogue effectively. It involves the ability to recognize and challenge self-limiting beliefs and negative thought patterns. This skill is crucial for maintaining a positive mindset, fostering resilience, and overcoming challenges.

Intrapersonal intelligence also plays a pivotal role in fostering emotional well-being. It involves the ability to regulate one's emotions, manage stress, and cultivate a sense of inner peace and contentment. This not only enhances mental and emotional health but also contributes to overall well-being and life satisfaction.

Intrapersonal intelligence is closely linked to motivation and self-drive. It involves the capacity to set and pursue meaningful goals, even in the face of obstacles or setbacks. Individuals with high intrapersonal intelligence are driven by a sense of purpose and derive satisfaction from achieving personal milestones.

Intrapersonal Intelligence in Leadership and Beyond

Intrapersonal intelligence is essential for effective leadership. Leaders who possess a deep understanding of themselves are better equipped to lead authentically and inspire others. They are aware of their strengths and areas for growth, enabling them to assemble complementary teams and delegate tasks effectively.

Intrapersonal intelligence:

- Fosters a growth mindset. It involves a willingness to learn, adapt, and continuously improve. Individuals with high intrapersonal intelligence are open to feedback, view challenges as opportunities for growth, and are committed to self-development.

- Enhances decision-making abilities. When individuals have a clear understanding of their values, priorities, and long-term objectives, they can make choices that align with their authentic selves. This leads to greater satisfaction and a sense of fulfillment in both personal and professional endeavors.

- Promotes a strong sense of self-confidence. Individuals who possess this intelligence recognize their worth and capabilities, allowing them to approach challenges with a positive outlook. This self-assuredness empowers them to take risks, pursue ambitious goals, and persevere in the face of adversity.

- Contributes to effective time management and productivity. By understanding their own working styles, preferences, and energy levels, individuals can structure their days in a way that optimizes their productivity. They are able to prioritize tasks, allocate resources efficiently, and achieve their goals with greater efficiency.

In personal and professional relationships, intrapersonal intelligence fosters authenticity. When individuals have a deep understanding of themselves, they are more likely to communicate openly and honestly. This level of authenticity cultivates trust and meaningful connections with others, both at home and at work.

When it comes to resilience and adaptability, intrapersonal intelligence is pivotal. Individuals who possess this intelligence are better equipped to bounce back from setbacks and adapt to change. They have a strong sense of self-belief and a clear sense of direction, which enables them to navigate challenges with grace and composure.

Intrapersonal intelligence also contributes to effective self-care practices. It involves recognizing one's own needs for rest, relaxation, and rejuvenation. This self-awareness allows individuals to implement self-care routines that promote physical, mental, and emotional well-being.

Overall, intrapersonal intelligence encompasses a comprehensive and multifaceted understanding of oneself that goes beyond the scope of Emotional Intelligence (EQ). It empowers individuals to navigate their inner landscapes, make informed decisions, set meaningful goals, and lead authentic and purpose-driven lives. This intelligence is a fundamental pillar of personal and professional success, contributing to self-confidence, effective communication, ethical decision-making, and overall well-being.

Interpersonal Intelligence Beyond EQ

Interpersonal intelligence goes beyond Emotional Intelligence (EQ) by encompassing a broader understanding of human interaction and relationships. While EQ focuses on individual emotions and their management, interpersonal intelligence delves into the dynamics of communication, empathy, and collaboration with others.

Dynamic Communication and Building Relationships

Effective communication is a central tenet of interpersonal intelligence. It involves not only expressing oneself clearly but also actively listening and understanding the perspectives of others. Individuals with high interpersonal intelligence are adept at adapting their communication style to suit different audiences and contexts.

Empathy is a key component of interpersonal intelligence. It involves the ability to understand and resonate with the emotions and experiences of others. This skill is essential for building trust, establishing rapport, and fostering positive relationships.

Interpersonal intelligence encompasses conflict resolution and negotiation skills. It involves the capacity to navigate disagreements, find common ground, and arrive at mutually satisfactory solutions. Leaders with high interpersonal intelligence are skilled at mediating conflicts within teams and facilitating productive discussions.

Moreover, interpersonal intelligence extends to cultural competence and inclusivity. It involves an awareness and appreciation of diverse perspectives, values, and cultural norms. Leaders with high interpersonal intelligence create inclusive environments where individuals from different backgrounds feel valued and respected.

Collaboration and teamwork are integral aspects of interpersonal intelligence. It involves the ability to work effectively with others towards a common goal. Leaders with high interpersonal intelligence are skilled at building cohesive teams, leveraging the strengths of team members, and fostering a culture of collaboration.

Interpersonal intelligence is crucial for networking and relationship-building. It involves the ability to establish and maintain meaningful connections with a diverse range of individuals. Leaders with high interpersonal intelligence are adept at building professional networks that can be leveraged for mutual benefit.

Leadership Beyond the Norms

Interpersonal intelligence plays a pivotal role in leadership influence and persuasion. It encompasses the ability to inspire and motivate others towards a shared vision or goal. Leaders with high interpersonal intelligence possess the charisma and communication skills to garner support and drive initiatives forward.

Interpersonal intelligence is instrumental in mentoring and coaching. It involves the capacity to understand the strengths and developmental areas of team members and provide constructive guidance for their growth. Leaders with high interpersonal intelligence are effective mentors who empower others to reach their full potential.

Adaptability in social situations is another hallmark of interpersonal intelligence. It involves the ability to read social cues and adjust one's behavior accordingly. Leaders with high interpersonal intelligence are perceptive to the needs and emotions of those around them, allowing them to navigate various social contexts with ease.

In group settings, interpersonal intelligence extends to emotional regulation. It involves the skill of maintaining composure and facilitating a positive emotional climate, even in challenging situations. Leaders with high interpersonal intelligence are adept at diffusing tension, promoting positivity, and creating a conducive atmosphere for collaboration.

Interpersonal intelligence aids in conflict prevention and management. It involves the ability to recognize potential sources of conflict and proactively address them. Leaders with high interpersonal intelligence are skilled at establishing open lines of communication and fostering a culture of transparency, which reduces the likelihood of conflicts arising.

Additionally, interpersonal intelligence is crucial in client and stakeholder relations. It encompasses the ability to understand and meet the needs of external parties, such as clients, customers, or stakeholders. Leaders with high interpersonal intelligence are adept at building and maintaining positive relationships that contribute to organizational success.

At a team and organizational level, interpersonal intelligence influences organizational culture and employee engagement. It involves creating an environment where individuals feel valued, heard, and supported. Leaders with high interpersonal intelligence prioritize employee well-being, leading to higher levels of job satisfaction, productivity, and retention.

Interpersonal intelligence also is integral in managing organizational change. It involves the ability to navigate the emotions and concerns of team members during periods of transition. Leaders with high interpersonal intelligence communicate change effectively, address concerns empathetically, and facilitate a smooth transition process.

Leaders with enhanced interpersonal intelligence are better at conflict transformation and peace-building. It involves the capacity to mediate and facilitate dialogue between groups or communities with differing perspectives or interests. This contributes to social cohesion and harmony within diverse contexts.

Thus, while Emotional Intelligence (EQ) is a vital component of effective leadership, Interpersonal Intelligence expands upon it by encompassing a comprehensive understanding of human interaction, relationships, and social dynamics. It empowers leaders to excel in:

- Communication

- Empathy

- Conflict resolution
- Cultural competence
- Collaboration
- Networking
- Influence
- Mentoring
- Adaptability
- Emotional regulation
- Conflict prevention
- Client relations
- Organizational culture
- Change management

It also empowers leaders to excel in even broader initiatives like conflict transformation and peace-building. By honing their Interpersonal Intelligence, leaders can truly excel in navigating the complex web of human relationships and interactions, ultimately driving success and positive impact within their organizations and communities.

Navigating Complex Challenges Beyond IQ and EQ

In the realm of leadership, navigating complex challenges requires a multifaceted approach that extends beyond the boundaries of intellectual intelligence (IQ) and emotional intelligence (EQ). In these situations, a blend of emotional resilience, practical intelligence, ethical intelligence, and other forms of intelligence proves indispensable.

One key limitation of relying solely on IQ and EQ is the potential oversight of practical intelligence (PQ), also known as "street smarts." Practical intelligence encompasses the ability to navigate real-world situations effectively, relying on adaptability, common sense, and the application of knowledge in practical contexts. This form of intelligence is particularly critical in dynamic, fast-paced environments where leaders must make quick, informed decisions based on a nuanced understanding of situational factors.

The exclusive focus on IQ and EQ may neglect the importance of cultural intelligence (CuQ) in today's globalized world. CuQ involves the ability to understand and effectively interact with people from diverse cultural backgrounds. Leaders who possess high CuQ are adept at navigating cultural nuances, demonstrating respect for diverse perspectives, and fostering inclusive environments. This form of intelligence is invaluable in international business settings and organizations with culturally diverse teams.

In addition to PQ and CuQ, ethical intelligence (EthQ) plays a pivotal role in guiding leaders through complex challenges. While IntraQ addresses emotional self-awareness and regulation, ethical intelligence delves into the realm of moral and principled decision-making. Leaders with high ethical intelligence demonstrate a strong sense of integrity, honesty, and a commitment to upholding ethical standards, even in the face of difficult choices. This form of intelligence serves as a compass for leaders, ensuring that their decisions align with values and principles.

Intrapersonal intelligence, which pertains to self-awareness and self-regulation, is a critical dimension that complements EQ. Leaders with high intrapersonal intelligence possess a deep understanding of their own emotions, strengths, weaknesses, and motivations. This self-awareness allows them to make informed decisions, manage stress, and navigate their own internal landscape effectively. Intrapersonal intelligence empowers leaders to lead authentically and with a clear sense of purpose.

Interpersonal intelligence, extending beyond EQ, focuses on understanding and navigating social dynamics, building and maintaining relationships, and influencing others positively. Leaders with high interpersonal intelligence excel in communication, negotiation, conflict resolution, and team building. They possess the ability to connect with others on a meaningful level, fostering a collaborative and productive work environment.

Additionally, analytical intelligence, encompassing critical thinking, logical reasoning, and problem-solving abilities, is an indispensable dimension in leadership. While IQ provides a foundation for analytical thinking, analytical intelligence involves the capacity to assess information, identify patterns, and make sound decisions based on evidence. Leaders who excel in analytical intelligence are adept at evaluating complex situations, identifying potential solutions, and making informed choices that drive organizational success.

While IQ and EQ are undoubtedly valuable components of leadership intelligence, they represent only a fraction of the broader spectrum of intelligences essential for navigating complex challenges. Practical intelligence, cultural intelligence, ethical intelligence, intrapersonal intelligence, interpersonal intelligence, and analytical intelligence collectively contribute to a leader's capacity to make informed, effective decisions. Embracing this multifaceted approach equips leaders with a diverse toolkit to address the intricacies of today's dynamic business landscape. By recognizing and cultivating these various intelligences, leaders can rise to the occasion, guiding their teams and organizations to success in the face of complexity and uncertainty.

Rethinking Leadership in the 21st Century

In the dynamic, interconnected world of the 21st century, leadership demands a more comprehensive and adaptable approach. This section emphasizes the need to move beyond singular intelligence models and embrace a multi-intelligence framework.

The Call for a Comprehensive Approach

As we continue to navigate the 21st century, the landscape of leadership has undergone a seismic shift. The demands placed on leaders today far exceed those of previous eras. In an age defined by rapid technological advancements, globalization, and unprecedented connectivity, leaders are tasked with navigating a complex web of challenges that require a nuanced and multifaceted approach.

The conventional models of leadership, which often emphasized hierarchical structures and top-down decision-making, are no longer sufficient. The call for a comprehensive approach to leadership arises from the recognition that the complexities of today's world necessitate a more inclusive, adaptable, and holistic style of leadership.

This rethinking of leadership extends beyond the confines of IQ and EQ, acknowledging that effective leadership encompasses a diverse array of intelligences. It acknowledges that leadership is not a one-size-fits-all endeavor, but rather a dynamic, context-dependent practice that demands a nuanced understanding of the ever-evolving organizational and global landscape.

The comprehensive approach to leadership embraces the notion that leaders are not solitary figures at the helm, but rather facilitators of collective intelligence and collaborative problem-solving. It recognizes that the strength of an organization lies not only in the capabilities of its individual leaders, but in the collective intelligence of its teams and the interconnectedness of its stakeholders.

This approach acknowledges that leadership is not confined to a select few at the top of the organizational hierarchy. Instead, it permeates every level of an organization, from frontline employees to middle management to executive leadership. Each member of the organization possesses a unique set of intelligences that, when harnessed effectively, contributes to the collective intelligence of the whole.

In this comprehensive paradigm, leaders are not solely defined by their titles or positions, but by their ability to inspire, empower, and facilitate growth and innovation within their teams. They are catalysts for positive change, fostering a culture of continuous learning, adaptability, and ethical conduct.

The call for a comprehensive approach also recognizes that leadership is not confined to the walls of the organization. Leaders must be attuned to the broader societal and global contexts in which their organizations operate. They must grapple with complex issues such as sustainability, diversity and inclusion, and ethical responsibility. This requires a heightened awareness of cultural, social, and political dynamics that impact the organization's mission and operations.

This approach emphasizes the importance of adaptability and agility in leadership. In a rapidly evolving world, leaders must be adept at responding to change, seizing opportunities, and navigating uncertainty. They must possess the capacity to pivot and recalibrate strategies in response to shifting market dynamics, technological disruptions, and unforeseen challenges.

The comprehensive approach to leadership is also rooted in the belief that leaders are not infallible, but are continuously learning and evolving. It encourages leaders to engage in ongoing self-reflection, seeking opportunities for growth and development. It invites leaders to be receptive to feedback, open to new perspectives, and willing to challenge their own assumptions and beliefs.

Indeed, the call for a comprehensive approach to leadership is an acknowledgement of the complexities and interdependencies of the 21st-century world. It calls upon leaders to transcend the confines of traditional models and embrace a more inclusive, adaptable, and holistic style of leadership. It challenges leaders to recognize and harness the diverse array of intelligences within themselves and their teams. In doing so, leaders can navigate the intricacies of today's dynamic business landscape with wisdom, agility, and a steadfast commitment to positive impact.

Embracing a Multi-Intelligence Framework

Embracing a multi-intelligence framework is the foundation of rethinking leadership in the 21st century. It signifies a departure from the traditional paradigm that narrowly defines intelligence as a singular, fixed entity. Instead, it heralds a new era of leadership that recognizes the diverse and dynamic nature of human capabilities.

This framework acknowledges that intelligence manifests in myriad forms, each with its unique strengths and contributions. From emotional resilience to practical wisdom, from creativity to analytical thinking, these intelligences collectively form a rich tapestry of human potential. Leaders who understand and leverage this diverse range of intelligences are poised to excel in the complex and rapidly evolving landscape of the modern world.

At the heart of the multi-intelligence framework lies the recognition that no single intelligence reigns supreme. Rather, each intelligence complements and augments the others, creating a synergistic effect that propels leaders to new heights of effectiveness. A leader may excel in emotional intelligence, for instance, but it is the integration of this emotional acumen with analytical thinking, resilience and practical wisdom that truly empowers them to make informed and impactful decisions.

The multi-intelligence framework invites leaders to recognize and cultivate the intelligences that may be less pronounced in their own skill set. It encourages a spirit of continuous learning and growth, as leaders seek to expand their proficiency across a broader spectrum of intelligences. This openness to development is a hallmark of agile and forward-thinking leadership.

Embracing a multi-intelligence framework also fosters a culture of inclusivity and diversity within organizations. It recognizes that individuals bring a wide array of intelligences to the table, and that the collective intelligence of a team is enriched by this diversity. Leaders who value and leverage the varied intelligences of their team members create environments where innovation thrives, and solutions emerge from a rich tapestry of perspectives.

This framework transcends the boundaries of organizational silos and hierarchies. It invites leaders to tap into the intelligences of stakeholders at every level, from front-line employees to middle management to executive leadership. By harnessing the collective intelligence of the entire organization, leaders can unlock a reservoir of creativity, problem-solving capacity, and adaptability.

One of the key tenets of the multi-intelligence framework is the acknowledgment that intelligence is not a fixed trait, but a malleable skill set that can be developed and refined over time. Through intentional practice, focused learning, reflective exercises, and more, leaders can enhance their proficiency across a range of intelligences. This commitment to growth is an essential characteristic of leaders who thrive in the dynamic and unpredictable landscape of the 21st century.

The multi-intelligence framework is deeply attuned to the human element of leadership. It recognizes that leadership is not solely about processes, systems, or metrics, but about the individuals who comprise an organization. It emphasizes the importance of understanding and connecting with the emotional, psychological, and social dimensions of leadership, recognizing that these factors profoundly influence organizational dynamics and outcomes.

Embracing a multi-intelligence framework is a paradigm shift that transcends the limitations of traditional models of leadership. It heralds an era of leadership that celebrates the diverse and dynamic nature of human potential. Leaders who adopt this framework are poised to excel in the complex and rapidly evolving landscape of the modern world. They are equipped to navigate uncertainty, inspire innovation, and foster cultures of continuous learning and growth. By embracing a multi-intelligence framework, leaders forge a path toward a new era of leadership excellence and impact.

Setting the Stage for a Holistic Approach

In the ever-evolving landscape of leadership, a holistic approach that integrates various dimensions of intelligence is crucial. This approach acknowledges that leadership is a multifaceted endeavor that transcends the boundaries of singular capabilities. Rather, it requires a dynamic interplay of intelligences, each contributing its unique strengths to the collective tapestry of leadership prowess.

By adopting this comprehensive approach, leaders leverage the synergy between emotional resilience and analytical thinking to achieve unprecedented success. Emotional resilience serves as the foundation for effective leadership, empowering leaders to navigate intricate and emotionally charged situations with grace and composure. It grants them the ability to endure challenges, recover from setbacks, and stay resolutely focused on the broader vision. When complemented by analytical thinking, this emotional fortitude transforms into a formidable tool for making informed decisions and crafting strategic plans.

Contrary to a common misconception, emotional resilience is not synonymous with imperturbability. It does not imply an absence of emotion, but rather the ability to understand, manage, and channel emotions constructively. A leader with emotional resilience recognizes that emotions are a natural part of the human experience, and that acknowledging and processing them is essential for effective leadership. This self-awareness empowers them to respond thoughtfully rather than react impulsively, fostering an environment of trust and stability.

Analytical thinking complements emotional resilience by providing a structured framework for processing information and making decisions. It involves the ability to critically evaluate data, discern patterns, and synthesize insights. When integrated with emotional resilience, analytical thinking ensures that decisions are not driven solely by emotion, but are informed by evidence and reason and not altered by setbacks or challenges. This synergy between emotional resilience and analytical thinking forms a central tenet of effective leadership.

The synergy between emotional resilience and analytical thinking transcends the confines of individual leadership. It permeates organizational culture, influencing how teams collaborate, make decisions, and respond to setbacks and challenges. A culture that values emotional resilience and analytical thinking fosters an environment where innovation flourishes, conflicts are resolved constructively, and individuals feel empowered to contribute their unique perspectives.

In times of crisis and change, the interplay of emotional resilience and analytical thinking is particularly salient. When faced with uncertainty or adversity, leaders must draw upon their emotional resilience to provide a steady and reassuring presence. Simultaneously, they must engage their analytical thinking to assess the situation, formulate a strategic response, and guide their team toward a positive outcome. This dynamic interplay ensures that decisions are not made impulsively or driven by fear, but are grounded in a clear understanding of the situation.

The dynamic relationship between emotional resilience and analytical thinking underscores the critical role of self-care for leaders. It recognizes that maintaining emotional well-being is not a luxury, but a strategic imperative. Leaders who make self-care a priority are better equipped to navigate the challenges of leadership and to model healthy coping mechanisms for their team. This commitment to self-care is a defining trait of leaders who lead with authenticity and long-term sustainability.

Setting the stage for a holistic approach to leadership involves recognizing the dynamic interplay between emotional resilience and analytical thinking. It acknowledges that effective leadership requires a nuanced understanding of emotions, coupled with a structured approach to decision-making. This interplay permeates organizational culture, influencing how teams collaborate and respond to challenges. In times of crisis and change, it provides a steady and strategic foundation for leadership.

This interplay underscores the importance of self-care, recognizing that a leader's emotional well-being is a critical factor in their ability to lead effectively. By embracing this holistic approach, leaders position themselves to excel in the complex and dynamic landscape of the 21st century.

Cultivating a Balanced Leadership Intelligence Profile

In the pursuit of effective leadership, it is imperative to recognize that intelligence is not a one-dimensional construct. Rather, it encompasses a diverse array of capacities that collectively contribute to a leader's proficiency. Cultivating a balanced leadership intelligence profile involves the deliberate development and integration of various intelligences, ensuring that they harmonize and complement one another.

Central to this endeavor is the recognition that emotional intelligence and intellectual intelligence are not mutually exclusive. They are not in opposition, but rather, they can coexist and mutually reinforce one another. Leaders with a balanced intelligence profile understand that emotions are not antithetical to reason, but rather, they provide vital information that informs rational decision-making. They recognize that intellect devoid of emotional insight can lead to decisions devoid of human context.

Beyond emotional resilience and analytical thinking, discussed in the previous section, a balanced leadership intelligence profile requires many things, including a commitment to ongoing self-reflection and development. It entails a willingness to engage in practices that enhance emotional resilience, such as mindfulness, stress management, and self-awareness exercises. It also involves honing analytical thinking skills through structured problem-solving, critical evaluation, and exposure to diverse perspectives. This dedication to self-improvement is not a static endeavor but an evolving journey.

A balanced leadership intelligence profile is characterized by adaptability and openness to new ideas. It recognizes that intelligence is not a fixed entity, but a malleable skill set that can be refined and expanded over time. Leaders with this profile approach challenges with a growth mindset, viewing setbacks as opportunities for learning and development. They embrace change as a catalyst for innovation, rather than a threat to the status quo.

In cultivating a balanced intelligence profile, leaders must also consider the role of practical intelligence. Often referred to as "street smarts," practical intelligence encompasses the ability to navigate real-world situations effectively. It involves skills such as adaptability, common sense, and the application of knowledge in practical contexts. Leaders with a balanced intelligence profile understand that success in the complex landscape of leadership requires more than theoretical knowledge—it demands a keen understanding of how to translate knowledge into action.

Cultural intelligence, another essential facet, is integral in today's globalized world. It encompasses the ability to understand and effectively interact with individuals from diverse cultural backgrounds. Leaders with a balanced intelligence profile approach cultural differences with curiosity and respect, recognizing that diverse perspectives enrich decision-making and problem-solving. They actively seek to bridge cultural divides, fostering environments of inclusivity and collaboration.

Intrapersonal intelligence, the capacity for self-awareness and self-regulation, is another linchpin of a balanced leadership intelligence profile. Leaders with this proficiency possess a deep understanding of their own emotions, strengths, weaknesses, and motivations. This self-awareness enables them to lead authentically, aligning their actions with their values and principles. It also empowers them to recognize when self-care is necessary, preventing burnout and fostering sustained effectiveness.

Interpersonal intelligence, extending beyond emotional intelligence, encompasses the ability to understand and navigate social dynamics. Leaders with a balanced intelligence profile excel in building and maintaining relationships, and they possess the capacity to positively influence others. This proficiency extends to skills such as effective communication, negotiation, and conflict resolution. It allows leaders to create environments where individuals thrive and collaborate harmoniously.

Ethical intelligence, anchored in principles of integrity, honesty, and responsibility, is the bedrock of a balanced leadership intelligence profile. It goes beyond theoretical knowledge of ethics and demands a commitment to ethical conduct in practice. Leaders with this proficiency consistently make decisions that align with their values, setting a standard of integrity for their team and organization.

A balanced leadership intelligence profile places a premium on analytical intelligence. This encompasses critical thinking, logical reasoning, and problem-solving abilities. Leaders with this proficiency excel in assessing information, identifying patterns, and making sound decisions based on evidence. They approach complex challenges with a methodical and analytical mindset, ensuring that decisions are well-informed and strategic.

Cultivating a balanced leadership intelligence profile involves a deliberate and holistic approach to leadership development. It recognizes the interplay of multi-intelligences, understanding that they can mutually reinforce one another. It embraces ongoing self-improvement and a growth mindset, viewing challenges as opportunities for learning. It integrates practical, cultural, intrapersonal, interpersonal, ethical, and analytical intelligences, recognizing their collective contribution to effective leadership. By nurturing a balanced intelligence profile, leaders position themselves to excel in the complex and dynamic landscape of the 21st century.

Holistic Intelligence—A Comprehensive Model of Intelligence

By now, it should be evident that while IQ measures cognitive abilities and EQ assesses emotional awareness, these metrics offer only a limited glimpse into human capabilities. The true nature of intelligence is remarkably diverse and intricate, spanning a spectrum of distinct dimensions. Visualizing this paradigm shift, Figure 3 illustrates how these multiple intelligences extend beyond the conventional EQ vs IQ framework, revealing a more comprehensive model of human intelligence, which we'll refer to as Holistic Intelligence.

Holistic Intelligence is a comprehensive model that demonstrates how the 8 Pillars of Intelligence transcend conventional notions of cognitive and emotional intelligence within leadership. This signifies that human intelligence is not confined to cognitive and emotional realms alone.

Holistic Intelligence

- Analytical Intelligence
- Ethical Intelligence
- Interpersonal Intelligence
- Intrapersonal Intelligence
- Cultural Intelligence
- Practical Intelligence
- Creative Intelligence
- Emotional Resilience

Emotional Intelligence (EQ) | Cognitive Intelligence (IQ)

Figure 3. Holistic Intelligence.

Positioned at the base of the diagram, IQ and EQ are acknowledged as crucial elements of intelligence. However, they are portrayed as foundational blocks rather than the sole determinants of a person's intellectual capacity.

By incorporating the eight pillars, the diagram advocates for a more holistic comprehension of intelligence. Each pillar represents a unique facet of human capability, including self-awareness, social adeptness, problem-solving skills, creativity, adaptability, cultural sensitivity, ethical decision-making, and emotional resilience.

The diagram illustrates that these multiple intelligences often intersect and interact, emphasizing the dynamic nature of human intelligence. For instance, emotional resilience intelligence may intertwine with interpersonal intelligence in scenarios requiring adept conflict resolution.

The diagram not only challenges the conventional EQ vs IQ paradigm but also serves as a visual representation of the rich tapestry of human intelligence. It invites us to recognize and celebrate the diversity of intelligences that collectively contribute to our multifaceted capacities. Embracing this expanded perspective empowers individuals to harness their full range of capabilities and fosters a deeper appreciation for the complexity of human potential.

Thus, 'holistic intelligence' refers to a comprehensive framework of intelligence, which embraces the spectrum of multi-intelligences. These include analytical intelligence, ethical intelligence, interpersonal intelligence, intrapersonal intelligence, cultural intelligence, practical intelligence, creative intelligence, and emotional resilience—collectively known as the '8 Pillars of Leadership.' Additionally, it encompasses both emotional and cognitive intelligence. Thus, holistic intelligence encapsulates a broad array of cognitive and emotional capacities, presenting not only a complete reflection of intelligence but also a nuanced understanding of what today's holistic leaders require for success in the dynamic landscape of leadership.

Transformative Potential: How Holistic Intelligence Can Reshape Lives

Never underestimate the transformative power of the leadership intelligence we explore in this book. It has the potential not only to elevate your professional life but also to profoundly impact your personal journey. Exceptional leaders, honing the multi-intelligences discussed in this book, have the capacity to become remarkable human beings. Grace and compassion, virtues the world thirsts for, can blossom in their wake. This sentiment finds resonance in a true story.

During our extensive travels, my wife and I found ourselves residing in a palace on the tranquil shores of Lake Constance in Germany. This choice was deliberate, as it provided us the opportunity to embark on diverse train journeys, each leading to unique destinations. It was during one of these vibrant train journeys, in a bustling carriage, that we had the privilege of encountering young Mateo, a curious soul of about five years. Seated across from us were his parents, flanked by his two adoring younger sisters.

Mateo was a whirlwind of activity, hardly sitting still. He clambered up and down seats, playfully jostling his sisters to make space for himself, navigating from one seat to the next with uncontainable exuberance. The father's expression betrayed a mix of exasperation and affectionate resignation, while the mother teetered on the brink of tears, her patience wearing thin. Unfazed, my wife and I observed the lively scene, unruffled by Mateo's spirited antics.

The mother, apologetic for Mateo's vivacity, finally confided, "It's the Down Syndrome. We struggle to contain him, and he seldom heeds our pleas. It's the Down Syndrome." With a quiet assurance, I responded, "It's alright. He's just a little boy, exuberant and full of energy. Boys, you know, love to engage with the world in their own dynamic way. They revel in playfully teasing their sisters."

At that moment, Mateo's mother broke into tears. Through her sobs, she confessed, "No, it's the Down Syndrome. We find it so hard to manage him, and he seems so distant. He has Downs." All along, I was aware of Mateo's condition, as my own daughter is blessed with the same extra chromosome. I gently took her hand in mine and murmured, "I understand. My daughter also has Down Syndrome. It's not the condition, it's just Mateo being himself, reveling in the joy of childhood."

More tears flowed from Mateo's mother. I knew that the country she hailed from in Europe offered scant support for parents of children with Down Syndrome. So, I began sharing the remarkable journey of my daughter, the challenges we've faced, and the triumphs we've celebrated together. Our conversation flowed seamlessly for about an hour, and when the train reached its final destination, Mateo's mother enveloped my wife and me in a warm embrace. Overflowing with gratitude, she thanked us for irrevocably altering her perspective, for we had gifted her a renewed understanding of resilience in the face of adversity, and a newfound appreciation for the beauty that radiates from every unique individual, regardless of their circumstances.

A New Era of Leadership

As we embark on this transformative journey into a new era of leadership, it is important to approach this endeavor with a sense of anticipation and purpose. The path that lies ahead promises to be one of profound growth, learning, and evolution. It is a journey that invites us to shed the constraints of outdated paradigms and embrace a more expansive and nuanced understanding of leadership intelligence.

This transformative journey begins with a willingness to challenge preconceived notions and question established norms. It calls for a departure from the familiar territories of IQ and EQ and invites us to explore the untapped potential of emotional resilience, practical intelligence, ethical intelligence, and cultural intelligence, among others. It beckons us to cultivate a deeper awareness of our own strengths, limitations, and motivations, laying the foundation for a more authentic and impactful leadership style.

As we navigate this transformative journey, we do so with a sense of curiosity and open-mindedness. We recognize that the landscape of leadership is dynamic and ever-evolving, shaped by an array of external forces, from technological advancements to shifts in societal values. This recognition prompts us to approach our roles as leaders with a spirit of continuous learning and adaptation.

The journey ahead also invites us to reflect on the profound impact that leadership can have on individuals, teams, and organizations. It underscores the responsibility we bear as stewards of collective progress and success. This awareness propels us to lead with a sense of purpose, guided by a commitment to ethical conduct, inclusivity, and the greater good.

Anticipating the transformative journey ahead, we acknowledge that it will not be without its challenges. It will call on us to confront our own biases and assumptions, to navigate the complexities of diverse perspectives, and to grapple with the inherent uncertainties of leadership. Yet, it is precisely through these challenges that we will find the richest opportunities for growth and development.

This transformative journey is not a solitary endeavor; it is a collective odyssey that we undertake in concert with our teams and organizations. It invites us to foster a culture of learning, empowerment, and mutual respect, where every individual has the opportunity to contribute their unique insights and talents. It is a journey that celebrates diversity of thought and perspective, recognizing that it is through this diversity that we unlock the full spectrum of human potential.

As we anticipate the transformative journey ahead, we do so with a sense of optimism and possibility. We recognize that the challenges we face are matched by the boundless opportunities for innovation, impact, and positive change. It is a journey that invites us to envision a future of leadership that transcends the confines of traditional paradigms, one that is characterized by adaptability, resilience, and a deep commitment to the well-being of all stakeholders.

Now as we stand on the threshold of this transformative journey, we do so with a sense of purpose and anticipation. Our mission extends beyond redefining leadership for the 21st century; we aspire to completely reimagine it. We are setting out to chart a course that not only acknowledges but celebrates the profound richness of human intelligence and potential. Together, we shall venture into uncharted territories, daring to break new ground. In doing so, we aim not only to be effective leaders in the traditional sense, but to also serve as inspirers, empowerers, and elevators of those we have the privilege to lead. The path that lies ahead is one of boundless possibility, and we approach it with open hearts and an unwavering commitment to the pursuit of excellence in leadership.

Part 3. Embracing Resilience for Success

As we delve into the heart of this book, you're about to embark on a profound exploration of emotional resilience for success in business leadership. This section is the comprehensive core, meticulously crafted to equip you with the invaluable insights and strategies needed to navigate the complexities of the business world with unwavering resilience. It's a transformative journey that will empower you to not only overcome challenges but to thrive in the ever-evolving landscape of modern leadership.

As you stand before these majestic peaks, let the grandeur of the Bernese Alps remind you of the heights you're capable of reaching. The mountains, resolute and unyielding, mirror the challenges that await in the realm of business leadership. Yet, like the clouds that dance around their summits, every obstacle is a passing moment in the broader expanse of your journey.

The midday sun casts its brilliance, illuminating the path ahead. Just as it pierces through the clouds, your resilience shines through adversity. This section, 'Embracing Resilience for Success in Business Leadership,' is your guide through the craggy terrains of the modern business world. It is meticulously crafted to fortify you with the wisdom and strategies needed to not only weather storms but to rise higher in the face of them.

With each page turned, you ascend further, drawing strength from the very challenges that stand before you. Remember, the summit is not the end but a vantage point for even greater vistas. Embrace this transformative journey, for within these pages lie the keys to thriving amidst the evolving landscape of modern leadership.

Cultivating Emotional Resilience

Now let's delve into the intricacies of cultivating emotional resilience in leadership. We cover the fundamental understanding of emotional resilience, its crucial role in navigating challenges, and provides actionable strategies and exercises for building and sustaining resilience over time. The addition of case studies and a section on measurement further enriches the content.

> **Author's Note** While we endeavor to cover Emotional Resilience comprehensively, it is an extensive topic that cannot be fully encapsulated within a single book. That's why you'll discover additional resources on this subject in my Empowered Leadership© & Inspirational Journeys© Mastery Series.

The Resilient Soul: A Guiding Affirmation

In the ebb and flow of life, I find my center. Through trials and triumphs, I stand strong, guided by an inner light. I trust in the wisdom of the universe, knowing that every challenge is a lesson, every setback a setup for a comeback. I am anchored in love, compassion, and grace, for these are the foundations of my resilience. With each breath, I embrace the present moment, surrendering the past and the future. I am a vessel of strength, a beacon of light, and I rise above adversity with grace and courage. I am resilient, I am whole, I am at peace.

Affirmation Instructions

1. **Find a Quiet Space**   Choose a quiet and comfortable space where you can sit or stand without distractions. This could be a corner of your room, a peaceful outdoor spot, or anywhere you feel at ease.
2. **Take a Moment to Breathe**   Begin by taking a few deep and calming breaths. Inhale slowly through your nose, allowing your lungs to fill with air, and then exhale gently through your mouth. Let go of any tension in your body.

3. **Repeat the Mantra Aloud or Silently** Start repeating the mantra either aloud or in your mind. Feel the words resonate within you. You can say it slowly and deliberately, or at a pace that feels natural to you.

4. **Focus on the Meaning** As you say the mantra, reflect on the meaning behind the words. Allow them to sink in and resonate with your inner being. Consider how each phrase relates to your own journey and experiences.

5. **Visualize Resilience** As you repeat the mantra, visualize yourself embodying resilience. Picture yourself facing challenges with strength, grace, and a sense of inner peace. See yourself rising above adversity.

6. **Embrace the Present Moment** Allow the mantra to ground you in the present moment. Let go of worries about the past or future, and simply be present with the affirmation of your own resilience.

7. **Close with Gratitude** When you feel ready, conclude the practice with a moment of gratitude. Acknowledge your own inner strength and the wisdom that guides you. Take this sense of resilience with you as you continue your journey.

8. **Return to the Mantra When Needed** Whenever you feel moments of doubt, stress, or a need for inner strength, return to this mantra. Use it as a source of inspiration and a reminder of your own capacity for resilience.

Remember, this mantra is a tool for self-reflection, empowerment, and renewal. Feel free to adapt it or personalize it to make it resonate more deeply with your own spiritual beliefs and experiences.

This mantra serves as a steadfast companion, offering you a focal point to keep your vision clear and your spirit resilient, especially during moments when you may need to regain your focus and inner strength.

Defining Emotional Resilience in Leadership

Emotional resilience is a bedrock of effective leadership. It encompasses the ability to weather storms, navigate uncertainties, and bounce back from challenges. In the context of leadership, emotional resilience goes beyond simply enduring; it involves maintaining composure, making reasoned decisions, and leading with clarity even amid intense pressure.

Emotional Resilience: A Dynamic Trait

At its essence, emotional resilience entails harnessing one's emotions as a source of strength and wisdom. It entails recognizing and processing difficult emotions rather than suppressing or being overwhelmed by them. Leaders with emotional resilience can remain steady and composed, inspiring confidence and trust in their team, even during turbulent times.

It's important to understand that emotional resilience does not imply an absence of emotions. Instead, it implies a healthy relationship with one's emotions. Leaders with high emotional resilience possess keen self-awareness regarding their emotional state and are adept at regulating their responses. They can distinguish between transient emotional reactions and more enduring emotional states, allowing them to make decisions with a clear mind.

In the realm of leadership, emotional resilience manifests in various ways. It empowers leaders to communicate effectively, even in challenging situations. It enables them to navigate conflicts and disagreements with grace and tact. It also facilitates the ability to motivate and inspire team members, providing a stabilizing force in times of uncertainty.

Emotional resilience is not a static quality but a dynamic trait that can be cultivated and strengthened over time. It involves the conscious development of emotional intelligence, which includes self-awareness, self-regulation, empathy, and interpersonal skills. Through deliberate practice and reflection, leaders can enhance their capacity for emotional resilience, enabling them to lead with greater efficacy and impact.

The Role of Emotional Resilience in Authentic Leadership

Emotional resilience is a foundational element of authentic leadership. It enables leaders to lead from a place of authenticity, remaining true to their values and principles even in the face of adversity. This authenticity fosters trust and credibility, which are essential for effective leadership.

Leaders who possess emotional resilience are also more adept at managing change and uncertainty. They have the capacity to adapt to evolving circumstances and guide their teams through transitions. This is particularly critical in today's fast-paced and constantly changing business environment, where the ability to navigate change is a key determinant of organizational success.

Defining emotional resilience in leadership is crucial to understanding its significance. It involves harnessing emotions as a source of strength and wisdom, rather than being dominated by them. This trait is characterized by self-awareness, self-regulation, empathy, and effective interpersonal skills. Cultivating emotional resilience is an ongoing process that requires conscious effort and reflection. As an essential component of authentic leadership, emotional resilience equips leaders to navigate challenges, inspire their teams, and drive organizational success. Understanding and cultivating emotional resilience is a crucial step toward becoming a more effective and impactful leader.

Key Components of Emotional Resilience

Emotional resilience is a multi-dimensional intelligence that pertains to an individual's capacity to bounce back from adversity, setbacks, and challenges. It encompasses a range of characteristics and skills that enable individuals to maintain their emotional well-being and effectively navigate high-pressure situations, including:

- **Adaptability**   Emotional resilience involves the ability to adapt to changing circumstances and remain composed under pressure. It allows individuals to think rationally and make sound decisions even in challenging situations.

- **Positive Outlook**   Resilient individuals tend to maintain a positive perspective even when faced with adversity. They possess an optimistic outlook, which helps them see opportunities in challenges.

- **Problem-Solving Skills**   Emotional resilience is associated with effective problem-solving abilities. Resilient individuals approach challenges with a solution-oriented mindset, seeking ways to overcome obstacles.

- **Emotional Regulation**   This aspect of resilience involves the ability to manage and regulate one's emotions. It enables individuals to maintain a level-headed approach, even in emotionally charged situations.

- **Persistence and Determination**   Resilient individuals demonstrate persistence and determination in the face of setbacks. They do not easily give up, but rather, they persevere in their efforts to achieve their goals.

- **Coping Mechanisms**   Emotional resilience involves having a repertoire of healthy coping mechanisms to manage stress and adversity. This may include practices such as mindfulness, exercise, or seeking support from others.

- **Self-Reflection**   Resilient individuals engage in self-reflection to gain insight into their emotions, behaviors, and thought patterns. This self-awareness helps them make adjustments and learn from challenging experiences.

- **Optimism and Hope** Emotional resilience is closely linked to an optimistic outlook and a sense of hope for the future. Resilient individuals believe in their ability to overcome challenges and move forward.

While emotional resilience and emotional intelligence (EQ) are related, they represent distinct dimensions of intelligence. Emotional intelligence provides critical insights into understanding and managing emotions; emotional resilience serves as the foundational strength that allows individuals and leaders to navigate the complexities and challenges of the modern world. Together, these intelligences form a powerful toolkit for personal and professional growth.

From Self-awareness to Empathy

At the core of emotional resilience is self-awareness. This involves recognizing and understanding one's own emotions, as well as how they influence thoughts, behaviors, and decision-making. Leaders with high levels of self-awareness are attuned to their emotional responses, allowing them to respond thoughtfully rather than react impulsively in challenging situations.

Emotional resilience also entails the ability to regulate one's emotions. This means being able to manage intense or distressing emotions in a constructive manner. Leaders who excel in emotional regulation can maintain composure under pressure, think clearly, and make well-considered decisions, even in high-stress situations.

Empathy is a critical component of emotional resilience, as it involves understanding and relating to the emotions and experiences of others. Leaders who demonstrate empathy are more adept at building strong, trusting relationships with their team members. This fosters a supportive and collaborative work environment, which is essential for weathering challenges collectively.

From Adaptability to Coping Mechanisms

Another key aspect of emotional resilience is adaptability. This component involves the capacity to adjust to changing circumstances and bounce back from setbacks. Leaders who are adaptable can navigate uncertainties with grace and maintain a forward-looking perspective, even in the face of adversity.

Optimism is the ability to maintain a positive outlook, even in challenging situations. It involves viewing setbacks as temporary and surmountable rather than insurmountable obstacles. Leaders who possess a healthy dose of optimism inspire hope and confidence in their team members, creating a more resilient and motivated workforce.

Emotional resilience encompasses the ability to employ constructive coping mechanisms in response to stress or adversity. This may include practices like mindfulness, deep breathing exercises, or engaging in activities that promote relaxation and self-care. These coping mechanisms help leaders recharge and regain perspective, enhancing their capacity to lead effectively.

From Problem-solving to Growth Mindset

Leaders with emotional resilience are adept problem solvers. They can approach challenges with a solution-oriented mindset, breaking down complex issues into manageable steps. This component is closely tied to analytical intelligence, as it involves critical thinking and logical reasoning to identify and implement effective solutions.

Having a strong support network is a crucial component of emotional resilience. This includes trusted colleagues, mentors, friends, and family members who can provide guidance, encouragement, and a listening ear during challenging times. Leaders who cultivate a supportive network are better equipped to navigate difficulties and maintain their emotional well-being.

Engaging in regular self-reflection and self-care practices is integral to emotional resilience. This involves taking time to assess one's emotions, experiences, and responses, as well as prioritizing activities that promote mental and emotional well-being. Leaders who prioritize self-care are better equipped to handle the demands of leadership with equanimity.

Emotional resilience is also associated with a growth mindset. Leaders who view challenges as opportunities for learning and growth are more likely to bounce back from setbacks and approach difficulties with a sense of curiosity and determination.

Thus, the components of emotional resilience encompass self-awareness, emotional regulation, empathy, adaptability, optimism, effective coping mechanisms, problem-solving skills, social support, reflection, and a growth mindset. These components work in tandem to equip leaders with the capacity to navigate challenges, inspire their teams, and lead with resilience and effectiveness. Understanding and cultivating these components is central to developing robust emotional resilience in leadership.

Differentiating Emotional Resilience from Emotional Intelligence

When we delve into the realm of teaching emotional resilience, it's not uncommon for individuals to draw parallels with discussions on Emotional Intelligence (EQ). They often remark, 'This sounds quite like a discussion on Emotional Intelligence, doesn't it?' To this, we nod in agreement, acknowledging the connection. Indeed, at its core, emotional resilience can be seen as an intelligence that encompasses EQ. However, it's vital to recognize that emotional resilience goes beyond EQ. It involves cognitive processes dedicated to comprehending and managing emotions, synergizes with various other intelligences, and ultimately transcends EQ itself.

Our intention isn't to replace or diminish the significance of what emotional intelligence teachings have brought to the world. Instead, we aim to underscore that when combined, emotional intelligence and emotional resilience form a dynamic duo for effective leadership and personal growth. With this perspective in mind, let's explore specific instances that vividly demonstrate how emotional resilience stretches beyond emotional intelligence. These instances equip individuals and leaders with the mindset and tools needed to not just navigate, but thrive in the face of challenging and demanding situations. In doing so, we'll underscore how this powerful combination drives effective leadership and fosters personal and professional growth.

ER vs. EQ: Understanding the Distinction

Emotional resilience is the capacity to navigate and bounce back from adversity, maintaining composure and effectiveness in high-pressure situations. It encompasses a range of attributes, including adaptability, stress management, problem-solving under pressure, and maintaining a positive outlook. Resilient individuals are able to persevere through challenges, utilizing healthy coping mechanisms and proactive growth strategies. They demonstrate a strong sense of determination and are adept at maintaining composure during crises, effectively communicating their decisions and inspiring confidence in others.

Emotional Intelligence, on the other hand, primarily focuses on the understanding, recognition, and management of one's own emotions, as well as the ability to recognize and influence the emotions of others. It involves self-awareness, self-regulation, empathy, and effective communication. Individuals with high EQ can navigate social situations adeptly, build strong interpersonal relationships, and exhibit a high degree of emotional self-control.

Emotional resilience goes beyond EQ in several key ways:

Scope of Application

- Emotional Resilience encompasses a broader set of skills and characteristics, extending beyond the realm of emotions to include adaptability, problem-solving, and decision-making under stress.
- Emotional Intelligence predominantly revolves around understanding and managing emotions, both within oneself and in interpersonal interactions.

Adaptability in Adversity

- Emotional Resilience primarily addresses how individuals respond to adversity and pressure. It focuses on one's ability to remain effective and composed during high-stress situations.
- Emotional Resilience involves the capacity to not only understand and manage emotions but also to adapt and bounce back from challenging situations. It focuses on maintaining a level of stability and effectiveness even in the midst of adversity.
- EQ primarily focuses on recognizing and managing emotions, without emphasizing the aspect of adaptability in the face of significant stress or difficulties.
- EQ emphasizes recognizing and managing emotions in various contexts, with a significant emphasis on interpersonal relationships.

Cognitive Processes and Understanding

- Emotional Resilience encompasses cognitive processes related to understanding and interpreting emotions in complex and demanding situations. It involves the ability to analyze, synthesize, and make decisions based on emotional information.

- EQ primarily centers on recognizing, understanding, and managing emotions at an individual level without necessarily delving into the cognitive dimensions involved in high-pressure scenarios.

Interaction with Other Intelligences

- Emotional Resilience recognizes that resilience, especially in emotionally charged situations, is not solely dependent on emotional intelligence. It incorporates cognitive processes related to understanding and managing emotions, alongside other forms of intelligence. It interacts with and leverages other intelligences, such as analytical intelligence, interpersonal intelligence, and practical intelligence, as necessary and appropriate.

- EQ focuses predominantly on emotions and interpersonal dynamics, without necessarily emphasizing the broader spectrum of intelligences that may be relevant in high-pressure situations.

- EQ primarily focuses on emotional understanding and management, often operating more independently from other forms of intelligence.

Thriving in the Face of Adversity

- Emotional Resilience places a strong emphasis on the ability to not only endure challenges but also to grow, learn, and even excel in the face of adversity. It involves a forward-looking approach to handling difficulties.

- While EQ provides tools for managing emotions, it may not inherently include the same degree of emphasis on the proactive pursuit of growth and excellence in challenging situations.

Comprehensiveness of Response

- Emotional Resilience addresses a wide range of emotional responses, from everyday stressors to significant life-altering events. It encompasses the ability to remain effective and composed in both minor and major adversity.

- EQ tends to focus on emotional responses in a broader sense, but may not provide the same depth of tools and strategies required for resilience in high-pressure scenarios.

Proactive Growth Orientation

- Emotional Resilience involves a proactive pursuit of growth and learning, even in the face of challenges. It sees adversity as an opportunity for development.

- Emotional Intelligence, while valuable, does not inherently emphasize this proactive growth orientation.

In essence, Emotional Resilience is a broader and more comprehensive intelligence that encompasses elements of Emotional Intelligence. While EQ is a crucial aspect of one's overall emotional makeup, Emotional Resilience extends beyond EQ by encompassing a wider array of attributes necessary for navigating complex and high-pressure situations effectively. Together, they form critical cornerstones of an individual's emotional and psychological well-being, each with its unique contributions to personal and professional success.

A More Comprehensive Look at Resilience

Now that we've established this, lets extend the basic characteristics of Emotional Resilience we discussed previously to include:

- **Self-Awareness and Emotional Insight** Emotional resilience involves a deep understanding of one's own emotions, including their triggers, patterns, and impact on behavior and decision-making.

- **Adaptability and Flexibility** Resilient individuals are adept at adapting to changing circumstances and bouncing back from setbacks. They remain agile and resourceful in the face of adversity.

- **Positive Outlook and Optimism**   Emotional resilience incorporates a positive outlook, allowing individuals to maintain hope and confidence, even when confronted with challenges.

- **Effective Stress Management**   Resilient individuals have robust stress management techniques. They can channel stress into productive energy and are less likely to be overwhelmed by pressure.

- **Problem-Solving and Decision-Making Under Stress**   Resilience encompasses the ability to make sound decisions and solve complex problems even in high-pressure situations. Resilient individuals remain effective and clear-headed.

- **Emotional Regulation and Control**   Emotional resilience involves the capacity to regulate emotions effectively. This allows individuals to maintain composure and make rational decisions, even when emotions are running high.

- **Healthy Coping Mechanisms**   Resilient individuals possess constructive coping mechanisms. They avoid harmful or self-destructive behaviors and seek positive ways to manage stress and emotions.

- **Perseverance and Determination**   Emotional resilience embodies a strong sense of perseverance. It enables individuals to stay committed to their goals, even when faced with significant obstacles.

- **Empathy and Understanding of Others**   Resilient individuals are empathetic and understand the emotions and perspectives of others. This enables them to navigate complex interpersonal dynamics, especially in high-stress environments.

- **Proactive Growth and Learning**   Emotional resilience encourages continuous learning and personal growth, even in the face of adversity. Resilient individuals view challenges as opportunities for development.

- **Maintaining Composure in Crisis**   Resilience allows individuals to remain composed and effective in the midst of crisis situations, providing stability and leadership to others.

- **Effective Communication Under Pressure**   Resilient individuals excel in communicating clearly and decisively, even in high-pressure scenarios. They can convey their message effectively and inspire confidence in others.

- **Balancing Emotions with Practical Considerations** Emotional resilience involves the ability to balance emotional responses with practical considerations. Resilient individuals make decisions that align with their goals and values, even when emotions are heightened.

Emotional resilience is distinct from emotional intelligence (EQ) in its emphasis on adaptability, cognitive processes related to understanding and managing emotions, interaction with other intelligences, and proactive pursuit of growth in the face of adversity. Emotional resilience is a critical asset in leadership and high-pressure contexts, enabling individuals to maintain effectiveness and make sound decisions even in the most challenging situations.

Synergy between Emotional Resilience and Emotional Intelligence

Emotional Resilience and Emotional Intelligence are not mutually exclusive; they complement each other. This synergy creates a powerful combination, enabling individuals to navigate complex situations with both emotional insight and resilience. Here are examples:

- **Enhanced Decision-Making** Emotional Intelligence equips individuals with the ability to make emotionally informed decisions and navigate social interactions effectively. When coupled with Emotional Resilience, individuals are not only attuned to their emotions but also possess the fortitude to make tough decisions under pressure.

- **Navigating Complex Relationships** Emotional Intelligence is crucial for building and maintaining positive relationships. However, it's Emotional Resilience that provides the strength to weather conflicts and challenges that inevitably arise in any relationship. Together, they form a robust foundation for healthy interpersonal dynamics.

- **Coping with Change and Uncertainty** Emotional Resilience is particularly instrumental in coping with significant changes or uncertainties, allowing individuals to adapt and bounce back from setbacks. Emotional Intelligence facilitates understanding and processing the emotions associated with change, creating a smoother transition.

- **Leadership Effectiveness**   In leadership roles, Emotional Intelligence is essential for inspiring and motivating teams. Emotional Resilience, on the other hand, ensures that leaders can maintain their effectiveness even in high-pressure situations or when facing challenges or adversity. Leaders with this combination of attributes can guide their teams through challenges with grace and determination.

- **Fostering a Growth Mindset**   Emotional Resilience fosters a growth mindset, where challenges are viewed as opportunities for learning and development. Emotional Intelligence supports this by providing the tools to understand and regulate emotions in the face of challenges, creating a positive feedback loop.

- **Adaptability and Innovation**   When individuals possess high Emotional Intelligence, they are adept at understanding the needs and emotions of others. Emotional Resilience further enhances this by fostering adaptability and promoting innovative thinking, which are essential skills in rapidly changing environments.

By recognizing the intricate interplay between Emotional Resilience and Emotional Intelligence, individuals can take deliberate steps to cultivate and harness both intelligences for maximum effectiveness in personal and professional endeavors. This integrated approach empowers individuals to navigate the complexities of the modern world with confidence, grace, and a heightened capacity for growth and success.

Lessons from Resilient Leaders

In the dynamic landscape of leadership, setbacks and adversities are inevitable. What sets exceptional leaders apart is their capacity to navigate these challenges with grace, determination, and a steadfast focus on their vision. Resilient leaders view setbacks not as insurmountable roadblocks, but as opportunities for growth, learning, and innovation. Through their experiences, they offer invaluable lessons on how to cultivate and apply emotional resilience in the face of adversity.

Resilient leaders possess a growth mindset, viewing challenges as opportunities for learning and development. They understand that setbacks are not indicative of personal failure, but rather a natural part of the leadership journey. This perspective empowers them to approach adversity with curiosity and a determination to emerge stronger.

One hallmark of emotional resilience is the ability to maintain composure in high-pressure situations. Resilient leaders do not succumb to panic or despair when confronted with adversity. Instead, they remain calm, think rationally, and make well-considered decisions, even in the most challenging circumstances.

Resilient leaders excel in adapting to change, recognizing it as an inherent aspect of progress and growth. They are agile in their approach, able to pivot and adjust strategies when necessary. This adaptability allows them to navigate unforeseen challenges and seize emerging opportunities.

Resilient leaders do not view failure as a final verdict, but as a temporary setback. They extract valuable lessons from their failures, using them as stepping stones toward future success. This capacity for introspection and learning from mistakes is a hallmark of emotional resilience.

Resilient leaders have a profound impact on their teams. Through their example, they inspire and motivate others to persevere in the face of adversity. They communicate a sense of optimism and confidence, instilling a collective belief in the team's ability to overcome challenges.

Emotional resilience is closely tied to emotional intelligence. Resilient leaders leverage their emotional intelligence to understand and manage their own emotions, as well as those of their team members. This enables them to foster a supportive and empathetic work environment, which is crucial for navigating challenges together.

Cultivating a Culture of Resilience

Within their organizations, resilient leaders recognize the importance of cultivating a culture of resilience. They prioritize open communication, provide opportunities for skill-building and development, and create a safe space for team members to voice concerns and seek support.

With a long-term perspective, resilience leaders recognize that setbacks are temporary and do not define the ultimate trajectory of their endeavors. They remain focused on their vision and are willing to endure short-term challenges for the sake of long-term success.

Resilient leaders are not afraid to seek mentorship and guidance from trusted advisors or colleagues. They understand the value of diverse perspectives and recognize that seeking support is a sign of strength, not weakness. This willingness to seek input and feedback contributes to their overall resilience.

Resilient leaders strike a balance between optimism and realism. While they maintain a positive outlook, they also approach challenges with a realistic assessment of the situation. This balanced perspective enables them to make informed decisions and take purposeful action.

Past successes are a source of confidence and motivation for resilience leaders. They remind themselves of previous achievements, using them as evidence of their ability to overcome challenges. This self-assurance bolsters their resilience in the face of new obstacles.

Resilient leaders surround themselves with a supportive network of colleagues, mentors, and friends. This network serves as a source of encouragement, advice, and perspective during challenging times. It provides a valuable sounding board for ideas and solutions.

Being Authentic in Leadership

Resilient leaders are not afraid to demonstrate authenticity and vulnerability. They acknowledge their own challenges and setbacks, creating an environment where team members feel comfortable doing the same. This openness fosters trust and strengthens the team's collective resilience.

Encouraging a growth mindset, is something resilient leaders actively encourage in their team members. They provide opportunities for skill development, offer constructive feedback, and create an environment where learning and growth are celebrated. This empowers team members to embrace challenges and persevere.

Resilient leaders understand the importance of celebrating small wins along the way. Acknowledging progress, no matter how incremental, provides a sense of accomplishment and reinforces the team's ability to overcome challenges.

> **Author's Note**   In the dynamic world of startups, acknowledging and celebrating small victories can be a strategic move. During my consulting experience, a remarkable scenario unfolded that highlighted the significance of recognizing these incremental achievements. At an internet startup, a junior leader displayed a keen understanding of the pivotal moments the company faced, particularly during challenging financial periods. She took it upon herself to publicly acknowledge and celebrate even the modest accomplishments achieved by her team.
>
> Curiously, this act of acknowledging small wins drew resentment from the senior executive team. They viewed it as an audacious display of self-promotion, failing to grasp the deeper intention behind the celebrations. Their perception was clouded by notions of attention-seeking and self-centeredness. Despite my efforts to elucidate the importance of such recognition, the senior executives remained obstinate in their stance.
>
> Regrettably, this disconnect culminated in the dismissal of the junior leader, leaving a void in the team. The aftermath was telling: the startup's morale plummeted, and its trajectory took a nosedive. The failure was not merely due to financial constraints, but it was

> exacerbated by a leadership vacuum at the helm. This episode serves as a stark reminder of the transformative impact that acknowledging small wins can have on team dynamics, especially in high-stakes environments.

Resilient leaders recognize that different situations may call for different leadership styles. They remain adaptable, tailoring their approach to suit the needs of the team and the demands of the situation. This flexibility enhances their effectiveness in navigating diverse challenges.

Navigating Setbacks and Adversities

Resilient leaders view setbacks as learning opportunities rather than setbacks. They approach challenges with a mindset of curiosity, seeking to understand what can be gleaned from the experience. This forward-looking perspective contributes to their ongoing growth and development.

Resilient leaders exhibit tenacity and perseverance in the face of adversity. They do not give up easily, but instead approach challenges with a determined resolve to find solutions and overcome obstacles.

Resilient leaders understand that failure can be a catalyst for innovation. They use setbacks as a springboard for creative problem-solving and innovation. Instead of viewing failure as a roadblock, they see it as an opportunity to explore new approaches, technologies, or strategies that may not have been considered otherwise. This innovative mindset propels them and their teams forward, even in the face of adversity.

Resilient leaders understand that change is a constant in the dynamic landscape of leadership. They do not shy away from it, but instead, they embrace it as an opportunity for growth and evolution. Their adaptability in the face of change positions them to effectively navigate even the most turbulent waters.

Resilient leaders recognize the importance of self-care in maintaining their emotional resilience. They prioritize activities that rejuvenate and replenish their mental and emotional well-being. Whether it's regular exercise, mindfulness practices, or spending quality time with loved ones, they understand that caring for themselves is essential for sustaining their resilience.

While resilient leaders maintain an optimistic outlook, they also balance it with a realistic assessment of the challenges they face. This balanced perspective allows them to approach adversity with a clear-eyed understanding of the situation, enabling them to make informed decisions and take purposeful action.

Resilient leaders actively cultivate a growth mindset in their team members. They create an environment where learning, experimentation, and growth are not only encouraged but celebrated. This mindset empowers team members to view setbacks as opportunities for learning and development.

Resilient leaders demonstrate empathy and understanding, both towards themselves and others. They recognize that everyone faces challenges and setbacks, and they extend compassion to those experiencing difficult times. This empathetic approach creates a supportive and inclusive work environment that fosters collective resilience.

Resilient leaders are committed to continuous learning and adaptation. They understand that the landscape of leadership is ever-evolving, and they proactively seek out new knowledge, skills, and perspectives. This dedication to growth equips them with the tools and insights needed to navigate an ever-changing professional landscape.

In navigating setbacks and adversities, resilient leaders exemplify a set of principles and practices that can be emulated and cultivated by others. Their ability to maintain composure, learn from failure, and inspire their teams sets them apart as exceptional leaders. By understanding and internalizing these lessons, aspiring leaders can cultivate their own emotional resilience, enabling them to effectively navigate the complex challenges of leadership.

Emotions as Catalysts: How Emotional Resilience Drives Effective Leadership

Emotionally resilient leaders possess a profound understanding of the dynamic nature of emotions. They recognize that feelings are not static, but rather, they ebb and flow in response to various stimuli and situations. This awareness empowers them to navigate their emotions with agility, ensuring that they do not become overwhelmed by negative feelings and can effectively harness the energy of positive emotions.

Honest Expression of Emotions

Viewing emotions as invaluable sources of information is important. Resilience leaders understand that emotions serve as signals, providing insights into their own state of mind and the emotional climate of their team or organization. By paying attention to these signals, they make informed decisions and take appropriate action.

Emotionally resilient leaders possess the ability to harness the energy carried by emotions. They know how to channel this energy in constructive ways, using it to fuel their motivation, creativity, and determination. This enables them to approach challenges with vigor and purpose, even in the face of adversity.

Their impact extends beyond their own actions; resilient leaders have a contagious effect on those around them. Their emotional resilience serves as a source of inspiration and motivation for their team members. By demonstrating composure in the face of challenges and maintaining a positive outlook, they instill confidence and a sense of purpose in others.

Recognizing the significance of creating a positive emotional climate, resilient leaders actively work to cultivate an environment where team members feel valued, supported, and motivated. This positive emotional climate not only enhances individual well-being but also contributes to higher levels of team performance and collaboration.

They encourage open and honest emotional expression within their team or organization. By creating a space for team members to share their thoughts, concerns, and feelings, resilient leaders foster a culture of trust and psychological safety. This open communication allows for the timely identification and resolution of issues, preventing them from escalating into larger challenges.

Understanding that authenticity and vulnerability are not signs of weakness, but rather, demonstrations of strength is crucial. Emotionally resilient leaders are not afraid to show vulnerability and authenticity, understanding that leadership is about being genuine and relatable. This authenticity builds trust and strengthens their connections with team members.

Being a Driving Force Behind Effective Leadership

Resilient leaders are adept at navigating difficult conversations. They approach these discussions with empathy, active listening, and a commitment to finding constructive solutions. Their emotional resilience enables them to maintain composure and focus on the best interests of all parties involved.

Balancing empathy with objectivity is another hallmark of emotionally resilient leaders. While they are attuned to the emotions of others, they also maintain an objective perspective, ensuring that decisions are made based on a clear assessment of the situation. This balanced approach allows them to lead with both compassion and sound judgment.

Resilient leaders actively work to inspire a culture of emotional resilience within their team or organization. They set the tone by modeling resilience in their own behavior and by providing the necessary support and resources for team members to develop their own emotional resilience. This culture of resilience becomes a foundation of the organization's overall success.

In essence, emotional resilience is not just a personal attribute of a leader, but a driving force behind effective leadership. Resilient leaders understand that emotions hold the potential to catalyze positive action and drive meaningful results. By embodying emotional resilience and fostering its development within their teams, leaders create a powerful foundation for individual and organizational success.

Building Blocks of Emotional Resilience

The essential building blocks that constitute emotional resilience include:

- Self-awareness, recognizing it as a crucial factor of resilience.

- Emotional regulation, emphasizing its critical role in managing responses in high-stress environments.

- Empathy and compassion, showcasing how these qualities foster meaningful connections in leadership.

Self-Awareness: The Foundation of Emotional Resilience

At the core of emotional resilience lies a profound and unwavering sense of self-awareness. This foundational attribute enables individuals to recognize, understand, and navigate their own emotions with clarity and insight. Self-awareness serves as the compass that guides emotional responses, allowing individuals to respond thoughtfully rather than react impulsively.

Developing self-awareness involves a deep exploration of one's own emotions, thoughts, and behaviors. It requires a willingness to engage in introspection and self-reflection, often delving into the underlying beliefs and assumptions that shape one's emotional responses. This introspective journey is not always easy, as it may unearth uncomfortable or challenging aspects of oneself. However, It Is through this process that individuals gain a comprehensive understanding of their emotional landscape.

One key aspect of self-awareness is the ability to accurately identify and label one's emotions. This goes beyond the basic recognition of broad emotions like "happy" or "sad." It involves discerning the nuanced variations within each emotional spectrum. For example, recognizing the subtle differences between frustration, disappointment, and irritation allows for more precise self-expression and targeted emotional regulation.

In addition to recognizing emotions, self-awareness extends to understanding the triggers and patterns that influence emotional responses. This involves identifying specific situations, environments, or interactions that evoke certain feelings. By pinpointing these triggers, individuals can proactively prepare for or navigate through potentially challenging situations, mitigating the risk of becoming overwhelmed.

Self-awareness also encompasses an awareness of one's physical and physiological responses to emotions. Emotions are not solely experienced in the mind; they manifest in the body as well. For instance, stress may be accompanied by muscle tension, a rapid heart rate, or shallow breathing. By tuning into these physical cues, individuals can gain early indicators of emotional responses, allowing them to intervene and regulate their emotions effectively.

Additionally, self-awareness involves an understanding of the narratives and stories that individuals construct around their experiences. These narratives shape perceptions of self and others, influencing emotional responses. For example, an individual who believes they are inherently "unworthy" may respond differently to praise or criticism than someone who views themselves as capable and deserving. By examining and, if necessary, reframing these narratives, individuals can cultivate more adaptive and resilient emotional responses.

A crucial aspect of self-awareness is the recognition of one's strengths and limitations. This involves an honest appraisal of one's capabilities, talents, and areas for growth. Understanding where one excels and where they may face challenges allows for more realistic goal-setting and a greater sense of agency in navigating life's challenges.

It is important to point out that self-awareness is not static; it is a continuous process of growth and self-discovery. As individuals evolve, their self-awareness deepens, leading to new insights and perspectives. It requires an ongoing commitment to introspection and a willingness to confront and integrate new aspects of oneself.

Cultivating self-awareness often involves various practices and techniques. Mindfulness meditation, journaling, and self-assessment tools can be invaluable resources in this journey. These practices provide structured avenues for self-reflection and offer a means of tracking personal growth over time.

As essential component of emotional resilience, self-awareness empowers individuals to navigate their emotional landscape with clarity, insight, and authenticity. By honing this foundational skill, individuals lay the groundwork for building resilience in the face of life's challenges, fostering a greater sense of well-being and personal agency.

Emotional Regulation: Manage Response in High-Stress Environments

Emotional resilience is not solely about experiencing or recognizing emotions; it also involves the ability to regulate them effectively. This critical skill allows individuals to respond to challenging situations in a balanced and adaptive manner, even in high-stress environments. Emotional regulation encompasses a range of strategies and techniques that enable individuals to modulate the intensity and duration of their emotional responses.

One key facet of emotional regulation is the capacity to calm the physiological arousal associated with heightened emotions. In high-stress environments, the body's stress response system may become activated, leading to increased heart rate, rapid breathing, and heightened muscle tension. Through practices such as deep breathing exercises, progressive muscle relaxation, and mindfulness techniques, individuals can mitigate the physical manifestations of stress, promoting a sense of calm and composure.

Another crucial aspect of emotional regulation involves the ability to shift one's attention and focus. In high-stress situations, individuals may become hyper-focused on the perceived threat or source of distress. This narrowed attentional scope can limit perspective and hinder problem-solving abilities. By consciously redirecting attention to other aspects of the situation or to positive and constructive thoughts, individuals can broaden their perspective and approach challenges with greater clarity.

The capacity to reframe or reevaluate challenging situations comes from emotional regulation as well. This involves shifting one's perspective to view a situation in a more constructive or positive light. For example, instead of viewing a setback as a failure, individuals may choose to see it as an opportunity for growth and learning. This cognitive reframing can transform the emotional impact of a situation and empower individuals to respond with greater resilience.

Emotional regulation encompasses the ability to delay impulsive reactions. In high-stress environments, there may be a tendency to react hastily in an attempt to alleviate discomfort or anxiety. However, this impulsive response may not align with one's long-term goals or values. Through practices such as "pause and reflect" techniques, individuals can create a moment of space between stimulus and response, allowing for more intentional and considered actions.

Emotional regulation involves the skill of assertive communication. In high-stress situations, effective communication can become challenging, as emotions may run high and clarity may be compromised. Assertive communication involves expressing oneself in a clear, direct, and respectful manner, even when emotions are heightened. This enables individuals to convey their needs, boundaries, and perspectives effectively, fostering healthy interactions and problem-solving.

Another key aspect of emotional regulation is the practice of setting and maintaining healthy boundaries. In high-stress environments, there may be external pressures or demands that can contribute to emotional overwhelm. By establishing clear boundaries around time, energy, and commitments, individuals can protect their well-being and allocate resources judiciously.

Emotional regulation encompasses the ability to engage in self-soothing activities. These are intentional practices that promote relaxation and a sense of well-being. This may include activities such as taking a warm bath, engaging in creative expression, or spending time in nature. Engaging in self-soothing practices provides individuals with a source of comfort and rejuvenation, enabling them to face challenges with greater equanimity.

In addition to these strategies, emotional regulation involves the recognition and validation of one's own emotions. It is important to acknowledge that all emotions, even those deemed "negative," serve a purpose and convey valuable information. By honoring and validating one's emotional experiences, individuals can cultivate a greater sense of self-compassion and emotional well-being.

As you can see, emotional regulation equips individuals with the tools and techniques needed to navigate high-stress environments with resilience and grace. It empowers individuals to respond thoughtfully rather than react impulsively, promoting a greater sense of control and agency. By honing this critical skill, individuals enhance their capacity to weather challenges and emerge from adversity with strength and adaptability.

Empathy and Compassion: Connecting Through Empathetic Leadership

Empathy and compassion are foundational building blocks of emotional resilience and effective leadership. These qualities enable leaders to connect with others on a deep and meaningful level, fostering a sense of trust, understanding, and collaboration. In high-stress environments, the ability to demonstrate empathy and compassion can be a powerful force for alleviating tension and creating a supportive work culture.

Empathy involves the capacity to understand and share the feelings and perspectives of others. It requires active listening, perspective-taking, and an open-hearted willingness to enter into the emotional experience of another person. Empathetic leaders tune into the needs and concerns of their team members, demonstrating genuine care and concern for their well-being. This fosters a sense of psychological safety and trust, enabling team members to express themselves openly and honestly.

Compassion goes beyond empathy, encompassing a genuine desire to alleviate the suffering of others. Compassionate leaders take action to support and uplift their team members, especially in times of difficulty or distress. This may involve offering words of encouragement, providing resources or assistance, or simply being present as a source of comfort and support. Compassion creates a culture of care and mutual support, reinforcing the sense of belonging and camaraderie within the team.

Empathetic leadership is particularly crucial in high-stress environments, where individuals may be grappling with heightened emotions, uncertainty, or challenging circumstances. By demonstrating empathy, leaders acknowledge the emotional experiences of their team members, validating their feelings and providing a sense of understanding. This can be immensely reassuring, helping team members feel seen, heard, and valued.

Empathetic leaders possess a keen awareness of non-verbal cues and emotional signals. They are attuned to the subtle shifts in body language, tone of voice, and facial expressions that convey underlying emotions. This heightened sensitivity allows them to pick up on the emotional states of their team members, even when words may not fully articulate their feelings. This awareness enables leaders to respond with greater nuance and attunement.

Empathetic leaders practice active listening, which involves not only hearing the words being spoken but also discerning the underlying emotions and needs. They create a space for team members to express themselves openly, without judgment or interruption. This fosters a sense of psychological safety, encouraging individuals to share their thoughts, concerns, and ideas freely.

Endeavoring to see situations from the vantage point of their team members, empathetic leaders engage in perspective-taking. This involves putting oneself in another's shoes, considering their experiences, challenges, and aspirations. By adopting this perspective, leaders gain valuable insights into the unique needs and perspectives of each team member, enabling them to tailor their leadership approach accordingly.

Empathetic leadership also involves the ability to regulate one's own emotions in response to the emotions of others. Leaders must be attuned to their own emotional reactions and be capable of managing them effectively. This ensures that their responses are thoughtful and constructive, rather than reactive or driven by their own emotional states. By maintaining a sense of equanimity, leaders can provide a stabilizing influence in high-stress situations.

Empathetic leaders prioritize open and transparent communication. They create an environment where team members feel comfortable expressing their thoughts, concerns, and emotions. This open dialogue builds trust and strengthens the sense of connection within the team. It also allows for constructive feedback and problem-solving, contributing to a culture of continuous improvement.

In high-stress environments, empathetic leaders acknowledge the challenges and pressures faced by their team members. They express genuine concern for their well-being and offer support and resources as needed. This may involve providing additional resources, adjusting workloads, or offering flexible solutions to accommodate individual needs. Through their compassionate actions, leaders demonstrate a commitment to the welfare of their team members.

As a key element of emotional resilience, empathetic leadership enables leaders to forge meaningful connections with their team members. By practicing empathy and compassion, leaders create a culture of care, trust, and mutual support. This not only enhances individual well-being but also contributes to a more resilient and cohesive team, capable of navigating challenges with unity and strength.

Mindfulness and Emotional Regulation Techniques

Cultivating emotional resilience is a dynamic process that requires intentional practices and techniques. Among the most powerful tools in this endeavor are mindfulness and emotional regulation techniques. These practices empower individuals to navigate their emotional landscape with greater awareness, equanimity, and effectiveness.

Mindfulness: Gaining a Deeper Understanding of Self

Mindfulness involves the intentional cultivation of present-moment awareness. It entails paying focused and non-judgmental attention to one's thoughts, emotions, bodily sensations, and the surrounding environment. By anchoring oneself in the present, individuals can gain a deeper understanding of their inner experiences, allowing for greater emotional clarity and self-regulation.

One of the foundational practices in mindfulness is meditation. This involves setting aside dedicated time to engage in focused awareness of the breath, bodily sensations, or specific thoughts and emotions. Through consistent meditation, individuals develop the capacity to observe their inner experiences without becoming overly identified with them. This detachment fosters a sense of spaciousness and freedom in relation to one's emotions.

Body scan exercises are another valuable form of mindfulness practice. These involve systematically directing attention to different areas of the body, noting any sensations or tensions present. By cultivating this somatic awareness, individuals can detect early signs of heightened emotional states and respond proactively. This practice also promotes a sense of embodiment and groundedness.

Mindfulness can be integrated into daily activities through practices like mindful eating or mindful walking. These involve bringing focused attention to ordinary activities, such as savoring each bite of food or feeling the sensations of walking. By infusing mindfulness into everyday experiences, individuals can cultivate a sense of presence and engagement, reducing the tendency to get swept up in emotional reactivity.

Breath awareness is a fundamental aspect of mindfulness practice. By attuning to the natural rhythm of the breath, individuals can anchor themselves in the present moment. The breath serves as a reliable point of reference, providing a source of calm and stability amidst the fluctuations of emotions. This practice can be particularly effective in moments of heightened stress or agitation.

Mindfulness extends beyond formal practices. In addition to structured mindfulness exercises, individuals have the opportunity to nurture mindfulness in their interactions with others. This entails wholeheartedly focusing on the person they are engaging with, listening attentively, and being completely present. By providing this level of attention, individuals communicate respect, empathy, and sincere concern, which in turn nurtures positive and harmonious relationships.

Emotional Regulation: Responding Skillfully to Challenging Situations

Emotional regulation techniques complement mindfulness practices by providing individuals with practical tools for managing their emotions. These techniques empower individuals to respond skillfully to challenging situations, rather than reacting impulsively or becoming overwhelmed. They contribute to a greater sense of emotional balance and stability.

One effective emotional regulation technique is deep breathing. By engaging in slow, deliberate breaths, individuals activate the body's relaxation response, reducing the intensity of emotional arousal. This technique can be particularly valuable in moments of heightened stress, anxiety, or anger. It provides a simple yet powerful means of returning to a state of equilibrium.

Progressive muscle relaxation is another valuable technique for emotional regulation. This involves systematically tensing and then releasing different muscle groups in the body. By doing so, individuals release physical tension, which is often associated with emotional arousal. This practice promotes a sense of calm and ease, facilitating greater emotional balance.

Grounding exercises are particularly useful for individuals experiencing intense emotions. These techniques involve directing attention to sensory experiences in the present moment, such as the sensation of the feet on the ground or the feel of an object in hand. By grounding themselves in these tangible experiences, individuals can regain a sense of stability and control.

Journaling serves as a powerful outlet for emotional expression and reflection. By putting pen to paper, individuals can articulate their thoughts and feelings, gaining clarity and insight into their inner experiences. This practice also provides a tangible record of one's emotional journey, allowing for reflection and growth over time.

Artistic expression, such as drawing, painting, or sculpting, can serve as a potent means of emotional release and self-discovery. Through the creative process, individuals can channel their emotions into a tangible form, providing a sense of catharsis and expression. This creative outlet can be particularly valuable for individuals who may find it challenging to verbalize their emotions.

Another effective emotional regulation technique is the use of positive affirmations. These are positive statements or phrases that individuals repeat to themselves, affirming their strengths, capabilities, and resilience. By regularly engaging with positive affirmations, individuals can cultivate a more optimistic and empowered mindset, which contributes to greater emotional well-being.

Engaging in physical activity and exercise also has profound effects on emotional regulation. Regular exercise releases endorphins, which are chemicals in the brain associated with feelings of pleasure and well-being. This natural mood elevation can serve as a powerful antidote to feelings of stress, anxiety, or low mood. Exercise provides a healthy outlet for pent-up emotions, promoting a sense of release and vitality as well.

Together mindfulness and emotional regulation techniques are indispensable tools for cultivating emotional resilience. These practices empower individuals to navigate their emotional landscape with greater awareness, equanimity, and effectiveness. By integrating these practices into their daily lives, individuals can foster a deeper sense of self-awareness, emotional balance, and overall well-being.

Developing Adaptive Coping Mechanisms

Cultivating emotional resilience involves equipping oneself with a diverse toolkit of adaptive coping mechanisms. These mechanisms serve as the foundation for effectively navigating challenges, setbacks, and stressors that are inherent to leadership roles. By adopting a proactive and strategic approach to coping, individuals can bolster their capacity to maintain composure and make sound decisions even in the face of adversity.

From Reframing Perception to Accepting Emotions

One key adaptive coping mechanism is cognitive reappraisal. This involves reframing or changing the way one perceives a situation. By shifting their perspective, individuals can alter the emotional impact of a given circumstance. For example, viewing a setback as an opportunity for growth rather than a failure can mitigate feelings of frustration or disappointment. Cognitive reappraisal empowers individuals to extract valuable lessons from challenging experiences.

Problem-solving skills are indispensable in cultivating emotional resilience. This involves the ability to analyze a situation, identify potential solutions, and take decisive action. By actively engaging in problem-solving, individuals regain a sense of agency and control, reducing feelings of helplessness or overwhelm. This adaptive coping mechanism enables leaders to approach challenges with a solution-oriented mindset.

An invaluable strategy for cultivating emotional resilience lies in the application of techniques rooted in Acceptance and Commitment Therapy (ACT). ACT provides a comprehensive framework that empowers individuals to embrace their emotions wholeheartedly, including those that may be uncomfortable or distressing, without resorting to suppression or avoidance.

This approach concurrently underscores the importance of dedicating oneself to actions that resonate with one's core values and aspirations. Essentially,

ACT encourages individuals to embark on a journey of self-discovery and self-acceptance, acknowledging that emotions, even the most challenging ones, are an integral part of the human experience.

To put this into practical terms, let's delve into some step-by-step examples:

- Mindful Recognition of Emotions:
    1. Start by taking a moment to pause and become aware of your current emotional state.
    2. Label the emotions you're experiencing. For instance, you might be feeling frustration, anxiety, or sadness.
    3. Remember, the goal is not to judge or change these emotions, but simply to acknowledge them.

- Identifying Core Values:
    1. Reflect on what truly matters to you in your personal and professional life. These are your core values.
    2. They could be integrity, compassion, growth, or any other principles that guide your actions.
    3. Write down your core values to solidify them in your mind.

- Connecting Actions to Values:
    1. Consider specific actions or behaviors that align with each of your identified core values.
    2. For example, if one of your core values is "collaboration," an associated action might be actively seeking input from team members.

- Acceptance and Letting Go:
    1. Practice accepting your emotions without judgment. Understand that they are a natural response to various situations.
    2. Imagine placing your emotions in a metaphorical boat and allowing them to float away. This signifies letting go of the need to control or suppress them.

- Setting Meaningful Goals:

1. Define objectives that resonate with your core values and aspirations.
2. These goals should be specific, measurable, achievable, relevant, and time-bound (SMART).

- Taking Committed Action:
    1. Actively engage in behaviors that are in alignment with your identified core values and goals.
    2. Even in the face of discomfort or adversity, remain committed to these actions.

By adopting an attitude of acceptance and commitment towards their emotions, individuals not only foster psychological flexibility but also fortify their resilience. This means that in the face of adversity or challenging situations, they are better equipped to adapt and bounce back, ultimately emerging as stronger and more resilient leaders. This process is akin to forging a mental and emotional armor, enabling leaders to navigate through turbulent times with grace and effectiveness.

The techniques of ACT, when applied consistently and with purpose, serve as a potent tool in developing the adaptive coping mechanisms essential for becoming an emotionally resilient leader.

From Gaining Perspective to Setting Realistic Expectations

Maintaining a sense of perspective is a crucial adaptive coping mechanism. This involves recognizing the relative importance of a given situation in the broader context of one's life and professional journey. By avoiding the tendency to catastrophize or magnify the significance of a challenge, individuals can approach it with greater equanimity and clarity. Perspective-taking allows leaders to discern what truly warrants their attention and energy.

Seeking social support is a powerful coping mechanism for cultivating emotional resilience. Connecting with trusted colleagues, mentors, or friends provides an invaluable outlet for sharing experiences, seeking guidance, and receiving emotional validation. This sense of connection can mitigate feelings of isolation or overwhelm, offering a source of comfort and perspective.

Moreover, it reinforces the understanding that one is not alone in facing challenges.

Engaging in self-care practices is fundamental to building emotional resilience. This involves prioritizing one's physical, emotional, and mental well-being through activities such as regular exercise, adequate sleep, balanced nutrition, and relaxation techniques. Self-care serves as a buffer against the negative effects of stress and fosters a sense of vitality and balance. By consistently tending to their well-being, individuals fortify their capacity to weather challenges.

Embracing a growth mindset is a pivotal adaptive coping mechanism. This mindset is characterized by a belief that abilities and intelligence can be developed through effort, learning, and perseverance. By viewing challenges as opportunities for growth rather than fixed limitations, individuals approach them with a sense of curiosity and determination. This perspective empowers leaders to cultivate new skills and capacities in the face of adversity.

Another effective coping mechanism is the practice of setting realistic expectations. This involves acknowledging one's limitations and recognizing that perfection is an unattainable standard. By setting achievable goals and accepting that setbacks are a natural part of any endeavor, individuals reduce the likelihood of experiencing undue stress or frustration. Realistic expectations provide a more balanced and sustainable approach to leadership.

From Time Management to Self-Compassion

Time management and prioritization skills play a crucial role in coping with the demands of leadership. Effectively allocating time and resources enables individuals to address challenges in a systematic and organized manner. By establishing clear priorities and allocating sufficient time for critical tasks, leaders can mitigate feelings of overwhelm and ensure that they can devote attention to what matters most.

Mindful self-compassion is a powerful adaptive coping mechanism that involves treating oneself with the same kindness, care, and understanding that one would offer to a dear friend. This practice acknowledges that experiencing challenges and setbacks is an inherent part of the human experience. By responding to oneself with compassion rather than self-criticism, individuals foster a sense of emotional resilience and well-being.

Reflective practices, such as journaling or self-reflection, serve as valuable tools for developing emotional resilience. These practices provide a structured means of processing experiences, emotions, and challenges. By engaging in regular reflection, individuals gain insight into their patterns of thinking and behavior, allowing for greater self-awareness and the identification of adaptive strategies.

Maintaining a sense of humor is a powerful adaptive coping mechanism. Humor serves as a natural stress reliever, diffusing tension and providing a fresh perspective on challenging situations. By finding moments of levity, individuals can lighten the emotional weight of a situation and approach it with a more balanced and constructive mindset. Humor fosters a positive and resilient outlook.

Setting boundaries is also crucial for preserving emotional resilience. This involves establishing clear limits on the demands and expectations placed upon oneself. By delineating what is feasible and sustainable, individuals protect their well-being and prevent burnout. Boundaries empower leaders to allocate their resources judiciously and ensure that they can continue to operate at their best.

Cultivating a sense of purpose and meaning is a foundational coping mechanism. Having a clear understanding of one's values and the larger mission or purpose behind their work provides a source of motivation and resilience. By aligning their efforts with a sense of purpose, individuals derive a deeper sense of fulfillment and are better equipped to navigate challenges with a sense of determination.

Practicing self-compassion involves treating oneself with the same kindness, care, and understanding that one would offer to a dear friend. This adaptive coping mechanism acknowledges that experiencing challenges and setbacks is an inherent part of the human experience. By responding to oneself with compassion rather than self-criticism, individuals foster a sense of emotional resilience and well-being.

As you can see, developing adaptive coping mechanisms is essential for cultivating emotional resilience in leadership. These strategies empower individuals to navigate challenges with greater awareness, equanimity, and effectiveness. By intentionally adopting and practicing these coping mechanisms, leaders fortify their capacity to maintain composure, make sound decisions, and lead with resilience even in the face of adversity.

Building a Supportive Network: The Power of Emotional Resilience in Teams

Emotional resilience is not solely an individual endeavor; it thrives within a supportive network, particularly in team settings. When individuals collectively cultivate and reinforce emotional resilience, the entire team benefits from a culture of mutual understanding, empathy, and shared coping strategies.

From Open Communication to Growth Mindset

Transparent and honest communication is essential in cultivating a resilient team, as is active listening, which shows empathy. Open dialogue builds trust and fosters a sense of belonging, allowing individuals to navigate difficulties together. It creates an environment where team members feel safe expressing their emotions, concerns, and challenges. By actively listening and showing genuine concern for the well-being of colleagues, team members create a supportive atmosphere where emotions are acknowledged and validated.

Psychological safety is the bedrock upon which emotional resilience in teams is built. It entails creating an environment where team members feel comfortable taking risks, sharing vulnerabilities, and expressing their true selves without fear of reprisal or judgment. This leads to more innovative and effective problem-solving.

Equipping team members with resources and training in emotional resilience-building techniques is instrumental. Workshops, seminars, and access to relevant literature and tools empower individuals to develop their emotional resilience, recognize their strengths, and identify areas for growth.

Well-designed workspaces that promote collaboration, creativity, and comfort contribute to a positive atmosphere. Additionally, access to natural light, green spaces, and ergonomic furniture can enhance the overall well-being of team members. The physical environment plays a significant role in fostering emotional resilience.

Recognizing both individual and collective achievements reinforces a sense of purpose and accomplishment within the team. Equally important is acknowledging challenges and setbacks. This normalization of adversity reduces the stigma associated with difficulties, encouraging a more open and supportive environment.

Clarity in roles and expectations reduces ambiguity and potential sources of stress within a team. When team members understand their responsibilities and how their contributions align with the team's goals, they are better equipped to manage challenges and navigate complex situations.

In today's dynamic work environment, adaptability is also a critical trait for emotional resilience. Encouraging flexibility in work arrangements, allowing for creative problem-solving, and supporting the exploration of new approaches empower team members to navigate change and uncertainty with greater ease.

Cultivating a growth mindset within a team encourages individuals to view challenges as opportunities for learning and development. This perspective shift empowers team members to approach difficulties with curiosity and a willingness to explore new solutions.

From Skill Development to Meaningful Contribution

Offering opportunities for skill development, whether through workshops, mentorship programs, or cross-functional projects, enables team members to enhance their emotional intelligence and resilience. By investing in their growth, organizations foster a culture of continuous learning and development.

Encouraging peer support systems within a team creates a network of individuals who can provide emotional validation and practical advice. These peer relationships offer an additional layer of support beyond formal channels, strengthening the team's collective resilience.

Recognizing the importance of work-life balance contributes to emotional resilience within a team. Encouraging reasonable work hours, offering flexible scheduling options, and providing resources for stress management and self-care demonstrate an organizational commitment to employee well-being.

Encouraging regular breaks, both short and extended, allows team members to recharge and maintain optimal levels of productivity and emotional well-being. Breaks offer moments of respite, enabling individuals to return to their tasks with renewed focus and clarity.

Helping team members connect their work to a broader sense of purpose and impact can be a powerful motivator. Understanding the meaningful contributions they make to the organization and society at large reinforces a sense of purpose and bolsters emotional resilience.

From Healthy Team Dynamics to Mental Health

Addressing conflicts openly and constructively is essential for maintaining a healthy team dynamic. Establishing clear conflict resolution mechanisms provides a structured process for addressing disagreements and working towards mutually agreeable solutions.

Promoting self-reflection among team members fosters self-awareness and emotional intelligence. Providing opportunities for individuals to reflect on their experiences, strengths, and areas for growth contributes to their overall emotional resilience.

Embracing diversity within a team enriches perspectives and promotes a culture of inclusivity. When team members feel valued and respected for their unique contributions, they are more likely to feel supported and empowered in their roles.

Regular feedback channels create opportunities for team members to receive constructive input on their performance and contributions. This feedback loop fosters a culture of continuous improvement and reinforces the value of each individual's contributions.

Promoting mental health awareness and providing resources for mental well-being demonstrates a commitment to the holistic health of team members.

This support system reduces the stigma associated with mental health challenges and encourages individuals to seek the assistance they may need.

Incorporating these strategies into team dynamics fosters an environment where emotional resilience thrives. By creating a culture of support, understanding, and growth, teams are better equipped to navigate challenges, make informed decisions, and achieve collective success. Building a supportive network amplifies the impact of individual resilience, resulting in a cohesive and high-performing team.

Practical Exercises for Strengthening Emotional Resilience

Now let's look at actionable exercises to actively strengthen emotional resilience. Here, individual reflection and journaling are introduced as a means to deepen self-awareness, allowing leaders to gain insights into their emotional responses. Afterward, group sharing and support activities are introduced to foster a culture of resilience within teams, creating a safe space for open communication.

Individual Reflection and Journaling: A Journey into Self-Awareness

Individual reflection and journaling are powerful tools for cultivating emotional resilience. They provide a structured means to explore one's thoughts, emotions, and experiences, ultimately leading to heightened self-awareness. This practice encourages individuals to engage in introspection, allowing them to process challenges, identify strengths, and set meaningful goals.

Embarking on a Journey of Reflection

Before embarking on the journey of reflection and journaling, it's essential to create a conducive environment. Find a quiet space free from distractions, where you can comfortably sit and focus. Consider dedicating a specific time each day for this practice to establish a routine.

To guide the reflection process, consider using prompts or questions. These prompts serve as catalysts for deeper exploration. For instance, you might begin with questions like, "What emotions am I experiencing today?" or "What challenges have I encountered recently?" Prompt-based reflection provides a framework for introspection.

A significant aspect of emotional resilience is understanding and navigating emotions. During reflection, allow yourself to fully acknowledge and experience your emotions. Consider the specific situations or triggers that evoked these feelings. This awareness lays the foundation for constructive emotional regulation.

Through consistent reflection, individuals can identify recurring patterns in their emotions and reactions. Recognizing specific triggers empowers individuals to develop targeted coping strategies. For example, if certain situations consistently lead to stress or frustration, proactive steps can be taken to mitigate their impact.

Reflection provides an opportunity to celebrate personal achievements and acknowledge individual strengths. Take time to document moments of success, no matter how small they may seem. Recognizing one's capabilities fosters a sense of competence and self-efficacy, both of which contribute to emotional resilience.

Making Progress on the Journey

Integrating reflection with goal-setting is a powerful combination. After gaining insights through reflection, individuals can set intentional, actionable goals. These goals might focus on personal growth, skill development, or navigating specific challenges. Setting clear objectives provides direction and purpose.

Reflection offers a platform to cultivate gratitude. Take time to acknowledge and appreciate the positive aspects of your life, both big and small. This practice reframes perspectives, shifting the focus towards elements that bring joy, fulfillment, and a sense of well-being.

Through reflection, individuals have the opportunity to consider different viewpoints. This can be particularly valuable in challenging situations where multiple perspectives may exist. By examining situations from various angles, individuals can develop a more comprehensive understanding.

Maintaining a journal allows for the tracking of personal progress and growth over time. By revisiting earlier entries, individuals can observe how their responses to challenges have evolved. This retrospective view reinforces a sense of accomplishment and provides motivation to continue on the path of growth.

Reflection encourages self-compassion, which involves treating oneself with the same kindness and understanding as one would offer to a friend. It involves acknowledging one's struggles and imperfections without self-judgment. Practicing self-compassion is a key component of emotional resilience.

Not only that, but reflection provides an opportunity to connect with one's core values and beliefs. Consider what matters most to you in various aspects of your life, such as work, relationships, and personal development. Aligning actions with core values enhances a sense of authenticity and purpose.

Why Use Reflection Journaling?

In times of challenge or adversity, reflection can serve as a platform for brainstorming and exploring potential solutions. Consider different approaches and strategies that align with your values and objectives. This proactive mindset empowers individuals to take constructive action.

Reflective journaling offers a safe space to process difficult or traumatic experiences. Writing about these events allows individuals to express their emotions, gain perspective, and begin the healing process. It can be a crucial step in building emotional resilience.

For some, verbal communication may not be the most comfortable or effective means of expression. Reflection through writing provides an alternative avenue for individuals to articulate their thoughts and emotions. This process of self-expression contributes to enhanced emotional well-being.

Regular reflection sharpens decision-making skills, fosters mindfulness, and present-moment awareness. By reviewing past choices and their outcomes, individuals can gain insights into their decision-making processes. This awareness enables more informed and effective decision-making in the future. Reflection encourages individuals to be fully engaged with their thoughts, emotions, and experiences. This practice of being present enhances overall well-being and contributes to emotional resilience.

Deepening the Journey

During times of change or transition, reflection serves as a valuable tool for adaptation. It allows individuals to process the emotions and challenges associated with change, facilitating a smoother transition process.

Incorporating creative elements into reflection, such as drawing, painting, or other forms of artistic expression, can deepen the introspective process. Creative outlets offer an alternative means of self-expression, allowing for a more holistic exploration of emotions and experiences.

Regular reflection can lead to profound self-discovery. It unveils layers of self-awareness, revealing hidden strengths, values, and aspirations. This process of self-discovery is integral to building emotional resilience.

Integrating reflection with a growth mindset encourages a perspective of continuous learning and development. It reframes challenges as opportunities for growth, instilling a sense of optimism and determination.

By engaging in individual reflection and journaling, individuals embark on a journey of self-discovery, enhanced self-awareness, and strengthened emotional resilience. This practice empowers individuals to navigate challenges with greater clarity, purpose, and adaptability, ultimately contributing to their overall well-being and success in leadership roles.

Group Sharing & Support: Foster a Culture of Emotional Resilience

In the journey to cultivate emotional resilience, the power of collective support and shared experiences cannot be underestimated. Group sharing and support exercises create a safe space for individuals to connect, empathize, and learn from one another. These exercises promote a culture of emotional resilience within teams and organizations, ultimately enhancing overall well-being and effectiveness.

Icebreaker Activities

Before engaging in group sharing and support exercises, it is crucial to establish an environment of trust and safety. Encourage open communication, active listening, and confidentiality. Emphasize that participants are free to share as much or as little as they feel comfortable.

Begin sessions with icebreaker activities and check-ins. These exercises set a positive tone, fostering a sense of camaraderie and connection among participants. Icebreakers can range from simple get-to-know-you games to activities that encourage self-expression and creativity.

Here are some icebreaker ideas along with examples:

- **Photo sharing**   Participants bring a photo that represents a meaningful moment or achievement in their life. They share the story behind the photo with the group. Example: A photo of a hiking trip with friends and the sense of accomplishment felt at the summit.

- **Strengths and appreciations**   Each participant shares a personal strength or skill they feel proud of. The group then expresses appreciation for that strength. Example: "I consider myself a good listener. I appreciate how you make people feel heard and valued."

- **Two truths and a lie**   Each participant shares two true statements about themselves and one false statement. The group tries to guess which statement is the lie. Example: "I've traveled to five different countries. I can play the piano. I've climbed a mountain."

- **Life timeline**   Participants draw a timeline of significant events in their life, both positive and challenging. They then share one event with the group and explain why it was impactful. Example: "One significant event was when I graduated from college. It was a proud moment for me and my family."

- **Gratitude journaling**   Participants take a few minutes to write down something they are grateful for. They can then choose to share it with the group if they feel comfortable. Example: "Today, I'm grateful for the support of my family during a challenging time."

- **Guided Visualization**   The facilitator guides participants through a relaxation exercise, asking them to visualize a place or scenario that brings them peace and comfort. Example: "Close your eyes and imagine a serene beach. Feel the warm sand beneath your feet and the gentle breeze against your skin..."

- **Personal symbols**   Participants choose an object or symbol that represents them in some way. They share why they picked that symbol and what it signifies to them. Example: "I chose a compass because it represents my love for exploration and finding new paths."

Remember, the key is to create an atmosphere of trust and respect, where participants feel comfortable sharing. Icebreakers should be inclusive and non-invasive, allowing individuals to reveal as much as they are comfortable with. These activities can set a positive tone for the session and promote a sense of unity among participants.

Sharing and Support

After the icebreaker, delve deeper into group sharing and support with a goal of fostering a culture of emotional resilience. Here are some sharing and support ideas:

- **Sharing personal resilience stories**   Invite participants to share their personal experiences of resilience. These stories serve as powerful examples of overcoming challenges and demonstrate the diverse ways in which emotional resilience can be applied. Encourage individuals to reflect on the specific strategies and mindsets that contributed to their resilience.

- **Empathetic listening and reflection**   Create opportunities for empathetic listening and reflection. Pair participants and provide them with a structured format for sharing. One person shares a personal challenge or experience, while the other listens attentively. Afterward, the listener offers reflections on what they heard, emphasizing understanding and validation.

- **Group discussions on resilience themes**   Facilitate group discussions on specific resilience themes or topics. These discussions provide a platform for participants to exchange insights, strategies, and perspectives related to emotional resilience. Encourage open dialogue, inviting participants to contribute their unique viewpoints.

- **Peer support circles**   Establish peer support circles within the group. These small, dedicated groups meet regularly to provide mutual encouragement, share experiences, and offer support. Peer support circles create a sense of belonging and camaraderie, reinforcing the notion that individuals are not alone in their challenges.

- **Collaborative problem-solving sessions**   Organize sessions focused on collaborative problem-solving. Present participants with hypothetical or real-life challenges, and encourage them to work together to generate solutions. This exercise promotes teamwork, creative thinking, and the application of emotional resilience in practical situations.

- **Guided visualization and mindfulness practices**   Incorporate guided visualization and mindfulness practices into group sessions. These exercises promote relaxation, self-awareness, and present-moment awareness. Guided visualization can help participants envision themselves successfully navigating challenges, bolstering their confidence and resilience.

- **Creative expression and art-based activities**   Integrate creative expression and art-based activities into group sessions. Participants can use various artistic mediums to convey their emotions, experiences, and resilience journeys. Creative outlets offer alternative forms of self-expression and promote emotional well-being.

- **Role reversal and perspective-taking**   Engage participants in role-reversal exercises that encourage them to view challenges from different perspectives. This fosters empathy and understanding, allowing individuals to gain insights into the experiences of others. It promotes a more holistic approach to emotional resilience.

- **Appreciative inquiry**   Incorporate the principles of appreciative inquiry, which focuses on identifying strengths and opportunities for growth. Participants engage in positive, forward-looking discussions that highlight successes and explore possibilities for building on them.

By incorporating these practical exercises into group sessions, individuals can actively contribute to a culture of emotional resilience. These activities promote connection, self-awareness, and the development of adaptive coping strategies. Participants emerge from these sessions with strengthened resilience skills and a deeper appreciation for the power of collective support.

Scenario Analysis: Enhancing Response Strategies

Next, we'll immerse ourselves in a series of meticulously curated real-world scenarios, each one carefully chosen to offer a diverse range of challenges and opportunities for growth. These scenarios serve as invaluable learning tools, enabling you to step into different roles and navigate complex situations with emotional resilience at the forefront.

For each scenario, you'll encounter the following components:

- **Introduction** We'll set the stage by introducing the scenario, providing you with context, and outlining the key players and their roles in the situation.

- **Reflective Questions** Before delving into the details, you'll be presented with thought-provoking questions designed to stimulate critical thinking and encourage you to consider potential approaches.

- **Detailed Scenario & Handling** We'll present the scenario in its entirety, offering a comprehensive view of the situation, the challenges it poses, and the dynamics at play. We'll provide you with an in-depth analysis of how this situation was handled in the real world. This includes a detailed account of the strategies employed, the decisions made, and the communication tactics used by those involved.

- **Outcome** You'll gain insight into the results and consequences of the actions taken in the real-world scenario. Understanding the outcomes, whether positive or with areas for improvement, is crucial in refining your own response strategies.

By engaging with these scenarios, you'll not only enhance your decision-making, communication, and adaptability skills, but also develop a deeper understanding of how emotional resilience can be applied in various professional contexts. Through active participation and reflection, you'll be better equipped to tackle similar challenges you may encounter in your own leadership journey.

Real-World Scenario 1: Crisis Management in the Financial Sector

In the wake of a major economic downturn, a prominent financial institution found itself grappling with unprecedented challenges. The CEO, an experienced leader known for his remarkable emotional resilience, was thrust into the center of a maelstrom. The financial sector was reeling, and stakeholders were seeking reassurance and stability.

Recognizing the critical role of middle management in executing the organization's strategy, the CEO invested significant effort in equipping these leaders with the tools and information they needed. He held regular meetings with department heads, providing them with a platform to voice their concerns and share insights. This inclusive approach ensured that decision-making was informed by a broad spectrum of perspectives, leading to more robust strategies.

Reflective Questions

1. Imagine you are the CEO in this scenario. What would be your initial thoughts and feelings when faced with such unprecedented challenges? How would you cultivate emotional resilience to navigate through them?
2. Consider the importance of middle management in executing the organization's strategy. What challenges might they face during a crisis like this, and how can their insights and perspectives be valuable in building organizational resilience?
3. Reflect on the delicate balance the CEO might strike between pragmatism and empathy. Why is it important for leaders to maintain this balance during times of crisis? Can you recall a situation where you had to make a similar decision, and how did emotional resilience play a role?
4. Think about why the CEO might focus on the long-term vision. Why is it crucial to balance immediate challenges with future positioning, and how might strategic thinking contribute to the organization's emotional resilience and overall resilience?

5. Consider the concept of emotional resilience. How do you define it, and why is it vital for leaders, especially in challenging times? Can you think of other instances where emotional resilience played a pivotal role in overcoming adversity?

Take some time to analyze the scenario presented. Consider the various elements, decisions, and challenges faced by the CEO and the financial institution. Jot down your thoughts and insights.

Scenario 1 In Full

In the wake of a major economic downturn, a prominent financial institution found itself grappling with unprecedented challenges. The CEO, an experienced leader known for his remarkable emotional resilience, was thrust into the center of a maelstrom. The financial sector was reeling, and stakeholders were seeking reassurance and stability.

Recognizing the critical role of middle management in executing the organization's strategy, the CEO invested significant effort in equipping these leaders with the tools and information they needed. He held regular meetings with department heads, providing them with a platform to voice their concerns and share insights. This inclusive approach ensured that decision-making was informed by a broad spectrum of perspectives, leading to more robust strategies.

Throughout the crisis, the CEO demonstrated a profound level of emotional resilience. While he made difficult decisions to stabilize the organization, such as restructuring and cost-cutting measures, he did so with a genuine understanding of the human impact. He sought to mitigate job losses wherever possible and provided support services for affected employees. This combination of decisive action and compassionate leadership was instrumental in maintaining morale.

In the midst of crisis management, the CEO maintained a steadfast focus on the long-term vision for the organization. He understood that while immediate challenges were pressing, it was equally important to position the institution for future success. This required strategic thinking and a commitment to innovation. He encouraged teams to explore new revenue streams and invest in areas with growth potential, demonstrating a forward-looking perspective.

Outcome

Under the CEO's guidance and exceptional emotional resilience, the financial institution not only weathered the storm but emerged with renewed strength. By navigating the crisis with emotional intelligence and resilience, he instilled confidence in stakeholders, preserved the organization's integrity, and positioned it for sustained success in the years that followed. This case study serves as a powerful example of the profound impact that emotional resilience can have on crisis management and organizational resilience. It underscores the importance of level-headed leadership in times of adversity and provides valuable lessons for leaders facing similar challenges.

Real-World Scenario 2: Leading Through a Global Pandemic

As the world grappled with the unprecedented challenges posed by a global pandemic, leaders across various industries were faced with the monumental task of navigating uncharted territory. In the healthcare sector, where the stakes were particularly high, a seasoned hospital administrator with a remarkable capacity for emotional resilience found herself at the forefront of the crisis.

With years of experience in healthcare administration, the hospital administrator was no stranger to high-pressure situations. However, the scale and complexity of the pandemic presented a unique set of challenges. Her response was characterized by a blend of emotional resilience, strategic thinking, and compassionate leadership.

Reflective Questions

1. Imagine yourself in the shoes of the hospital administrator. What emotions and thoughts might you experience when faced with the challenges of a global pandemic? How would you cultivate emotional resilience to navigate through them?
2. Why is clear communication crucial in a crisis, particularly in a healthcare setting? How can transparency build trust and unity among a community?
3. Reflect on why the administrator might use an empathetic leadership style. Why is it important for leaders to be empathetic, especially in high-stress situations? Can you recall a time when empathy made a significant difference in a crisis?
4. Consider the administrator's ability to make decisive decisions and adapt to evolving circumstances. Why is this skill set vital in crisis management? How do you think her collaboration with medical experts contributed to effective decision-making?
5. Reflect on what measures might be taken to prioritize the safety of healthcare workers. Why is ensuring the safety of frontline workers a critical aspect of crisis response?

6. Why is it important for leaders to engage with the broader community during a crisis? How might collaboration with various stakeholders enhance the effectiveness of a response?

7. Consider the emphasis on staff education and training. Why is ongoing professional development important, especially in rapidly evolving situations like a pandemic?

Take some time to analyze the scenario provided. Consider the strategies employed by the hospital administrator and the impact they had on the hospital's response to the pandemic. Jot down your thoughts and insights.

Scenario 2 In Full

As the world grappled with the unprecedented challenges posed by a global pandemic, leaders across various industries were faced with the monumental task of navigating uncharted territory. In the healthcare sector, where the stakes were particularly high, a seasoned hospital administrator with a remarkable capacity for emotional resilience found herself at the forefront of the crisis.

With years of experience in healthcare administration, the hospital administrator was no stranger to high-pressure situations. However, the scale and complexity of the pandemic presented a unique set of challenges. Her response was characterized by a blend of emotional resilience, strategic thinking, and compassionate leadership.

Recognizing the critical importance of clear communication during a crisis, the administrator prioritized transparency. She established regular communication channels to keep staff, patients, and stakeholders informed of the evolving situation. This included daily briefings, email updates, and town hall meetings. Her transparent approach helped to alleviate anxiety and fostered a sense of trust and unity among the hospital community.

The administrator demonstrated exceptional empathy, recognizing the emotional toll the pandemic was taking on her team. She actively listened to the concerns and fears of staff members, providing a supportive space for them to express themselves. She implemented initiatives to bolster mental health resources, offering counseling services and stress-relief activities. This empathetic approach not only supported the well-being of her team but also enhanced their resilience in the face of adversity.

In the early stages of the pandemic, uncertainty loomed large. The administrator's ability to make swift, well-informed decisions was instrumental. She worked closely with medical experts to develop and implement robust protocols for patient care, staff safety, and resource allocation. As the situation evolved, she remained adaptable, adjusting strategies in response to emerging data and best practices.

The safety of healthcare workers was of utmost concern. The administrator took proactive measures to secure personal protective equipment (PPE) and implement rigorous infection control protocols. She also established dedicated COVID-19 units and isolation areas within the hospital, minimizing the risk of transmission. These measures were crucial in safeguarding the well-being of frontline workers.

Recognizing the broader impact of the pandemic on the community, the administrator took steps to engage with local stakeholders. She collaborated with public health authorities, government agencies, and community organizations to coordinate efforts and share resources. Additionally, she facilitated initiatives to support vulnerable populations, such as providing free testing and telehealth services.

In the face of rapidly evolving medical knowledge about the virus, the administrator prioritized staff education and training. She facilitated regular workshops and seminars, ensuring that healthcare professionals were equipped with the latest information and best practices. This investment in professional development not only bolstered the hospital's response to the pandemic but also enhanced the skill sets of its staff for the long term.

Outcome

Through her unwavering leadership, the hospital administrator successfully guided her team through the challenges of the global pandemic. The hospital not only maintained its commitment to high-quality patient care but also emerged as a source of strength and support for the community. This case study exemplifies the power of emotional resilience, empathy, and strategic decision-making in navigating unprecedented crises. It serves as a testament to the pivotal role that leaders play in times of adversity and provides valuable insights for those facing similar challenges.

Real-World Scenario 3: Navigating a Complex Merger

In the fast-paced world of global finance, mergers and acquisitions are commonplace. However, when two financial powerhouses embarked on a merger, they faced a confluence of complexities. The task at hand was not only to blend their extensive operations seamlessly but also to do so in a way that preserved client trust and upheld regulatory compliance.

At the helm of this ambitious undertaking were two Chief Executive Officers, each known for their distinct leadership styles. The first, renowned for a visionary approach, was adept at steering organizations through transformative change. The second, known for his astute operational expertise, was skilled at optimizing processes for efficiency and profitability. Together, the two Chief Executive Officers formed a formidable leadership team tasked with guiding the merger. Recognizing the emotional toll that mergers can take on employees, the CEOs prioritized emotional resilience.

Reflective Questions

1. Put yourself in the shoes of the CEOs. What emotions and thoughts might you experience when tasked with guiding a complex merger of financial powerhouses? How would you cultivate emotional resilience to navigate through them?
2. Consider the distinct leadership styles of the two CEOs. How might their individual strengths contribute to the success of the merger? How could potential differences be leveraged for positive outcomes?
3. Reflect on the CEOs' emphasis on emotional resilience. Why is this particularly important in the context of mergers and acquisitions? Can you think of a similar situation where emotional resilience played a pivotal role?
4. Reconciling disparate organizational cultures is a significant challenge. Why is this important for the success of a merger? How might employee involvement in this process contribute to a unified culture?
5. Consider the CEOs' approach to decision-making. Why is it crucial to strike a balance between long-term vision and short-term imperatives during a merger?

6. Why is preserving client trust crucial in a merger? Can you think of a scenario where client confidence played a pivotal role in a business transition?

7. Reflect on the importance of regulatory compliance in the context of a merger. Why is meticulous due diligence and risk mitigation strategies crucial for success?

8. Why is talent retention key to a successful merger? Can you recall a situation where a comprehensive employee development program contributed to the success of a transition?

Take some time to analyze the scenario provided. Consider the strategies employed by the CEOs and their impact on the merger process. Jot down your thoughts and insights.

Scenario 3 In Full

In the fast-paced world of global finance, mergers and acquisitions are commonplace. However, when two financial powerhouses embarked on a merger, they faced a confluence of complexities. The task at hand was not only to blend their extensive operations seamlessly but also to do so in a way that preserved client trust and upheld regulatory compliance.

At the helm of this ambitious undertaking were two Chief Executive Officers, each known for their distinct leadership styles. The first, renowned for a visionary approach, was adept at steering organizations through transformative change. The second, known for his astute operational expertise, was skilled at optimizing processes for efficiency and profitability. Together, the two Chief Executive Officers formed a formidable leadership team tasked with guiding the merger. Recognizing the emotional toll that mergers can take on employees, the CEOs prioritized emotional resilience.

They understood that open communication, empathy, and managing resistance were critical to success. They embarked on a comprehensive communication strategy, addressing concerns, and providing regular updates to staff at all levels. In addition to transparency, they emphasized adaptability, encouraging teams to embrace change and view it as an opportunity for growth.

One of the primary challenges in any merger is reconciling disparate organizational cultures. The CEOs took a deliberate approach, involving employees from both companies in the process. They held workshops and town hall meetings, allowing staff to voice their perspectives and concerns. This inclusive approach not only fostered a sense of ownership but also laid the foundation for a unified culture.

The CEOs recognized the need for strategic decision-making that balanced long-term vision with short-term imperatives. They established cross-functional teams to assess the impact of various integration strategies. These teams conducted thorough analyses, evaluating the potential benefits and risks associated with each option. This rigorous approach ensured that decisions were rooted in data and aligned with the overall merger objectives.

Preserving client trust was crucial in the merger process. The CEOs understood that clients were closely monitoring the transition and that any disruptions could erode confidence. They implemented a client communication strategy that provided transparency about the merger's progress and outlined the benefits it would bring. Additionally, they established a dedicated client support team to address inquiries and concerns promptly.

Navigating the complex landscape of regulatory compliance was a critical aspect of the merger. The CEOs assembled a specialized team focused on ensuring adherence to all relevant regulations. This team conducted extensive due diligence, identifying potential compliance risks and implementing robust risk mitigation strategies. Their meticulous approach helped to safeguard the merger process from legal and regulatory pitfalls.

Recognizing that talent retention was key to a successful merger, the CEOs prioritized employee development. They launched a comprehensive training program, equipping staff with the skills and knowledge needed to thrive in the merged entity. Additionally, they implemented retention incentives, ensuring that key talent remained engaged and committed throughout the transition. They also established channels for feedback, allowing employees to express concerns and suggestions, further enhancing their resilience in the face of change.

Outcome

Through meticulous planning, strategic decision-making, and a steadfast commitment to emotional resilience, the CEOs successfully navigated the complex merger. The merged entity emerged as a stronger, more competitive player in the financial sector, seamlessly integrating operations and delivering enhanced value to clients. This case study serves as a testament to the transformative power of effective leadership in the context of mergers and acquisitions, offering valuable insights for leaders embarking on similar endeavors.

Real-World Scenario 4: Crisis Response in the Public Sector

In a rapidly changing world, governmental organizations face an array of challenges, from natural disasters to public health emergencies. This case study centers on a public health crisis that required swift, coordinated action across multiple agencies and levels of government. A novel infectious disease emerged, rapidly spreading within the community. The crisis necessitated a multi-agency response, involving local, state, and federal entities. The crisis management team comprised leaders from various sectors, including healthcare, emergency management, law enforcement, and public communication.

Recognizing the emotional toll that such crises can take on both responders and the affected community, leaders prioritized emotional resilience. They understood that open communication, empathy, and managing resistance were crucial to success. The leaders created a supportive environment that encouraged team members to express their concerns and emotions, providing resources for mental health support. This proactive approach not only fortified the emotional well-being of their teams but also enhanced their capacity to cope with the challenges at hand.

Reflective Questions

1. Put yourself in the shoes of one of the leaders in this scenario. What would be your initial thoughts and emotions when faced with such a rapidly unfolding public health crisis? How would you cultivate emotional resilience to navigate through them?
2. Reflect on the importance of emotional resilience in managing a crisis. Why is it crucial for leaders to prioritize open communication, empathy, and active listening during high-stress situations? Can you think of a situation where emotional resilience played a pivotal role?
3. Consider the role of clear and transparent communication in a crisis. Why is this particularly important in a public health emergency? Can you recall a situation where communication played a pivotal role in crisis response?
4. Reflect on the need for collaborative decision-making in a complex crisis. Why is it valuable to gather diverse perspectives and expertise

when making critical decisions? Can you think of a scenario where collaborative decision-making was instrumental?

5. Why is it essential to engage and empower the affected community during a crisis? How might involving community leaders and organizations enhance the effectiveness of response efforts?

6. Consider the importance of efficient resource allocation in crisis management. Why is it critical to assess and prioritize resource needs? Can you recall a situation where resource allocation was a significant factor in a crisis response?

7. Reflect on the power of data in crisis response. Why is it crucial to collect and analyze data for decision-making? Can you think of a scenario where data-driven insights played a pivotal role in crisis management?

8. Why is it important to conduct a thorough review and analysis after a crisis? How can lessons learned inform future preparedness and response efforts?

Take some time to analyze the scenario provided. Consider the strategies employed by the crisis management team and their impact on the public health crisis. Jot down your thoughts and insights.

Scenario 4 In Full

In a rapidly changing world, governmental organizations face an array of challenges, from natural disasters to public health emergencies. This case study centers on a public health crisis that required swift, coordinated action across multiple agencies and levels of government. A novel infectious disease emerged, rapidly spreading within the community. The crisis necessitated a multi-agency response, involving local, state, and federal entities. The crisis management team comprised leaders from various sectors, including healthcare, emergency management, law enforcement, and public communication.

Recognizing the emotional toll that such crises can take on both responders and the affected community, leaders prioritized emotional resilience. They understood that open communication, empathy, and managing resistance were crucial to success. The leaders created a supportive environment that encouraged team members to express their concerns and emotions, providing resources for mental health support. This proactive approach not only fortified the emotional well-being of their teams but also enhanced their capacity to cope with the challenges at hand.

In the midst of a crisis, clear and transparent communication is essential. The crisis management team recognized that effective communication could make a significant difference in the community's response. They established a dedicated communication center staffed with trained communicators and subject-matter experts. This team worked tirelessly to disseminate accurate and timely information to the public. They held regular press briefings, providing updates on the situation, safety measures, and resources available. By addressing concerns directly and honestly, they fostered trust and confidence in their response efforts.

The complexity of the crisis necessitated collaborative decision-making. The leaders understood that no single individual possessed all the answers. They valued the expertise of their team members and ensured that everyone's voice was heard. They convened daily strategy sessions, where experts from various fields shared insights and recommendations. This collaborative approach ensured that decisions were well-informed and collectively endorsed, instilling a sense of collective ownership and shared responsibility.

Engaging the affected community was essential to an effective response. Leaders established community outreach teams comprised of trained personnel who were not only knowledgeable about the crisis but also skilled in offering emotional support. These teams provided information, resources, and assistance directly to residents. Additionally, they empowered community leaders and organizations to play an active role in the response efforts. This approach not only bolstered community resilience but also ensured that response strategies were culturally sensitive and tailored to local needs.

Efficient resource allocation is critical in crisis management. Leaders conducted rigorous assessments to identify and prioritize resource needs. They established centralized warehouses for medical supplies, protective equipment, and essential supplies. Additionally, they coordinated with private sector partners to ensure a steady supply chain and seamless distribution of resources. This meticulous approach not only ensured that resources were available where they were needed most but also demonstrated a commitment to effective and responsible resource management.

In a rapidly evolving crisis, data is a powerful tool for decision-making. Leaders implemented robust data collection and analysis systems to monitor the spread of the disease, track resource utilization, and assess the effectiveness of interventions. Data-driven insights informed real-time adjustments to response strategies, allowing for agile and targeted actions. This evidence-based approach not only instilled confidence in their decision-making but also enabled them to adapt swiftly to the evolving nature of the crisis.

As the crisis abated, leaders conducted a thorough review of their response efforts. They identified successes, areas for improvement, and lessons learned. This post-crisis evaluation informed updates to emergency response plans, resource allocation strategies, and communication protocols, ensuring greater preparedness for future crises. By maintaining a forward-looking perspective, they reinforced their organization's resilience and readiness for future challenges.

Outcome

Through a combination of emotional resilience, collaborative decision-making, and data-driven response, the crisis management team effectively navigated the public health crisis. Their coordinated efforts led to a controlled containment of the disease, minimizing its impact on the community. This case study serves as a testament to the power of effective leadership in crisis response, providing valuable insights for leaders facing similar challenges in the public sector.

Real-World Scenario 5: Innovating in the Technology Sector

The technology sector is known for its rapid pace of innovation, demanding leaders who can navigate complex landscapes while fostering creativity and adaptability. This case study focuses on a leading technology company facing a critical turning point in the industry. The company, a prominent player in the tech sector, found itself at a crossroads. Disruptive technologies were reshaping the industry, and competition was fiercer than ever. The leadership team recognized the need for a transformative approach to stay relevant and maintain their position as industry leaders.

Understanding that innovation often requires a delicate balance of risk-taking, creativity, and collaboration, the leadership team placed a strong emphasis on emotional resilience. They knew that in the face of uncertainty and the need for bold steps, emotional resilience would be crucial for themselves and their teams. They fostered a culture of psychological safety, where employees felt encouraged to share ideas and take calculated risks without fear of retribution. This approach fueled a culture of innovation, as team members felt empowered to explore new possibilities.

Reflective Questions

1. Put yourself in the shoes of one of the leaders in this scenario. What might be your initial thoughts and emotions when faced with the need for transformative change in a rapidly evolving tech industry? How would you cultivate emotional resilience to navigate through them?
2. Reflect on the importance of emotional resilience in fostering innovation. Why is it crucial for leaders to create a culture of psychological safety for risk-taking and creativity? Can you think of a scenario where emotional resilience played a pivotal role in driving innovation?
3. Consider the role of experimentation and learning from failures in fostering innovation. Why is it important for organizations to create environments where employees can take calculated risks? Can you recall a situation where experimentation led to a breakthrough?

4. Reflect on the value of cross-functional collaboration in driving innovation. Why is it beneficial for teams from diverse departments to come together for ideation? Can you think of a scenario where interdisciplinary collaboration resulted in a groundbreaking solution?

5. Why is it important for innovation to be embedded throughout the organization, not just at the leadership level? Can you recall a time when an employee-led innovation significantly impacted an organization's trajectory?

6. Reflect on the significance of designing innovations with the customer in mind. Why is it crucial for solutions to address real-world problems and meet customer needs? Can you think of a scenario where a customer-centric approach led to a successful innovation?

7. Consider the dynamic nature of the tech industry. Why is it essential for organizations to be adaptable and stay ahead of market trends? Can you recall a situation where a company successfully navigated market shifts?

8. Reflect on the importance of tracking and measuring innovation efforts. Why is a data-driven approach valuable in assessing the impact of innovation initiatives? Can you think of a scenario where data-driven insights guided an organization's innovation strategy?

Take some time to analyze the scenario provided. Consider the strategies employed by the leadership team and their impact on the technology company's innovation efforts. Jot down your thoughts and insights.

Scenario 5 In Full

The technology sector is known for its rapid pace of Innovation, demanding leaders who can navigate complex landscapes while fostering creativity and adaptability. This case study focuses on a leading technology company facing a critical turning point in the industry. The company, a prominent player in the tech sector, found itself at a crossroads. Disruptive technologies were reshaping the industry, and competition was fiercer than ever. The leadership team recognized the need for a transformative approach to stay relevant and maintain their position as industry leaders.

Understanding that innovation often requires a delicate balance of risk-taking, creativity, and collaboration, the leadership team placed a strong emphasis on emotional resilience. They knew that in the face of uncertainty and the need for bold steps, emotional resilience would be crucial for themselves and their teams. They fostered a culture of psychological safety, where employees felt encouraged to share ideas and take calculated risks without fear of retribution. This approach fueled a culture of innovation, as team members felt empowered to explore new possibilities.

Innovation thrives in environments that encourage experimentation and learning from failures. The company not only provided resources for experimentation but also openly acknowledged that not every experiment would yield immediate success. They celebrated the lessons learned from failures and saw them as critical stepping stones toward breakthroughs. This culture of experimentation not only led to innovations but also instilled a mindset of continuous learning and adaptation.

Recognizing that the most innovative solutions often emerge at the intersection of different disciplines, the leadership team encouraged cross-functional collaboration. They organized regular forums where teams from diverse departments could come together to brainstorm, ideate, and co-create. This approach sparked interdisciplinary collaborations that resulted in groundbreaking products and solutions. They understood that this kind of collaboration required resilience in adapting to new perspectives and approaches.

The company understood that innovation is not solely the responsibility of the leadership team, but should be embedded in the DNA of the entire organization. They implemented innovation challenges and competitions, inviting employees at all levels to submit their ideas for evaluation. This approach not only unearthed hidden talents and perspectives but also instilled a sense of ownership and pride in the organization's innovation journey. This sense of ownership was a testament to the emotional resilience of the employees.

Innovation is most impactful when it addresses real-world problems and meets the needs of customers. The company adopted a customer-centric design thinking approach, conducting extensive user research and feedback sessions. This human-centered approach ensured that their innovations were not just technologically advanced, but also provided meaningful solutions to their customers' pain points. It required resilience to pivot and refine solutions based on user feedback.

The technology sector is inherently dynamic, with market trends and consumer preferences evolving rapidly. The leadership team maintained a keen awareness of market shifts and emerging technologies. They established a dedicated team responsible for trend analysis and market intelligence, ensuring that the company remained ahead of the curve in anticipating and responding to industry changes. This proactive approach required a level of emotional resilience to navigate uncertainties and make strategic decisions.

Innovation efforts were tracked and measured against key performance indicators (KPIs) aligned with the company's strategic objectives. This data-driven approach allowed the leadership team to assess the impact of their innovation initiatives, identify areas for optimization, and allocate resources effectively. It required resilience to face the data, even if it pointed to areas that needed improvement, and to make adjustments accordingly.

Outcome

By prioritizing emotional resilience, fostering a culture of experimentation, and embracing cross-functional collaboration, the technology company successfully navigated the challenges of the rapidly evolving industry. Their commitment to innovation not only ensured their continued relevance but also solidified their position as industry trailblazers, setting a benchmark for excellence in the technology sector. This case study exemplifies the power of innovative leadership in driving organizational success in the fast-paced world of technology.

Real-World Scenario 6: Resilience in Educational Leadership

Educational leadership plays a pivotal role in shaping the learning experiences and outcomes of students. This case study examines a school district facing multifaceted challenges, where resilient leadership was instrumental in driving positive change. The school district served a diverse student population, with varying socioeconomic backgrounds and learning needs. Limited resources, coupled with external pressures such as standardized testing and evolving curriculum requirements, created a complex environment for educational leaders. The district faced the challenge of ensuring equitable access to quality education while navigating budget constraints and policy changes.

Recognizing the importance of empathy, understanding, and effective communication in educational leadership, the district's leadership team placed a strong emphasis on emotional resilience. They knew that in the face of uncertainty and the need for bold steps, emotional resilience would be crucial for themselves and their teams. They prioritized creating a supportive and inclusive school culture, where both students and staff felt valued and heard. They recognized that resilience was not only about overcoming challenges, but also about fostering an environment where everyone could thrive.

Reflective Questions

1. Place yourself in the shoes of one of the leaders in this scenario. What might be your initial thoughts and emotions when faced with the need for transformative change in a rapidly evolving tech industry? How would you cultivate emotional resilience to navigate through them?

2. Reflect on the importance of emotional resilience in fostering innovation. Why is it crucial for leaders to create a culture of psychological safety for risk-taking and creativity? Can you think of a scenario where emotional resilience played a pivotal role in driving innovation?

3. Consider the role of experimentation and learning from failures in fostering innovation. Why is it important for organizations to create

environments where employees can take calculated risks? Can you recall a situation where experimentation led to a breakthrough?

4. Reflect on the value of cross-functional collaboration in driving innovation. Why is it beneficial for teams from diverse departments to come together for ideation? Can you think of a scenario where interdisciplinary collaboration resulted in a groundbreaking solution?

5. Why is it important for innovation to be embedded throughout the organization, not just at the leadership level? Can you recall a time when an employee-led innovation significantly impacted an organization's trajectory?

6. Reflect on the significance of designing innovations with the customer in mind. Why is it crucial for solutions to address real-world problems and meet customer needs? Can you think of a scenario where a customer-centric approach led to a successful innovation?

7. Consider the dynamic nature of the tech industry. Why is it essential for organizations to be adaptable and stay ahead of market trends? Can you recall a situation where a company successfully navigated market shifts?

8. Reflect on the importance of tracking and measuring innovation efforts. Why is a data-driven approach valuable in assessing the impact of innovation initiatives? Can you think of a scenario where data-driven insights guided an organization's innovation strategy?

Take some time to analyze the scenario provided. Consider the strategies employed and their impact. Jot down your thoughts and insights.

Scenario 6 In Full

Educational leadership plays a pivotal role in shaping the learning experiences and outcomes of students. This case study examines a school district facing multifaceted challenges, where resilient leadership was instrumental in driving positive change. The school district served a diverse student population, with varying socioeconomic backgrounds and learning needs. Limited resources, coupled with external pressures such as standardized testing and evolving curriculum requirements, created a complex environment for educational leaders. The district faced the challenge of ensuring equitable access to quality education while navigating budget constraints and policy changes.

Recognizing the importance of empathy, understanding, and effective communication in educational leadership, the district's leadership team placed a strong emphasis on emotional resilience. They knew that in the face of uncertainty and the need for bold steps, emotional resilience would be crucial for themselves and their teams. They prioritized creating a supportive and inclusive school culture, where both students and staff felt valued and heard. They recognized that resilience was not only about overcoming challenges, but also about fostering an environment where everyone could thrive.

Investing in the professional development of teachers and staff was an essential component of the district's approach. They provided ongoing training in areas such as trauma-informed teaching, culturally responsive pedagogy, and social-emotional learning. This equipped educators with the tools and strategies to address the diverse needs of their students effectively. They understood that resilience also meant being adaptable and equipped to support students facing a wide range of challenges.

The district encouraged collaboration among teachers, fostering a culture of shared learning and best practice exchange. They implemented regular professional learning communities (PLCs) where educators could collaborate on curriculum development, assessment strategies, and innovative teaching methods. This collaborative approach not only strengthened instructional practices but also built a sense of collective responsibility for student success. It required resilience to adapt teaching methods based on feedback and evolving educational approaches.

Understanding that each student's journey is unique, the district implemented a range of student-centered interventions. They established support systems such as mentoring programs, academic tutoring, and counseling services to address the individual needs of students facing academic, social, or emotional challenges. This personalized approach required resilience to navigate the complexities of each student's situation and find tailored solutions.

Recognizing the crucial role of parents and the broader community in a child's educational journey, the district actively sought to engage families in the learning process. They organized regular parent-teacher conferences, workshops, and community events to facilitate open communication and collaboration. This approach fostered a sense of partnership in supporting students' academic and personal growth. It required resilience to navigate potential communication challenges and ensure that all voices were heard.

The district remained attuned to shifts in educational policy, curriculum standards, and technological advancements. They established a dedicated team responsible for monitoring changes in the educational landscape and providing guidance on implementation strategies. This proactive approach ensured that the district remained aligned with evolving best practices. It required resilience to adapt to new policies and approaches while maintaining a focus on student success.

The district employed a balanced approach to assessment, incorporating both standardized testing and holistic measures of student success. They tracked academic progress, attendance rates, and social-emotional development indicators to gain a comprehensive understanding of each student's growth. This data-driven approach informed instructional decisions and allowed for targeted interventions when needed. It required resilience to interpret and act on data, even when it revealed areas that needed improvement.

Outcome

Through a combination of emotional resilience, professional development, collaborative learning communities, student-centered interventions, and community engagement, the school district achieved notable improvements in student outcomes. Graduation rates increased, standardized test scores improved, and students reported feeling more supported and engaged in their learning. This case study exemplifies the transformative impact of resilient educational leadership on the overall success and well-being of students. It serves as a testament to the potential for positive change when educational leaders prioritize empathy, collaboration, and student-centered approaches.

Measuring and Monitoring Emotional Resilience

In the realm of leadership, especially when it comes to emotional intelligence and resilience, measurement and assessment are critical. It allows leaders to understand their strengths, identify areas for improvement, and track progress over time. In this section, we delve into the metrics and indicators of individual emotional resilience, offering practical tools for leaders to evaluate and enhance this crucial aspect of their leadership capacity.

Defining Metrics for Emotional Resilience

Measuring emotional resilience requires a nuanced approach. It encompasses various dimensions, including self-awareness, adaptability, and the ability to bounce back from adversity. Metrics for emotional resilience should be designed to capture these facets comprehensively.

Here are some strategies for assessing emotional resilience, whether it's within yourself or in others within your organization:

- **Self-Assessment Tools** One of the fundamental ways to measure emotional resilience is through self-assessment tools. These may take the form of surveys or questionnaires that prompt individuals to reflect on their responses to challenging situations. Questions may explore their emotional reactions, coping mechanisms, and perceptions of their own resilience.

- **360-Degree Feedback** Gathering feedback from peers, subordinates, and superiors can provide valuable insights into an individual's emotional resilience. This 360-degree approach offers a well-rounded perspective on how a leader's emotional responses impact those around them. It also highlights areas where improvement may be needed.

- **Emotional Intelligence Assessments** There are established assessments that specifically measure emotional intelligence, which is closely linked to emotional resilience. These assessments often explore competencies such as self-awareness, self-regulation, empathy, and relationship management.

Scores on these assessments can serve as indicators of a leader's overall emotional resilience.

- **Behavioral Observations**   Observing how a leader handles challenging situations in real-time provides a dynamic measure of their emotional resilience. This can be done through structured scenarios or by paying close attention to how a leader responds to unexpected events. Behavioral observations offer valuable insights into the practical application of emotional resilience.

- **Physical and Psychological Health Indicators**   Emotional resilience is closely tied to both physical and psychological well-being. Indicators such as stress levels, sleep quality, and overall mental health can serve as proxies for emotional resilience. Leaders who exhibit good physical and psychological health are often better equipped to navigate challenges.

- **Adaptability in Dynamic Environments**   Measuring how well a leader adapts to change and uncertainty is a key component of emotional resilience. This can be assessed by evaluating their track record in leading teams through periods of transition, as well as their willingness to embrace new approaches and ideas.

- **Response to Feedback and Criticism**   A leader's ability to receive and act upon feedback is indicative of their emotional resilience. Leaders who are open to constructive criticism and demonstrate a willingness to learn and grow are often more emotionally resilient. Their capacity to view feedback as an opportunity for growth is a positive sign.

- **Resilience in the Face of Setbacks**   Assessing how a leader handles setbacks and failures is a direct measure of their emotional resilience. Leaders who are able to bounce back from adversity, learn from their experiences, and maintain a forward-looking perspective demonstrate a high level of emotional resilience.

- **Long-Term Consistency in Emotional Responses**   Consistency in emotional responses over time is a reliable indicator of emotional resilience. Leaders who exhibit stability in their emotional reactions, regardless of external circumstances, demonstrate a strong foundation of emotional resilience.

Measuring and monitoring emotional resilience is an essential component of effective leadership development. By utilizing a combination of self-assessment tools, feedback mechanisms, behavioral observations, and health indicators, leaders can gain valuable insights into their emotional resilience. These metrics serve as a roadmap for targeted development efforts, ultimately enhancing a leader's capacity to navigate challenges with grace and effectiveness.

Cultivating a Resilient Organizational Climate: Tools for Assessment

An organization's resilience is intrinsically linked to the collective emotional resilience of its members. Assessing and cultivating a resilient organizational climate is crucial for long-term success and adaptability. Tools and approaches that leaders can employ to evaluate and enhance the emotional resilience of their organizations include:

- **Surveys and Questionnaires**   Surveys and questionnaires are valuable tools for assessing the emotional climate within an organization. These tools can be designed to gather feedback from employees on various aspects, including their perception of support systems, stress levels, and their ability to cope with challenges. The data collected provides quantitative insights into the emotional well-being of the workforce.

- **Employee Engagement Surveys**   Employee engagement surveys often include questions related to emotional well-being and job satisfaction. By analyzing responses to these specific questions, leaders can gain a deeper understanding of how employees perceive their emotional experiences within the organization. Low scores in this area may indicate a need for targeted interventions.

- **Focus Groups and Interviews**   Engaging employees in open-ended discussions through focus groups or one-on-one interviews can yield qualitative insights into the emotional climate. This approach allows for a deeper exploration of specific issues and the identification of potential solutions. It also provides employees with a platform to voice their concerns and ideas for improvement.

- **Observations of Team Dynamics**   Leaders can assess team dynamics to gain insights into the emotional climate of their organization. Observations may focus on aspects such as communication styles, conflict resolution, and the overall cohesion of teams. Patterns of positive or negative emotional interactions can shed light on areas for improvement.

- **Analysis of Employee Feedback Channels**   Examining feedback received through various channels, such as suggestion boxes, anonymous reporting systems, or digital platforms, can provide valuable data on the emotional experiences of employees. Leaders can analyze trends and themes to identify areas where emotional support or intervention may be required.

- **Turnover and Retention Rates**   High turnover rates can be indicative of underlying issues related to the emotional climate within an organization. Leaders should monitor turnover and retention rates, particularly in high-stress or high-pressure environments. A spike in turnover may signal the need for interventions to enhance emotional resilience.

- **Absenteeism and Presenteeism Patterns**   Patterns of absenteeism and presenteeism (employees attending work despite being unwell or experiencing high levels of stress) can offer insights into the emotional well-being of the workforce. High levels of absenteeism or widespread presenteeism may signal emotional challenges that need to be addressed.

- **Utilization of Employee Assistance Programs (EAPs)**   The utilization rates of EAPs can provide a gauge of the emotional support being accessed by employees. Analyzing the reasons for seeking assistance through these programs can shed light on prevalent emotional challenges within the organization.

- **Feedback on Organizational Policies and Practices**   Employees' perceptions of organizational policies and practices can greatly impact their emotional well-being. Gathering feedback on areas such as work-life balance initiatives, conflict resolution processes, and support systems can help identify areas for improvement.

- **Analysis of Performance Reviews and Feedback**   Performance reviews often include assessments of behavioral competencies, including emotional intelligence and resilience. Analyzing feedback from performance evaluations can offer insights into how emotional resilience is valued and assessed within the organization.

Assessing the emotional resilience of an organization is a multifaceted endeavor that requires a combination of quantitative and qualitative approaches. By leveraging surveys, interviews, observations, and feedback channels, leaders can gain a comprehensive understanding of the emotional climate. This insight serves as a foundation for targeted interventions and initiatives aimed at cultivating a resilient organizational culture. Ultimately, a resilient organizational climate empowers employees to navigate challenges with confidence and adaptability, contributing to the overall success and longevity of the organization.

Sustaining Emotional Resilience Over Time

We'll conclude this section by emphasizing the need for continuous learning and adaptation in the journey towards emotional resilience. We encourage leaders to view resilience-building as an ongoing process, one that requires dedication and commitment. This section also provides additional leadership practices to foster a resilient organizational culture, ensuring that the benefits of emotional resilience are sustained over time.

Continuous Learning and Adaptation: A Resilience-Building Journey

Emotional resilience is not a static trait; it is a dynamic skill that requires continuous learning and adaptation. Sustaining emotional resilience over time necessitates a commitment to personal growth, skill development, and a willingness to embrace change. In this section, we delve into strategies and practices that support the ongoing cultivation of emotional resilience.

Emotional resilience is not a static trait; it is a dynamic skill that requires continuous learning and adaptation. Sustaining emotional resilience over time necessitates a commitment to personal growth, skill development, and a willingness to embrace change. In this section, we delve into strategies and practices that support the ongoing cultivation of emotional resilience.

Here are some strategies for continuous learning and adaptation, whether it's within yourself or in others within your organization:

- **Embracing a Growth Mindset** A growth mindset is the belief that abilities and intelligence can be developed through dedication and hard work. Embracing this perspective fosters a sense of agency and empowerment, crucial elements of emotional resilience. Leaders can encourage a growth mindset within their teams by providing opportunities for skill-building, acknowledging efforts, and celebrating progress.

- **Prioritizing Self-Care**   Self-care is foundational to maintaining emotional resilience. It encompasses practices that nurture physical, mental, and emotional well-being. This may include regular exercise, proper nutrition, adequate sleep, and engaging in activities that bring joy and relaxation. Leaders play a pivotal role in promoting self-care by modeling these behaviors and creating a supportive environment that prioritizes well-being.

- **Engaging in Reflective Practices**   Reflective practices, such as journaling, meditation, or mindfulness exercises, provide individuals with an opportunity to process their experiences and emotions. Regular reflection fosters self-awareness, a key element of emotional resilience. Encouraging team members to engage in these practices can enhance their ability to navigate challenges effectively.

- **Continual Skill Development**   Building emotional resilience requires the acquisition of specific skills, such as emotional regulation, effective communication, and stress management. Leaders can facilitate skill development through training programs, workshops, and coaching opportunities. Providing access to resources and mentorship further supports ongoing growth.

- **Fostering a Supportive Community**   A sense of belonging and a supportive community are invaluable for sustaining emotional resilience. Leaders can create an environment where team members feel valued, heard, and supported. Encouraging open communication, celebrating successes, and providing avenues for feedback all contribute to a sense of community within the organization.

- **Encouraging Lifelong Learning**   Emotional resilience is fortified by a commitment to lifelong learning. This encompasses both formal education and informal learning opportunities. Leaders can foster a culture of curiosity and continuous learning by providing access to relevant resources, encouraging skill-building, and supporting professional development endeavors.

- **Promoting Flexibility and Adaptability**   The ability to adapt to change is a crucial aspect of emotional resilience. Leaders can create an organizational culture that values flexibility and encourages adaptability. This may involve revisiting and revising strategies, being open to new ideas, and empowering team members to navigate change effectively.

- **Setting Realistic Expectations**   Maintaining emotional resilience requires a realistic understanding of one's capabilities and limitations. Leaders can support their teams by setting achievable goals, providing clear expectations, and offering constructive feedback. Avoiding overburdening individuals and acknowledging their efforts fosters a sense of accomplishment and resilience.

- **Balancing Challenge and Support**   A balance between challenge and support is essential for sustained emotional resilience. Leaders should provide opportunities for growth and development while ensuring that team members have the resources and support they need to succeed. This equilibrium fosters a sense of competence and confidence.

- **Cultivating a Learning Culture**   A learning culture promotes continuous improvement and growth. Leaders can cultivate this culture by encouraging curiosity, recognizing and celebrating learning achievements, and providing opportunities for skill-building and knowledge-sharing. A learning-focused environment reinforces the importance of ongoing development.

- **Embracing Change as an Opportunity**   Change is a constant in any organizational setting. Leaders can help their teams view change as an opportunity for growth and development rather than a source of stress or uncertainty. Providing a clear vision, communicating effectively, and involving team members in the change process can mitigate resistance and enhance resilience.

Sustaining emotional resilience over time is a dynamic and ongoing journey. Leaders play a pivotal role in supporting this process by fostering a growth mindset, prioritizing self-care, and providing opportunities for skill development and lifelong learning. Creating a supportive community, promoting adaptability, and setting realistic expectations further contribute to the sustained growth of emotional resilience within the organization. By embracing continuous learning and adaptation, individuals and teams can navigate challenges with confidence and thrive in an ever-evolving professional landscape.

Foster a Resilient Culture: Leadership Practices for Long-Term Success

Sustaining emotional resilience over time extends beyond individual efforts; it requires the cultivation of a resilient organizational culture. Leaders play a pivotal role in shaping this culture through their practices, behaviors, and values. In this section, we explore key leadership practices that contribute to the establishment and perpetuation of a resilient culture for long-term success.

Here are some strategies for long-term success fostering a resilient culture within your organization:

- **Modeling Resilience**   Leaders serve as role models for their teams. By demonstrating emotional resilience in the face of challenges, leaders inspire and empower others to develop their own resilience. This modeling can take the form of maintaining composure under pressure, acknowledging and managing emotions, and approaching setbacks with a solutions-oriented mindset.

- **Creating Psychological Safety**   Psychological safety is the belief that one will not be penalized or humiliated for speaking up with ideas, questions, concerns, or mistakes. A psychologically safe environment fosters trust, open communication, and a willingness to take risks. Leaders can establish psychological safety by actively listening, valuing diverse perspectives, and responding constructively to feedback.

- **Encouraging Autonomy and Empowerment**   Empowering team members to make decisions and take ownership of their work contributes to a culture of resilience. Leaders can provide guidance and support while also allowing individuals the autonomy to problem-solve and make choices. This sense of ownership instills confidence and builds resilience in team members.

- **Promoting Transparent Communication**   Clear and transparent communication is fundamental to a resilient culture. Leaders should provide regular updates, share organizational goals, and ensure that information flows freely. Transparent communication builds trust, reduces uncertainty, and enables team members to adapt effectively to change and challenges.

- **Nurturing a Growth Mindset**   Leaders can foster a growth mindset within the organization by promoting the belief that abilities and intelligence can be developed through dedication and effort. Encouraging a culture of continuous learning, acknowledging effort and improvement, and providing opportunities for skill development all contribute to a growth-oriented mindset.

- **Recognizing and Celebrating Resilience**   Acknowledging and celebrating instances of resilience reinforces its value within the organization. Leaders can publicly recognize individuals and teams who demonstrate resilience in the face of challenges. This recognition not only affirms the importance of resilience but also encourages others to develop and showcase their own resilient capabilities.

- **Providing Access to Resources and Support**   Leaders must ensure that team members have access to the resources, tools, and support they need to navigate challenges effectively. This may include training programs, mentorship opportunities, and avenues for seeking assistance. By equipping individuals with the necessary resources, leaders empower them to build and sustain resilience.

- **Creating Opportunities for Reflection and Learning**   Regular reflection and learning opportunities contribute to the ongoing development of emotional resilience. Leaders can facilitate these practices by encouraging team members to engage in self-reflection, participate in workshops or training, and share experiences and insights. Creating space for reflection supports continuous growth.

- **Embracing Diversity and Inclusion**   A diverse and inclusive work environment contributes to a resilient culture. Leaders should actively promote diversity of thought, background, and experience. Embracing different perspectives fosters creativity, adaptability, and a broader range of problem-solving approaches, all of which contribute to organizational resilience.

- **Fostering a Sense of Purpose and Meaning**   Connecting individual roles to a broader organizational purpose instills a sense of meaning and significance. Leaders can articulate and reinforce the organization's mission, vision, and values. When team members understand how their contributions contribute to larger goals, they are more likely to approach challenges with determination and resilience.

- **Encouraging Proactive Problem-Solving** Promoting proactive problem-solving encourages individuals to address challenges before they escalate. Leaders can foster a culture of initiative by recognizing and rewarding proactive behavior. Encouraging team members to identify and tackle potential issues demonstrates a collective commitment to resilience.

- **Building Trust and Rapport** Trust is the foundation of a resilient culture. Leaders must invest time in building strong relationships with team members based on mutual respect, integrity, and authenticity. Trusting relationships create an environment where individuals feel safe to take risks, share concerns, and seek support when needed.

- **Promoting Work-Life Balance** Balancing professional responsibilities with personal well-being is crucial for sustaining emotional resilience. Leaders should model and support healthy work-life integration by respecting boundaries, encouraging time off, and promoting practices that support overall well-being. A balanced approach to work and life contributes to sustained resilience.

- **Encouraging Cross-Functional Collaboration** Collaboration across different departments and teams enhances collective problem-solving and resilience. Leaders can facilitate cross-functional interactions by creating opportunities for collaboration, breaking down silos, and recognizing the value of diverse expertise. Cross-functional collaboration expands the collective intelligence available to tackle challenges.

- **Adapting Organizational Policies and Practices** Leaders should be willing to adapt organizational policies and practices to better support resilience. This may involve revisiting performance metrics, adjusting workloads, or implementing flexible work arrangements. By aligning policies with the goal of fostering resilience, leaders demonstrate a commitment to the well-being of their teams.

- **Providing Constructive Feedback and Coaching** Effective feedback and coaching contribute to the development of individual and team resilience. Leaders should offer specific, actionable feedback that helps team members learn and grow. Additionally, coaching conversations can provide guidance on building resilience skills and navigating challenges effectively.

- **Creating Opportunities for Skill Development** Leaders should actively support skill development that enhances emotional resilience. This may involve providing access to relevant training, workshops, or coaching. By investing in the development of resilience-related skills, leaders empower their teams to navigate challenges effectively.

Fostering a resilient culture requires intentional leadership practices that prioritize trust, learning, empowerment, and well-being. By modeling resilience, creating a psychologically safe environment, and supporting ongoing growth, leaders lay the foundation for long-term organizational success. Embracing diversity, promoting transparency, and adapting policies further contribute to the resilience of the organization. Through these practices, leaders cultivate a culture that thrives in the face of challenges and adapts to an ever-evolving professional landscape.

Case Studies: Applying Resilience in Leadership

Embark on a journey through a series of meticulously selected real-world case studies, each chosen to present a diverse array of challenges and opportunities for professional growth. These case studies are more than narratives; they are dynamic learning tools designed to immerse you in the complexities of leadership, with a focus on applying emotional resilience.

As we delve into these case studies, you'll step into the shoes of accomplished leaders facing pivotal moments in their careers. Their experiences have been carefully curated to provide you with valuable insights and practical takeaways. Through these scenarios, you'll sharpen your decision-making, communication, and adaptability skills, all while honing your emotional resilience.

These case studies are not just stories; they're opportunities to engage with real-world challenges and apply emotional intelligence in your own leadership journey. Let's explore these scenarios, drawing inspiration from the leaders who faced them head-on.

> **Disclaimer** The case studies are based on real-world events and involve actual individuals and organizations. The views and opinions expressed in the case studies are those of the author and do not necessarily reflect the official policy or position of any person or entity mentioned herein. The author and the editorial team have made every attempt to ensure accuracy and reliability of the information provided; however, they accept no responsibility or liability for any errors or omissions, or for any actions taken based on the information in these case studies.

Case Study Instructions

For each case study, you will find the following components:

Introduction   Provides context and background information about the individual or organization featured in the case study. It outlines the challenges they faced and the pivotal moments in their leadership journey.

Background   A detailed overview of the leader's role and the circumstances they encountered. This sets the stage for understanding the challenges they had to navigate.

Problem/Objective Statement   Articulates the specific issue or objective that the leader faced. It highlights the central challenge or opportunity that demanded their attention and action.

Reflective Questions   Before delving into the details, you will be presented with thought-provoking questions designed to stimulate critical thinking. Consider these questions as prompts for your analysis and reflection on the case.

Analysis and Discussion   Offers a comprehensive view of how the leader handled the situation. It includes a detailed account of the strategies employed, the decisions made, and the communication tactics used. This analysis provides valuable insights into their approach.

Conclusion with Key Findings   Discusses the outcomes and consequences of the leader's actions. Understanding the results, whether positive or with areas for improvement, is crucial in refining your own response strategies. Also highlights key takeaways and lessons that can be applied to your own leadership journey. Consider how the leader's actions and decisions can inform your approach to similar challenges.

By engaging with these case studies, you will not only enhance your decision-making, communication, and adaptability skills, but also develop a deeper understanding of how emotional resilience can be applied in various professional contexts. Through active participation and reflection, you will be better equipped to tackle similar challenges you may encounter in your own leadership journey.

Case Study Analysis 1: Mary Barra - General Motors

The case study examines Mary Barra's exemplary leadership during the General Motors ignition switch crisis, highlighting her demonstration of emotional resilience and decisive action under intense pressure.

Background

Mary Barra, the CEO of General Motors, confronted a critical crisis when it was revealed that a defective ignition switch had caused accidents, injuries, and fatalities. This crisis posed a severe threat to GM's reputation and raised crucial questions about the company's safety protocols.

Problem/Objective Statement

The objective was to address the ignition switch crisis swiftly, rectify the fault, and restore public trust in GM's commitment to safety.

Reflective Questions

1. How did Barra's transparent and accountable approach impact GM's reputation during the crisis?
2. What were the key factors that allowed Barra to make decisive decisions under immense pressure?
3. How did Barra's victim compensation fund demonstrate a commitment to stakeholders' well-being?
4. In what ways did Barra's leadership contribute to the company's long-term recovery and improvement?

Analysis and Discussion

Barra's response to the crisis demonstrated exceptional emotional resilience and effective leadership. Her swift and transparent action, establishment of a victim compensation fund, and commitment to safety reforms showcased her ability to lead decisively under pressure. Her unwavering composure and focus amidst intense scrutiny played a pivotal role in stabilizing the company.

Leadership Under Pressure   Barra's response to this crisis exemplified emotional resilience. Instead of evading responsibility, she took immediate and transparent action. She publicly acknowledged the issue, accepted accountability on behalf of the company, and expressed genuine remorse for the lives lost.

Swift and Decisive Action Barra understood the urgency of the situation. She initiated a massive recall of affected vehicles, swiftly rectifying the faulty ignition switch. This demonstrated her ability to make difficult decisions under immense pressure, prioritizing the safety and well-being of customers.

Transparency and Open Communication In times of crisis, open communication is crucial. Barra ensured that GM's response was transparent, providing regular updates on progress. She maintained clear and honest communication with stakeholders, including customers, employees, and the public. This transparency helped rebuild trust and confidence in the company.

Victim Compensation Fund Barra's emotional resilience was further evident in her decision to establish a victim compensation fund. This demonstrated her commitment to providing support and compensation to those affected by the faulty ignition switch, regardless of legal implications. It showcased a genuine concern for the well-being of the victims and their families.

Composure Under Scrutiny Throughout the crisis, Barra remained composed and focused, despite the intense public scrutiny and media attention. Her ability to handle herself under such pressure was crucial in maintaining a sense of stability within the company and among stakeholders.

Learning and Rebuilding Barra used this crisis as an opportunity for learning and improvement. She implemented significant changes in the company's safety protocols, ensuring that such a tragedy would not occur again. This proactive approach demonstrated her commitment to continuous improvement and her determination to turn a crisis into an opportunity for growth.

Impact and Legacy Barra's handling of the ignition switch crisis significantly impacted GM's reputation and future. Her emotional resilience and decisive action played a pivotal role in rebuilding trust and re-establishing GM as a responsible and safety-conscious automaker.

Conclusion with Key Findings, Decisions, or Outcomes

Mary Barra's leadership successfully navigated General Motors through the ignition switch crisis. Her decisive actions, transparency, and prioritization of stakeholders led to the restoration of public trust. The establishment of a victim compensation fund demonstrated her commitment to the well-being of those affected.

Taking Ownership   Barra's response highlighted the importance of acknowledging and taking ownership of organizational mistakes, even in the face of a crisis.

Transparency Builds Trust   Open and honest communication is essential for rebuilding trust and credibility with stakeholders.

Prioritizing Stakeholders   Barra's victim compensation fund exemplified the significance of prioritizing the well-being of affected individuals, even when faced with legal and financial implications.

Turning Crisis into Opportunity   Barra's proactive approach to safety reforms showcased the potential for growth and improvement following a major crisis.

Leading with Integrity   Barra's unwavering commitment to doing what was right, regardless of external pressures, underscores the importance of leading with integrity.

Mary Barra's handling of the General Motors ignition switch crisis serves as an inspirational case study in crisis management and leadership under pressure. Her demonstration of emotional resilience, transparent communication, and proactive problem-solving offers valuable insights for leaders facing challenging situations.

Case Study Analysis 2: Elon Musk - Tesla and SpaceX (USA)

The case study delves into Elon Musk's remarkable leadership during the development of the Model 3 car and the Falcon 9 rocket, illustrating his emotional resilience and determination in the face of significant technical challenges and tight deadlines.

Background

Elon Musk, the visionary CEO of Tesla and SpaceX, undertook two pivotal projects - the development of the Model 3 car at Tesla and the creation of the Falcon 9 rocket at SpaceX. These projects were marked by intricate technical complexities, stringent timelines, and immense scrutiny due to their critical significance in their respective industries.

Problem/Objective Statement

The objective was to successfully develop and launch the Model 3 car and the Falcon 9 rocket, despite formidable technical challenges, while adhering to tight project schedules.

Reflective Questions

1. How did Musk's transparent communication approach impact stakeholder trust and project progress?
2. What strategies did Musk employ to maintain a positive outlook and keep teams motivated amidst setbacks?
3. How did Musk's hands-on problem-solving approach contribute to overcoming technical complexities?
4. What lessons can be drawn from Musk's ability to balance audacious goals with practical constraints?

Analysis and Discussion

Musk's approach to these projects demonstrated remarkable emotional resilience and effective leadership. His transparent communication, optimistic outlook, hands-on technical involvement, and ability to balance realism with ambition were pivotal in surmounting challenges.

Leadership Under Pressure   Musk's response to these challenges exemplified emotional resilience. He didn't shy away from acknowledging setbacks and obstacles. Instead, he maintained a forward-thinking and determined mindset, showing an unwavering commitment to achieving his goals.

Transparent Communication   Musk understood the importance of transparent communication. He provided regular updates to stakeholders, including employees, investors, and the public, about the progress and challenges faced by both Tesla and SpaceX. This openness built trust and allowed stakeholders to have realistic expectations.

Positive Outlook in the Face of Setbacks   Despite encountering numerous setbacks, Musk remained optimistic and focused on finding solutions. He consistently conveyed confidence in the ultimate success of the projects, instilling a sense of belief and determination in his teams.

Meeting Tight Deadlines   Both the Model 3 and Falcon 9 projects had ambitious timelines. Musk's emotional resilience was evident in his ability to keep teams motivated and aligned with the goals, ensuring that everyone worked tirelessly to meet the deadlines.

Technical Problem-Solving   The projects involved complex technical challenges. Musk's emotional resilience was demonstrated in his hands-on approach to problem-solving. He actively engaged with engineering teams, contributing to the development of innovative solutions.

Handling Public Scrutiny   As a high-profile figure, Musk faced intense public scrutiny. His emotional resilience allowed him to withstand criticism, maintain his vision, and continue driving forward despite external pressures.

Balancing Innovation with Realism   Musk's emotional resilience was also evident in his ability to balance ambitious innovation with practical realism. He set audacious goals while remaining grounded in the technical realities and resource constraints.

Delivering on Commitments   Ultimately, Musk's emotional resilience played a crucial role in the successful launch of the Model 3 and the Falcon 9. He demonstrated the ability to lead teams through adversity and deliver on commitments that were critical to the success of both companies.

Legacy and Impact   Musk's emotional resilience in the face of formidable challenges has solidified his reputation as a visionary leader. His ability to drive innovation, navigate complex projects, and inspire teams has had a profound impact on the automotive and aerospace industries.

Conclusion with Key Findings, Decisions, or Outcomes

Elon Musk's leadership proved instrumental in the successful development and launch of both the Model 3 car and the Falcon 9 rocket. His emotional resilience, coupled with his innovative vision, played a pivotal role in achieving these milestones, solidifying his legacy as a transformative figure in the automotive and aerospace industries.

- **Transparency Fosters Trust**   Musk's open communication style with stakeholders built and sustained trust, even during challenging phases.

- **Maintain a Positive Outlook**   Musk's unwavering optimism and belief in project success inspired and motivated teams, reinforcing their determination.

- **Hands-On Problem-Solving**   Musk's direct involvement in technical challenges exemplified his dedication and provided a model for leadership in crisis situations.

- **Balancing Realism with Ambition**   Musk's ability to strike a balance between audacious goals and practical constraints is a critical aspect of effective project management.

- **Embrace Setbacks as Learning Opportunities**   Musk's willingness to acknowledge and glean insights from setbacks contributed significantly to the ultimate success of both projects.

Elon Musk's handling of the Model 3 and Falcon 9 projects serves as a compelling case study in emotional resilience and leadership under pressure. His ability to lead with transparency, maintain an unwavering positive outlook, and deliver on ambitious goals stands as a powerful testament to effective leadership in the face of adversity.

Case Study Analysis 3: Christine Lagarde - European Central Bank

The case study examines Christine Lagarde's tenure as President of the European Central Bank, a period marked by unprecedented economic challenges exacerbated by the COVID-19 pandemic. Lagarde's leadership played a pivotal role in guiding the Eurozone through a period of substantial economic uncertainty and volatility.

Background

Christine Lagarde assumed the role of President of the European Central Bank during a time of profound economic crisis. The COVID-19 pandemic had brought about multifaceted economic challenges, necessitating swift and effective responses to stabilize the Eurozone.

Problem/Objective Statement

The objective was to lead the Eurozone through an unprecedented economic crisis exacerbated by the COVID-19 pandemic, implementing policies and strategies to stabilize economies, support member countries, and foster sustained economic recovery.

Reflective Questions

1. How did Lagarde's transparent communication approach impact stakeholder trust and the ECB's effectiveness in addressing economic challenges?
2. What strategies did Lagarde employ to balance short-term economic stabilization efforts with a long-term vision for sustained growth?
3. In what ways did Lagarde's empathy-driven approach contribute to effective leadership and stakeholder engagement during the crisis?
4. How did Lagarde adapt her strategies to evolving economic conditions, and what lessons can be drawn from her flexibility in leadership?

Analysis and Discussion

Lagarde's leadership demonstrated exceptional emotional resilience and effective decision-making during an unprecedented economic crisis. Her transparent communication, decisive actions, empathetic engagement, and adaptability were instrumental in stabilizing the Eurozone.

Leadership Under Pressure   Lagarde's response to the crisis exemplified emotional resilience. She was confronted with multifaceted economic challenges and complex decisions that required quick and effective responses. Her ability to maintain composure and provide steady leadership was critical.

Clear Communication   Lagarde recognized the importance of clear and transparent communication. She engaged with the public, financial institutions, and member countries to provide updates on the ECB's strategies and measures. This transparency helped in building confidence and trust in her leadership.

Decisive Action   In the face of economic turmoil, Lagarde demonstrated the ability to make tough decisions. She implemented policies aimed at stabilizing the Eurozone and mitigating the impact of the crisis. Her decisiveness provided a sense of direction during a period of uncertainty.

Expressing Empathy   Lagarde displayed a high degree of empathy towards those affected by the economic crisis. She acknowledged the human impact of the challenges faced by individuals, businesses, and communities. This empathetic approach resonated with people and demonstrated her genuine concern.

Support for Member Countries   Recognizing the diverse challenges faced by Eurozone member countries, Lagarde worked to provide support tailored to each nation's unique circumstances. She fostered a spirit of collaboration and unity among member countries to collectively address the economic challenges.

Maintaining a Long-Term Perspective   While addressing immediate economic concerns, Lagarde also emphasized the importance of long-term planning and stability. She articulated a vision for the Eurozone's future and implemented measures to lay the foundation for sustained economic growth.

Building Alliances   Lagarde actively engaged with international institutions, policymakers, and leaders from around the world. Her efforts to build alliances and collaborate on global economic strategies contributed to a more coordinated and effective response to the crisis.

Adapting to Evolving Circumstances   The dynamic nature of the crisis required Lagarde to be adaptable and flexible in her approach. She was responsive to evolving economic conditions and adjusted strategies as needed to address new challenges.

Measuring Impact and Adjusting Course   Lagarde continuously monitored the impact of ECB policies and initiatives. She was willing to adjust course when necessary, demonstrating a commitment to data-driven decision-making and a willingness to learn from outcomes.

Legacy and Impact   Christine Lagarde's tenure at the European Central Bank during the COVID-19 crisis showcased her exceptional emotional resilience and leadership skills. Her ability to provide clear communication, make decisive decisions, and express genuine empathy left a lasting impact on the Eurozone's economic recovery.

Conclusion with Key Findings, Decisions, or Outcomes

Christine Lagarde's tenure at the European Central Bank left a profound impact on the Eurozone's economic recovery. Her transparent communication, decisive policy implementation, and genuine empathy contributed significantly to stabilizing economies and fostering a path to sustained growth.

Transparency Builds Trust   Lagarde's open and honest communication style played a pivotal role in gaining public and stakeholder confidence during a period of economic uncertainty.

Empathy Drives Effective Leadership Demonstrating genuine concern for the well-being of those affected by the crisis fosters trust and creates a more supportive environment.

Balancing Short-Term Solutions with Long-Term Vision Effective leaders must address immediate challenges while also planning for the future to ensure sustained success.

Flexibility is Key Adapting to changing circumstances is a vital leadership trait, especially in times of crisis where conditions are highly dynamic.

Christine Lagarde's leadership at the European Central Bank serves as a compelling case study in emotional resilience and effective crisis management. Her ability to provide clear communication, make tough decisions, and show genuine empathy contributed significantly to navigating the Eurozone through a period of economic uncertainty.

Case Study Analysis 4: Jack Ma - Alibaba Group

The case study analyzes the response of Jack Ma, the founder of Alibaba Group, when the highly anticipated IPO for Ant Group encountered unexpected regulatory obstacles in China. The crisis presented a significant challenge for Ma and the company, requiring decisive leadership and emotional resilience.

Background

Jack Ma, the visionary founder of Alibaba Group, faced a critical hurdle when the anticipated IPO for Ant Group encountered regulatory challenges in China. This unforeseen setback posed a substantial challenge for both Ma and the company.

Problem/Objective Statement

The objective was to navigate the unexpected regulatory obstacles surrounding the Ant Group IPO and sustain Alibaba's growth trajectory by demonstrating resilience, effective communication, and strategic adaptability.

Reflective Questions

1. How did Jack Ma's transparent communication style impact stakeholder trust and Alibaba's effectiveness in addressing the regulatory challenges?
2. What strategies did Jack Ma employ to balance short-term diversification efforts with a long-term vision for sustained growth and stability?
3. In what ways did Jack Ma's empowerment of his leadership team contribute to problem-solving and adaptability within the organization?
4. How did Jack Ma's collaborative approach with regulatory authorities influence the outcome of the regulatory challenges?

Analysis and Discussion

Jack Ma's response to the regulatory setback demonstrated exceptional emotional resilience and effective crisis management. His transparent communication, strategic diversification efforts, empowerment of his team, and collaborative approach with regulators were instrumental in navigating the crisis.

Leadership Under Pressure   Ma's response to the crisis exemplified emotional resilience. Faced with a sudden and complex regulatory issue, he demonstrated the ability to maintain composure and provide steady leadership during a turbulent period for the company.

Open Communication   Ma recognized the importance of open and honest communication. He addressed the regulatory concerns directly, providing clarity to stakeholders and the public. This transparent approach helped to manage expectations and maintain trust amidst the uncertainty.

Confidence in the Future   Despite the setback, Ma expressed confidence in the long-term prospects of both Ant Group and Alibaba. His unwavering belief in the potential of the company reassured employees, investors, and partners, reinforcing his role as a resilient leader.

Diversification Strategy   In response to the regulatory challenges, Ma spearheaded efforts to diversify Alibaba's offerings. This strategic shift allowed the company to explore new avenues and reduce its reliance on any single business unit, demonstrating Ma's agility and adaptability.

Seeking Collaborative Solutions   Rather than viewing the regulatory hurdles as insurmountable, Ma actively engaged with regulatory authorities and sought collaborative solutions. His willingness to work with regulators to address concerns reflected a constructive and forward-thinking approach.

Empowering the Team   During this period of uncertainty, Ma empowered his leadership team and employees to take initiative and contribute to finding solutions. This decentralized approach encouraged creativity and resourcefulness within the organization.

Resilience in Innovation   Ma's response to the regulatory challenge underscored his innovative mindset. He leveraged the setback as an opportunity to explore new business models and technologies, showcasing his ability to turn adversity into a catalyst for innovation.

Balancing Optimism with Realism   While maintaining a positive outlook, Ma also acknowledged the gravity of the situation. He provided a realistic assessment of the challenges ahead while instilling confidence in the company's ability to overcome them.

Adaptability and Learning   The crisis prompted Ma to reevaluate and adapt his leadership strategies. He demonstrated a willingness to learn from the experience and implement changes to strengthen the company's resilience in the face of future challenges.

Legacy and Impact   Jack Ma's handling of the regulatory setback at Ant Group demonstrated his exceptional emotional resilience and leadership skills. His ability to communicate effectively, maintain confidence in the company's future, and drive strategic diversification left a lasting impact on Alibaba's trajectory.

Conclusion with Key Findings, Decisions, or Outcomes

Jack Ma's handling of the regulatory challenges at Ant Group left a profound impact on Alibaba's trajectory. His transparent communication, strategic diversification, and collaborative approach with regulators were crucial in overcoming the crisis and maintaining the company's growth trajectory.

Transparent Communication is Key   Open and honest communication is crucial in maintaining trust and confidence during times of crisis.

Innovation in Adversity   Resilient leaders view setbacks as opportunities for innovation and transformation, leveraging challenges to drive positive change.

Empowerment Drives Solutions   Empowering teams to take initiative fosters a culture of creativity and resourcefulness, enabling the organization to adapt and thrive.

Collaboration Yields Results Actively engaging with stakeholders and seeking collaborative solutions, even in the face of regulatory challenges, can lead to constructive outcomes.

Jack Ma's response to the regulatory setback at Ant Group showcases emotional resilience in high-pressure situations. His ability to communicate transparently, maintain confidence, and drive strategic shifts in the company's direction exemplifies his exceptional leadership skills.

Case Study Analysis 5: Marillyn Hewson - Lockheed Martin

The case study analyzes the leadership of Marillyn Hewson, the former CEO of Lockheed Martin, during a period of heightened geopolitical tensions and budget constraints in the defense industry. Hewson's response to these challenges demonstrated exceptional emotional resilience and strategic leadership.

Background

Marillyn Hewson led Lockheed Martin through a complex period characterized by geopolitical tensions and stringent budgetary constraints in the defense sector. This demanding environment presented significant challenges for both Hewson and the organization.

Problem/Objective Statement

The objective was to navigate the complexities of the defense industry amidst geopolitical tensions and budgetary limitations while maintaining Lockheed Martin's competitiveness and global impact.

Reflective Questions

1. How did Marillyn Hewson's emphasis on innovation contribute to Lockheed Martin's ability to adapt and thrive in a challenging economic environment?
2. What were the key cost-effective measures implemented by Hewson, and how did they impact Lockheed Martin's competitiveness and profitability?
3. How did Hewson's diplomatic finesse in negotiations with government agencies and international partners contribute to securing critical contracts and alliances for Lockheed Martin?
4. In what ways did Marillyn Hewson's ethical leadership and unwavering commitment to integrity influence the organizational culture within Lockheed Martin?

Analysis and Discussion

Marillyn Hewson's response to the challenges in the defense industry showcased exceptional emotional resilience and strategic leadership. Her emphasis on innovation, cost-effective measures, diplomatic negotiation skills, and ethical leadership were instrumental in navigating the complexities of the geopolitical landscape.

Leadership Under Pressure   Hewson's response to the complex geopolitical landscape exemplifies emotional resilience. Faced with an intricate web of international relations and budgetary limitations, she demonstrated the ability to maintain focus and provide steadfast leadership during a turbulent period for the defense industry.

Strategic Innovation   Recognizing the need for innovation, Hewson championed research and development efforts within Lockheed Martin. She prioritized the development of cutting-edge technologies and solutions, positioning the company as a leader in the defense sector. This emphasis on innovation showcased her forward-thinking and adaptive approach.

Cost-Effective Solutions   In light of budget constraints, Hewson implemented cost-effective measures without compromising on the quality and efficacy of Lockheed Martin's products and services. Her strategic cost management approach ensured the company's competitiveness in a challenging economic environment.

Complex Negotiations and Diplomacy   Hewson skillfully navigated intricate negotiations with government agencies, international partners, and stakeholders. Her diplomatic finesse played a pivotal role in securing critical contracts and alliances, demonstrating her ability to handle high-pressure situations with grace and acumen.

Visionary Leadership   Throughout her tenure, Hewson maintained a clear vision for Lockheed Martin's growth and global impact. Her unwavering commitment to the company's mission and objectives provided stability and direction during uncertain times, solidifying her legacy as a resilient leader.

Empowering the Workforce   Hewson recognized the significance of an empowered and motivated workforce. She fostered a culture of innovation, collaboration, and inclusivity within Lockheed Martin, ensuring that employees felt valued and engaged in the company's mission.

Continuous Learning and Adaptation   In response to the rapidly evolving geopolitical landscape, Hewson exhibited a willingness to adapt and learn. She encouraged a culture of continuous improvement and supported initiatives aimed at enhancing Lockheed Martin's capabilities and competitiveness.

Ethical Leadership and Integrity   Throughout her leadership, Hewson maintained a commitment to ethical conduct and integrity. Her unwavering adherence to ethical standards provided a strong foundation for trust and credibility within the organization and among external stakeholders.

Legacy and Impact   Marillyn Hewson's tenure as CEO of Lockheed Martin stands as a testament to her exceptional emotional resilience and leadership skills. Her emphasis on innovation, cost-effectiveness, strategic negotiation, and visionary leadership left an enduring impact on the company's trajectory.

Conclusion with Key Findings, Decisions, or Outcomes

Marillyn Hewson's tenure as CEO of Lockheed Martin left a lasting impact on the company's trajectory. Her emphasis on innovation, cost-effective strategies, diplomatic negotiation, and unwavering commitment to ethical leadership solidify her legacy as an exceptional leader.

Innovation Drives Resilience   Prioritizing innovation enables organizations to adapt and thrive, even in challenging environments.

Strategic Cost Management   Effective cost management is essential for competitiveness, especially in industries with budgetary constraints.

Diplomacy and Negotiation Skills   Skillful negotiation and diplomacy are critical in navigating complex geopolitical landscapes.

Vision and Commitment   A clear and unwavering vision provides stability and direction during times of uncertainty.

Marillyn Hewson's leadership at Lockheed Martin exemplifies emotional resilience in high-pressure situations. Her strategic approach, diplomatic finesse, and unwavering commitment to the company's mission solidify her legacy as an exceptional leader.

Case Study Analysis 6: Carlos Ghosn - Nissan-Renault-Mitsubishi

The case study examines the leadership of Carlos Ghosn, the former CEO of the Nissan-Renault-Mitsubishi Alliance, during a high-stakes situation involving his arrest in Japan on charges of financial misconduct. Ghosn's response to this crisis demonstrates exceptional emotional resilience and strategic leadership.

Background

Carlos Ghosn, a prominent figure in the automotive industry, faced a severe crisis when he was arrested in Japan on allegations of financial misconduct. This high-profile situation posed significant threats to Ghosn's reputation and the stability of the Nissan-Renault-Mitsubishi Alliance.

Problem/Objective Statement

The objective was to navigate a complex legal situation while maintaining personal composure and professional stewardship of the Nissan-Renault-Mitsubishi Alliance, all in the face of intense public scrutiny and complex stakeholder dynamics.

Reflective Questions

1. How did Carlos Ghosn's transparent communication about the allegations contribute to his resilience and credibility during the crisis?
2. What strategies did Ghosn employ to effectively manage the intricate legal proceedings and stakeholder relationships in multiple countries?
3. How did Ghosn's ability to balance personal and professional struggles impact his resilience as a leader during the crisis?
4. In what ways did Carlos Ghosn's strategic decision-making and advocacy for his version of events contribute to his legal acquittal and reputation rebuilding?

Analysis and Discussion

Carlos Ghosn's response to the crisis showcased exceptional emotional resilience and strategic leadership. His transparent communication, adept legal defense, cultural intelligence, and ability to manage complex stakeholder dynamics were instrumental in navigating the complex legal situation and maintaining organizational stability.

Leadership Under Pressure   Ghosn's response to the legal predicament showcases emotional resilience. Faced with the weight of serious allegations and intense public scrutiny, he maintained composure and resolve, demonstrating an ability to navigate a high-pressure environment.

Maintaining Public Image   Despite the legal challenges, Ghosn adeptly managed his public image. He articulated his version of events, maintaining his innocence, and addressing the charges with transparency. This approach demonstrated his commitment to communicating directly with stakeholders, thereby exhibiting emotional resilience in the face of adversity.

Strategic Legal Defense   Ghosn engaged a legal team to navigate the complex and multifaceted legal proceedings. His strategic approach to the legal defense showcased a capacity to make calculated decisions under immense pressure, reinforcing his image as a resilient leader.

Navigating Cultural Differences   The arrest and subsequent legal proceedings took place in a foreign country with distinct legal, cultural, and linguistic nuances. Ghosn's ability to navigate these complexities demonstrated his adaptability and cultural intelligence, essential traits for leaders facing high-pressure situations on the global stage.

Continued Advocacy   Throughout the ordeal, Ghosn remained steadfast in advocating for his version of events. He engaged with the media, conducted interviews, and utilized various platforms to present his perspective. This unwavering commitment to his narrative illustrated his resilience in defending his reputation and legacy.

Balancing Personal and Professional Struggles   The crisis not only impacted Ghosn professionally but also personally. He had to navigate the emotional and logistical challenges of an arrest and legal battle, all while maintaining a public-facing role. Ghosn's ability to balance these aspects showcased his emotional resilience and fortitude.

Strategic Organizational Stewardship   While facing legal challenges, Ghosn continued to provide strategic direction to the Nissan-Renault-Mitsubishi Alliance. He ensured that the companies under the alliance remained focused on their objectives and operational targets, demonstrating his ability to compartmentalize and make critical decisions amidst adversity.

Complex Stakeholder Management   The crisis involved a multitude of stakeholders including shareholders, employees, partners, and government officials. Ghosn's adept management of these relationships during this tumultuous period showcased his capacity to handle intricate stakeholder dynamics.

Legal Acquittal and Rebuilding Reputation   Following his escape from Japan and subsequent legal battles, Ghosn aimed to rebuild his reputation. His successful legal acquittal and subsequent public appearances signaled a resurgence of his public image, illustrating his unwavering determination and emotional resilience.

Conclusion with Key Findings, Decisions, or Outcomes

Carlos Ghosn's successful legal acquittal and subsequent public appearances signaled a resurgence of his public image, illustrating his unwavering determination and emotional resilience. His ability to balance personal and professional struggles while providing strategic direction to the alliance underscored his resilience as a leader.

Transparent Communication   In times of crisis, transparent and direct communication is crucial for maintaining credibility and trust.

Cultural Intelligence   Understanding and navigating cultural differences is imperative, especially in high-pressure situations with global implications.

Balancing Personal and Professional Struggles   Leaders must find ways to manage personal challenges while fulfilling their professional responsibilities.

Advocacy and Strategic Decision-Making   Resilience requires a combination of advocacy for one's position and strategic decision-making to navigate complex situations.

Carlos Ghosn's response to the legal challenges he faced exemplifies emotional resilience in high-pressure situations. His strategic approach to legal defense, transparent communication, and ability to manage complex stakeholder dynamics underscore his resilience as a leader.

Part 4. Emotional Resilience Self-Assessment

Here we are, back at the boardwalk. This place, once a symbol of beginnings, now stands as a testament to your journey—a journey through pages, through insights, and through the boundless realm of leadership intelligence.

Remember those first steps you took? Each one was a choice, a commitment to growth, a pledge to become the resilient leader you aspired to be. Milestones passed, challenges faced, and triumphs celebrated—they all became threads woven into the tapestry of your leadership odyssey.

Much like the tides that shape the estuary, experiences have molded your path. Shadows and light, challenges and triumphs, they've all left their marks, painting a dynamic landscape of growth and resilience.

And as you stand here, looking ahead, remember this: Every footfall you've taken has contributed to a story—a story of leadership, of growth, of transformation. The boardwalk beneath your feet is more than just a path; it's a canvas, waiting for your unique vision to leave its indelible mark.

With an open heart and an unyielding spirit, you've navigated this journey. The boardwalk stretches ahead, disappearing into the horizon, much like your leadership potential. The distant pagoda-like structure, once an aspiration, is now a tangible testament to your growth.

As we pause here, take a moment to reflect on the miles you've traveled, the insights you've gained, and the leader you've become. Then, with renewed purpose, let's continue our journey—a journey that brings us to the heart of emotional resilience, a cornerstone of leadership strength, an assessment of your emotional resilience.

The Power of Self-Assessment: Unveiling Paths to Growth

In the journey of self-improvement, one of the most influential tools at our disposal is self-assessment. This introspective exercise allows us to gain insight into our strengths, weaknesses, and areas for growth. However, to truly unlock the potential for positive change, it's crucial to approach this process with unwavering honesty.

1. **A Personal Endeavor.** Self-assessment is a deeply personal endeavor. It's a private reflection, devoid of external judgment or scrutiny. No one is peering over your shoulder, and there's no need to present a polished facade. It's a sacred space for candid introspection.

2. **Navigating the Inner Landscape.** Honesty in self-assessment is akin to donning a pair of glasses that allow us to see our inner landscape with utmost clarity. It provides an unobstructed view of our emotional responses, coping mechanisms, and behavioral patterns.

3. **Recognizing Strengths and Growth Areas.** When we answer each question truthfully, we lay bare our true inclinations and tendencies. This process unveils not only our strengths but also highlights areas where growth and refinement are possible.

4. **Cultivating Authenticity.** Embracing honesty in self-assessment fosters authenticity. It allows us to acknowledge areas where we may be struggling or facing challenges. This authenticity becomes the bedrock upon which genuine and lasting growth can be built.

5. **A Foundation for Constructive Change.** Imagine a builder working on a house. They must first assess the structural integrity before making any improvements. Similarly, honest self-assessment serves as the foundation upon which constructive and sustainable change can be made.

6. **Overcoming Cognitive Biases.** Human nature often inclines us towards perceiving ourselves in a favorable light. This cognitive bias can inadvertently obscure areas that require attention. By embracing honesty, we dismantle these biases and see ourselves more objectively.

7. **Strengthening Emotional Resilience.** Emotional resilience, one of the cornerstones of personal development, is built on a foundation of self-awareness and authenticity. Being honest in self-assessment is the

cornerstone of this foundation, allowing us to identify and address areas for improvement.

8. **Fostering a Growth Mindset.** Honesty in self-assessment aligns seamlessly with a growth mindset—a belief that abilities and intelligence can be developed. It sets the stage for embracing challenges and viewing failures as stepping stones to success.

9. **Celebrating Progress.** When we approach self-assessment with honesty, we set a benchmark against which we can measure progress. This empowers us to celebrate our achievements, no matter how small, and reinforces our commitment to personal growth.

The act of answering self-assessment questions with honesty is a profound act of self-compassion and a testament to our dedication to personal growth. It's an intimate conversation with ourselves, a sanctuary for self-improvement, and the foundation upon which we can build a more resilient, authentic, and empowered self. So, embrace this process with an open heart and an honest spirit, and watch as it becomes a powerful catalyst for your personal evolution.

Self-Assessment 1-2-3!

Before you lies a powerful tool—the Emotional Resilience Self-Assessment©—a 35-question survey forged from millions of words written by our author on the subjects of technology, leadership, and intelligence, and refined through hundreds of questionnaires. It stands as a guiding compass on your journey toward becoming a more resilient leader.

This assessment is meticulously crafted to help you discern your strengths and areas for growth in emotional resilience. Remember, this self-assessment is not just a series of questions; it's a transformative tool designed to deepen your understanding of emotional resilience and empower you on your leadership journey. The insights you gain will serve as a valuable foundation for your growth as a resilient leader.

> **Author's Note** The Emotional Resilience Self-Assessment© tests dozens of resilient characteristics and represents years of research. While comparable intelligence and leadership assessments often come with price tags ranging from $65 to $350, we're pleased to offer our assessment to you completely free of charge. Furthermore, we're actively developing a more dynamic online version of this assessment to enhance your experience even further, and we're committed to trying to provide it to you without any cost. This dynamic platform is anticipated to be available in the near future, providing you with an automated and seamless process to uncover your emotional resilience insights. Keep an eye out for updates on our website for the latest developments.
>
> Please note that the timing of the enhanced online version's release will be influenced by the total readership of this book. The more readers who embark on this transformative journey, the greater resources we can allocate to expedite its development. Your engagement and support play a crucial role in bringing this valuable tool to fruition.
>
> **Note** The Emotional Resilience Self-Assessment© is a copyrighted professional tool intended for individual use. If you wish to utilize it within your organization, a licensing fee per user is required. For licensing inquiries and further details, please visit **williamrstanek.com/licensing/**. Thank you for respecting the intellectual property rights associated with this valuable resource.

Instructions for the Self-Assessment:

Here are the instructions for taking and scoring the self-assessment:

1. Go online to **williamrstanek.com/resilient/**. For a seamless experience, we've developed an online version that automates the process, providing you with automated progress, score tracking and result totaling. To access this digital version and unlock the full potential of this assessment, visit williamrstanek.com/resilient/ and embark on a dynamic exploration of your emotional resilience. When you finish the online self-assessment continue through the book.

2. **Read Each Statement:** Read each statement carefully and honestly consider how well it reflects your own behavior, thoughts, and feelings.

3. **Rate Yourself:** Assign a rating to each statement based on the scale provided:

    - **Rarely (1)**   This rating suggests that you perceive the characteristic described in the statement to apply to you in a very limited or infrequent way. It is not a common occurrence in your behavior, thoughts, or feelings.

    - **Sometimes (2)**   You believe that the characteristic does apply to you, but it is not a consistent or regular part of your behavior or mindset. It occurs periodically or in specific situations.

    - **Often (3)**   This rating signifies that the characteristic is a frequent occurrence in your behavior, thoughts or feelings. It is a regular part of how you approach situations and challenges.

    - **Absolutely (4)**   This rating indicates that the characteristic strongly resonates with you. It is a significant and consistent part of your behavior, mindset, or self-perception, influencing how you approach various situations and challenges in a profound and reliable manner.

    - **Innate (5)**   This rating signifies that the characteristic is not only deeply ingrained but also an essential and natural part of your behavior, mindset, or self-perception. It reflects a fundamental aspect of who you are, influencing how you approach various situations and challenges in a consistent and profound manner.

4. **Be Honest**   Be truthful in your assessment. There are no right or wrong answers, and this self-assessment is for your personal reflection.

5. **Avoid Overthinking**   Trust your initial instinct when choosing a rating. Do not spend too much time deliberating.

6. **Complete All Questions**   Ensure you respond to all 35 statements.

Author's Note   Select the value that most accurately represents your feelings or behaviors for each characteristic, ranging from 1 'Rarely' to 5 'Absolutely.' If this scale doesn't align with your perspective or the question/statement, consider it as ranging from 1 'Absolutely Disagree' to 5 'Absolutely Agree' for an alternate interpretation, as in:

1) Disagree   I disagree with this statement. It is not a common occurrence in my behavior, thoughts, or feelings.

2) Mixed   I have mixed feelings about this statement, neither entirely in agreement nor disagreement. It occurs periodically or in specific situations.

3) Agree   This statement aligns well with my beliefs and experiences, but without absolute certainty. It is a regular part of my behavior, thoughts, or feelings.

4) Absolutely Agree   This statement strongly resonates with my viewpoint and I wholeheartedly endorse it. It is a significant and consistent part of my behavior, mindset, or self-perception.

5) Innate   This statement reflects a pervasive and inherent part of my behavior, mindset, or self-perception. It is naturally occurring and a core aspect of my behavior, mindset, or self-perception.

Scoring the Self-Assessment

After completing the assessment, add up your scores to get a sense of your overall emotional resilience. The higher the score, the stronger the indication of emotional resilience in the assessed characteristics. Remember, the goal isn't to achieve a perfect score, but rather to gain insights into areas where one may excel and where there might be room for growth.

1. **Total the Scores:** Add up the scores you assigned to each statement. The highest possible score is 175.
2. **Interpretation:**

    35 - 59   Very Low Emotional Resilience

    60 - 84   Low Emotional Resilience

    85 - 109   Moderate Emotional Resilience

    110 - 134   Average Emotional Resilience

    135 - 159   Above Average Emotional Resilience

    160 - 172   High Emotional Resilience

    173 - 175   Exceptional Emotional Resilience

Your rating allows you to quantify and compare your perceived level of proficiency or behavior. Keep in mind that your rating serves as a starting point for personal growth and development, not an endpoint.

Making the Most of Your Self-Assessment Score

In the upcoming sections, you'll discover actionable strategies tailored to enhance your resilience, aligning with your self-assessment score. These recommendations complement the comprehensive insights already covered in this book, which you should continue to revisit and integrate into your leadership journey.

Interpretation of Scores:

- **Very Low Emotional Resilience (35 - 59)**   This range suggests that you will greatly benefit from developing deeper emotional resilience. Consider focusing on building specific characteristics like endurance, acceptance of failure, and patience can be particularly beneficial.

- **Low Emotional Resilience (60 - 84)**   This range suggests that while you have some level of emotional resilience, there are many areas where there is room for growth and improvement. Identifying and developing these areas will enhance your overall emotional resilience.

- **Moderate Emotional Resilience (85 - 109)**   Falling in this range suggests that you have a moderate level of emotional resilience. This is a fair foundation, and you likely demonstrate some strength in managing challenges and setbacks. There are certain areas where you are okay but need improvement, and many other areas where there's significant room for improvement.

- **Average Emotional Resilience (110 - 134)**   This range suggests that you possess average emotional resilience. You demonstrate some strength in managing challenges and setbacks, and this can be a notable asset at times. While you demonstrate reasonable strength in multiple areas, there is considerable room for continued growth.

- **Above Average Emotional Resilience (135 - 159)**   This range suggests that you possess above-average emotional resilience. You demonstrate strength in managing challenges and setbacks, and this is a notable asset. While you excel in multiple areas, there is always room for continued growth.

- **High Emotional Resilience (160 - 172)**   Congratulations! Falling within this range indicates that your emotional resilience is at a high level. You demonstrate a significant degree of adaptability and effectiveness in dealing with challenges. This is a commendable strength.

- **Exceptional Emotional Resilience (173 - 175)** Congratulations! Falling within this range indicates that your emotional resilience is at a high level. You demonstrate a significant degree of adaptability and effectiveness in dealing with challenges. This is a commendable strength.

Remember, this self-assessment is a tool for self-reflection and personal development. It provides insights into your emotional resilience across various characteristics. Use it as a starting point for further exploration and growth in this area.

Very Low Emotional Resilience: Embarking on the Resilience Journey

If your emotional resilience falls within the very low range (35 - 59), it indicates an area with significant potential for growth and development. This range signals an opportunity to cultivate and fortify essential characteristics like endurance, acceptance of failure, and patience, all of which are pivotal in building robust emotional resilience.

If you find yourself in this range, it's important to understand that this is a pivotal moment for your personal and professional development. It's an opportunity to embark on a journey towards deeper emotional resilience. By committing to targeted strategies and consistent practice, you can steadily strengthen your capacity to navigate challenges with greater confidence and effectiveness.

Next, we'll delve into specific strategies designed to empower individuals in the very low range of emotional resilience. These actionable steps are tailored to help you build a solid foundation for emotional well-being. Remember, your progress in enhancing emotional resilience is a testament to your dedication to personal growth. Let's embark on this transformative journey together.

A tailored plan to significantly enhance your emotional resilience follows:

Develop Mindfulness Practices   Engage in mindfulness meditation, deep breathing exercises, or yoga. These practices can help you stay present and manage stress effectively.

Enhance Emotional Awareness   Practice identifying and labeling your emotions. Understanding what you're feeling is the first step in managing your responses.

Cultivate a Growth Mindset   Embrace challenges as opportunities for learning and growth. Focus on solutions and view setbacks as temporary.

Set Realistic Goals   Break down larger goals into smaller, manageable steps. Celebrate your achievements, no matter how small.

Build a Support System   Surround yourself with positive, supportive individuals who can offer encouragement and perspective during challenging times.

Seek Professional Help   Consider speaking with an individual, team, or organizational trainer like the ones at Stanek & Associates! They can provide guidance and techniques to enhance emotional resilience.

Practice Self-Compassion   Treat yourself with kindness and understanding, especially during difficult moments. Avoid self-criticism.

Improve Problem-Solving Skills   Enhance your ability to analyze challenges and come up with effective solutions. Consider taking a problem-solving course or seeking advice from experienced individuals.

Foster a Growth-Oriented Environment   Surround yourself with opportunities for personal and professional development. Attend workshops, seminars, or engage in relevant courses.

Engage in Physical Activity   Regular exercise can help reduce stress, improve mood, and increase overall resilience.

Practice Gratitude   Regularly acknowledge and appreciate the positive aspects of your life. This can help shift your focus from challenges to opportunities.

Build Coping Strategies   Identify healthy ways to cope with stress, such as journaling, engaging in hobbies, or spending time in nature.

Learn from Setbacks   View failures as learning experiences. Reflect on what went wrong and how you can apply those lessons moving forward.

Manage Time Effectively   Prioritize tasks and allocate time appropriately. Avoid overloading yourself with commitments.

Develop Healthy Habits   Ensure you get enough sleep, maintain a balanced diet, and stay hydrated. Physical well-being contributes to emotional resilience.

Practice Assertiveness   Learn to communicate your needs and boundaries effectively. This can reduce stress related to interpersonal relationships.

Remember, building emotional resilience is a gradual process. Be patient with yourself and celebrate your progress along the way. Consistent effort and a positive mindset will contribute to meaningful improvements over time. In 'Emotional Resilience Now—A Resilience Action Plan for Leaders,' you will delve deep into these concepts and explore a wealth of others, all designed to empower you on your journey to greater resilience.

Low Emotional Resilience: Cultivating Foundational Resilience

If your emotional resilience falls within the low range (60 - 84), it signifies a foundational level of emotional strength. While you possess a certain degree of emotional resilience, there remain numerous untapped areas for growth and refinement. Recognizing and cultivating these areas holds the key to elevating your overall emotional well-being.

Here, we focus on providing you with tailored strategies to bolster your emotional resilience. These actionable steps are specifically designed to address the unique needs and opportunities present in the low range. By committing to these targeted approaches, you're taking a proactive step towards nurturing a more robust and adaptable mindset.

Acknowledging your current level of resilience is the first step towards transformation. Embrace this opportunity for growth and development, and let's embark on this journey together. Through focused effort and a positive mindset, you'll steadily amplify your capacity to face challenges with greater confidence and effectiveness.

A tailored plan to further enhance your emotional resilience follows:

Strengthen Emotional Awareness Continue practicing recognizing and labeling your emotions. The more you understand your feelings, the better you can manage them.

Build a Support Network Cultivate and maintain strong relationships with friends, family, and colleagues. These connections can provide valuable emotional support during challenging times.

Develop Mindfulness and Stress-Reduction Techniques Engage in regular mindfulness practices, deep breathing exercises, or progressive muscle relaxation. These techniques can help you stay centered and manage stress effectively.

Foster a Growth Mindset Embrace challenges and view failures as opportunities for growth. Focus on solutions and maintain a positive outlook.

Set Clear Goals Establish specific, achievable goals for various aspects of your life. This provides direction and a sense of accomplishment.

Cultivate Resilience-Building Habits Engage in activities that promote resilience, such as regular exercise, healthy eating, and quality sleep.

Enhance Problem-Solving Skills Continue to refine your ability to analyze challenges and develop effective solutions. Seek out opportunities to practice this skill.

Practice Self-Compassion   Be kind and understanding to yourself, especially during difficult moments. Avoid self-criticism and negative self-talk.

Seek Personal Growth Opportunities   Pursue activities that challenge you and contribute to your personal development. This could include taking on new responsibilities at work or exploring new hobbies.

Foster Flexibility and Adaptability   Embrace change as a natural part of life and be open to adjusting your plans or strategies as needed.

Build Resilient Coping Mechanisms   Identify and utilize healthy coping strategies, such as journaling, practicing mindfulness, or engaging in creative activities.

Set Boundaries Effectively   Clearly communicate your needs and limits to others. This helps prevent burnout and maintains healthy relationships.

Learn from Setbacks   Reflect on failures and setbacks to extract valuable lessons. Apply these insights to future endeavors.

Enhance Assertiveness Skills   Practice assertive communication to express your needs and boundaries confidently, reducing potential stress from miscommunication.

Nurture Emotional Intelligence   Continue to develop your ability to understand and manage emotions, as this complements emotional resilience.

Remember, progress in building emotional resilience is a journey. Consistency and a positive mindset are key. Celebrate your successes along the way and stay committed to your personal growth and well-being. In 'Emotional Resilience Now—A Resilience Action Plan for Leaders,' you will delve deep into these concepts and explore a wealth of others, all designed to empower you on your journey to greater resilience.

Moderate Emotional Resilience: Building a Stronger Foundation

If your emotional resilience falls within the moderate range (85 - 109), it signifies a commendable, but incomplete, foundation in managing challenges and setbacks. This is an encouraging start, indicating that you possess some, albeit limited, strengths in dealing with adversity. While you demonstrate proficiency in several aspects, there are many specific areas that hold potential for improvement and growth.

Here, we delve into strategies tailored to elevate your emotional resilience. These targeted approaches are designed to capitalize on your existing strengths while addressing areas that warrant further development. By engaging with these practices, you're taking deliberate steps towards fortifying your emotional well-being.

Recognize that being in the moderate range represents a valuable platform for growth. Embrace this opportunity to refine your resilience and build on your existing capabilities. With focused effort and a constructive outlook, you'll forge a path towards even greater proficiency in navigating life's challenges.

A tailored plan to further enhance your emotional resilience follows:

- **Practice Micro-Moments of Reflection**   Take short breaks during the day to check in with your emotions. Ask yourself how you're feeling and why.

- **Journaling for Emotional Clarity**   Regularly jot down your thoughts and emotions. This practice can help you gain deeper insights into your emotional landscape.

- **Strengthening Stress Management Techniques**   Explore mindful breathing by incorporating brief breathing exercises into your daily routine to stay centered and manage stress effectively. Explore progressive muscle relaxation by learning and practicing this technique to release tension and promote relaxation.

- **Cultivating Flexibility and Adaptability**   Embrace change deliberately by seeking out opportunities to adapt to new situations or approaches and practicing being open to adjustments in your plans. Enhance problem-solving skills by taking on complex challenges to sharpen your skills.

- **Engage in Creative Activities**   Participate in activities like painting, writing, or music, which serve as powerful coping mechanisms.

- **Deepening Emotional Intelligence**   Reflect on interpersonal dynamics by paying close attention to the emotions and reactions of those around you, and practicing empathy and consider different perspectives.

- **Nurture Growth Mindset**   Embrace stretch goals by setting ambitious yet achievable goals that push you beyond your comfort zone. Focus on continuous improvement and learning.

- **Fostering Self-Compassion**   Use affirmations and positive self-talk by integrating affirmations into your daily routine, and speaking to yourself with the same kindness and encouragement you offer to others.

- **Cultivating Inner Fortitude**   Prioritize physical wellness by regular exercise, balanced nutrition, and adequate rest provide a foundation for emotional resilience.

- **Improve Assertiveness Skills**   Practice clear communication by regularly expressing your needs and boundaries with confidence and clarity. This skill strengthens your interpersonal relationships.

- **Seek Constructive Feedback**   Welcome feedback as an opportunity for growth. Use it to refine your skills and enhance your emotional resilience.

- **Foster a Growth Mindset in Others**   Encourage colleagues and team members to embrace challenges as opportunities for learning and development.

- **Strengthen Decision-Making Skills**   Hone your ability to make informed decisions, especially in high-pressure situations.

- **Cultivate Emotional Regulation in Team Settings**   Model and encourage healthy emotional expression within your team or organization.

- **Embrace Continuous Learning**   Engage in ongoing professional development to expand your skill set and knowledge base.

- **Foster Flexibility in Problem-Solving**   Be open to exploring unconventional solutions to challenges.

- **Set Realistic Expectations**   Avoid setting overly ambitious goals that may lead to unnecessary stress. Focus on achievable milestones.

- **Celebrate Achievements, Big or Small**   Acknowledge your accomplishments, no matter how minor. This builds a positive reinforcement loop.

- **Maintain a Growth-Oriented Network**   Surround yourself with individuals who encourage personal and professional development.

- **Engage in Community Service or Volunteer Work**   Contributing to a cause you care about can provide a sense of purpose and fulfillment.

Remember, building emotional resilience is a gradual process. Be patient with yourself and celebrate your progress along the way. Consistent effort and a positive mindset will contribute to meaningful improvements over time. In 'Emotional Resilience Now—A Resilience Action Plan for Leaders,' you will delve deep into these concepts and explore a wealth of others, all designed to empower you on your journey to greater resilience.

Average Emotional Resilience: Elevating Your Resilience Quotient

If your emotional resilience falls within the average range (110 - 134), it indicates that you possess a commendable level of proficiency in managing some of the challenges and setbacks you've faced. This can be a notable asset at times, demonstrating your capacity to navigate adversity in certain situations. While you exhibit strength in various areas, there remains ample room for further growth in many other areas.

Here, we focus on strategies tailored to amplify your emotional resilience within the average range. These specialized approaches build upon your existing capabilities and aim to refine your responses to life's trials. By engaging with these practices, you're embarking on a journey towards heightened emotional well-being.

Acknowledge that being in the average range signifies a solid foundation for growth. Embrace this opportunity to cultivate your resilience and maximize your existing strengths. With dedicated effort and a forward-looking perspective, you'll forge a path towards even greater adeptness in facing life's challenges.

A tailored plan to further enhance your emotional resilience follows:

Leverage Your Existing Strengths   Reflect on the areas where you already demonstrate emotional resilience. This awareness will be a foundation for further growth.

Deepen Emotional Awareness   Continue to work on recognizing and labeling your emotions. This practice helps you understand your feelings and respond to them effectively.

Expand Your Support Network   Strengthen existing relationships and seek out new connections. A robust support system provides valuable emotional backing during challenges.

Diversify Mindfulness and Stress-Reduction Techniques   Explore various mindfulness practices and stress-reduction techniques to find what resonates best with you. Consistent engagement in these activities can enhance your resilience.

Embrace a Growth Mindset Wholeheartedly   Approach challenges with a growth-oriented perspective. View setbacks as opportunities for learning and development.

Set Clear, Specific Goals   Establish achievable objectives in various aspects of your life. This provides direction and a sense of accomplishment.

Cultivate Resilience-Building Habits Consistently   Engage in activities that promote resilience, such as regular exercise, balanced nutrition, quality sleep, and other self-care practices.

Enhance Problem-Solving Skills through Practice   Actively seek opportunities to analyze challenges and find effective solutions. Practice is key in refining this skill.

Foster Self-Compassion and Positive Self-Talk   Be kind and understanding to yourself, especially during difficult moments. Avoid self-criticism and replace it with positive, encouraging self-talk.

Pursue Personal Growth Opportunities Actively   Challenge yourself with new responsibilities at work or explore new hobbies and interests. This contributes to personal development and resilience.

Strengthen Flexibility and Adaptability   Embrace change as an integral part of personal and professional growth. Be open to adjusting your plans or strategies as needed.

Continue Building Resilient Coping Mechanisms   Identify and utilize healthy coping strategies, such as journaling, practicing mindfulness, or engaging in creative activities.

Establish and Communicate Boundaries Clearly   Clearly express your needs and limits to others. This helps prevent burnout and maintains healthy relationships.

Extract Lessons from Setbacks and Failures   Reflect on failures and setbacks to gain valuable insights. Apply these lessons to future endeavors for continued growth.

Hone Assertiveness and Effective Communication Skills   Practice assertive communication to confidently express your needs and boundaries, reducing potential stress from miscommunication.

Nurture and Further Develop Emotional Intelligence   Continue enhancing your ability to understand and manage emotions, as this complements emotional resilience.

Remember, possessing average emotional resilience is a commendable starting point. You already demonstrate strength in managing challenges, and this can be a notable asset. However, there is considerable room for continued growth. By focusing on specific areas of improvement and maintaining a growth-oriented mindset, you have the opportunity to elevate your resilience to new heights. Celebrate your progress and stay committed to your journey towards greater emotional resilience. In 'Emotional Resilience Now—A Resilience Action Plan for Leaders,' you'll explore these concepts in depth and find a wealth of resources to empower you further.

Above Average Emotional Resilience: Getting to Resilience Excellence

If your emotional resilience falls within the above average range, it suggests that you possess notable strength in managing challenges and setbacks. However, there is always room for continued growth.

If your emotional resilience falls within the above-average range (135 - 159), it suggests that you possess notable strength in managing most challenges and setbacks. This is a commendable strength, showcasing your capacity to navigate adversity with effectiveness in many situations. While you excel in multiple areas, the journey of growth is not complete, and there is room for further refinement.

Here, we focus on specialized strategies designed to refine and amplify your emotional resilience. These tailored approaches build upon your existing strengths and aim to elevate your responses to life's trials. By engaging with these practices, you're embarking on a journey towards heightened emotional well-being.

Recognize that being in the above-average range is a testament to both your strengths and areas for growth. Embrace this opportunity to continue refining your resilience and maximizing your existing capabilities. With dedicated effort and a forward-looking perspective, you'll further fortify your ability to face life's challenges with confidence and effectiveness.

A tailored plan to further enhance your emotional resilience follows:

- **Acknowledge and Celebrate Your Strengths**   Recognize the areas where you excel in emotional resilience. This awareness is a testament to your progress.

- **Deepen Emotional Awareness**   Continue to work on recognizing and labeling your emotions. This practice helps you understand your feelings and respond to them effectively.

- **Expand Your Support Network**   Strengthen existing relationships and seek out new connections. A robust support system provides valuable emotional backing during challenges.

- **Diversify Mindfulness and Stress-Reduction Techniques**   Explore various mindfulness practices and stress-reduction techniques to find what resonates best with you. Consistent engagement in these activities can enhance your resilience.

- **Embrace a Growth Mindset Wholeheartedly**   Approach challenges with a growth-oriented perspective. View setbacks as opportunities for learning and development.

- **Set Clear, Specific Goals**   Establish achievable objectives in various aspects of your life. This provides direction and a sense of accomplishment.

- **Cultivate Resilience-Building Habits Consistently**   Engage in activities that promote resilience, such as regular exercise, balanced nutrition, quality sleep, and other self-care practices.

- **Enhance Problem-Solving Skills through Practice**   Actively seek opportunities to analyze challenges and find effective solutions. Practice is key in refining this skill.

- **Foster Self-Compassion and Positive Self-Talk**   Be kind and understanding to yourself, especially during difficult moments. Avoid self-criticism and replace it with positive, encouraging self-talk.

- **Pursue Personal Growth Opportunities Actively**   Challenge yourself with new responsibilities at work or explore new hobbies and interests. This contributes to personal development and resilience.

- **Strengthen Flexibility and Adaptability** Embrace change as an integral part of personal and professional growth. Be open to adjusting your plans or strategies as needed.

- **Continue Building Resilient Coping Mechanisms** Identify and utilize healthy coping strategies, such as journaling, practicing mindfulness, or engaging in creative activities.

- **Establish and Communicate Boundaries Clearly** Clearly express your needs and limits to others. This helps prevent burnout and maintains healthy relationships.

- **Extract Lessons from Setbacks and Failures** Reflect on failures and setbacks to gain valuable insights. Apply these lessons to future endeavors for continued growth.

- **Hone Assertiveness and Effective Communication Skills** Practice assertive communication to confidently express your needs and boundaries, reducing potential stress from miscommunication.

- **Nurture and Further Develop Emotional Intelligence** Continue enhancing your ability to understand and manage emotions, as this complements emotional resilience.

Remember, building emotional resilience is a continual journey. Celebrate your achievements and stay committed to your personal growth and well-being. In 'Emotional Resilience Now—A Resilience Action Plan for Leaders,' you will delve deep into these concepts and explore a wealth of others, all designed to empower you on your journey to even greater resilience.

High Emotional Resilience: Optimizing Peak Resilience Potential

Congratulations on achieving a high level of emotional resilience! This significant accomplishment means your emotional resilience falls within the 160 – 172 range and reflects your exceptional adaptability and effectiveness in dealing with life's challenges. Your ability to navigate adversity with skill and confidence is a commendable strength.

Here, we provide specialized strategies to help you further leverage and refine your already exceptional emotional resilience. These tailored approaches are designed to maximize your existing capabilities and empower you to face even the most demanding situations with confidence and grace.

Recognize that being in the high range is a testament to your extraordinary strength and adaptability. This is an opportunity to continue refining your resilience, ensuring that you're equipped to handle any challenge that comes your way. With dedicated effort and a forward-looking perspective, you'll fortify your position as a leader who thrives in the face of adversity.

A tailored plan to further enhance your emotional resilience follows:

- **Deepen Emotional Awareness**   Continue to refine your ability to recognize and label your emotions. This heightened awareness will serve as a foundation for advanced emotional management.

- **Expand Your Support Network**   Strengthen existing relationships and actively seek out new connections. A robust support system provides invaluable emotional backing during both everyday situations and significant challenges.

- **Explore Advanced Mindfulness and Stress-Reduction Techniques**   Delve into advanced mindfulness practices, deep breathing exercises, and other stress-reduction techniques. Mastery of these practices will further enhance your centeredness and stress management capabilities.

- **Elevate Your Growth Mindset**   Embrace challenges wholeheartedly, viewing them as opportunities for continuous learning and development. Maintain a forward-thinking, optimistic outlook.

- **Set Ambitious and Strategic Goals**   Establish challenging yet achievable objectives in various facets of your life. This provides clear direction and fosters a sense of continuous accomplishment.

- **Champion Resilience-Building Habits with Precision**   Engage in activities that promote resilience, such as regular exercise, balanced nutrition, quality sleep, and other self-care practices. Fine-tune these habits for maximum impact.

- **Master Problem-Solving with Finesse**   Seek out complex challenges and opportunities to apply your problem-solving skills. Develop creative and effective solutions, honing this skill to an advanced level.

- **Foster a Culture of Self-Compassion and Positive Self-Talk**   Be exceptionally kind and understanding to yourself, particularly during challenging moments. Replace self-criticism with an unwavering stream of positive, affirming self-talk.

- **Pursue Cutting-Edge Personal Growth Opportunities**   Embrace endeavors that demand a high level of adaptability, innovation, and leadership. Challenge yourself to lead initiatives that catalyze personal and professional growth.

- **Cultivate Unparalleled Flexibility and Adaptability**   Embrace change as a fundamental aspect of growth, consistently demonstrating your ability to adjust strategies and plans as needed.

- **Refine and Expand Your Resilient Coping Mechanisms**   Identify and master advanced coping strategies that resonate with your unique style. Leverage these techniques to swiftly navigate even the most complex challenges.

- **Set and Communicate Boundaries with Expertise**   Clearly articulate your needs and limits to others, demonstrating a masterful command of boundary-setting for maximum effectiveness and well-being.

- **Extract Deeper Insights from Setbacks and Failures**   Reflect on setbacks and failures with an eye for extracting the most profound lessons. Apply these insights to future endeavors, leveraging them for even greater success.

- **Demonstrate Exceptional Assertiveness and Communication Skills**   Practice assertive communication with an unparalleled level of confidence. Your ability to express your needs and boundaries will inspire and influence those around you.

- **Elevate Your Emotional Intelligence to Mastery**   Continue to refine your ability to understand and manage emotions, reaching an advanced level of mastery that complements your exceptional emotional resilience.

Remember, maintaining and advancing emotional resilience is a dynamic, ongoing process. Your high level of emotional resilience positions you as a role model and influencer in your personal and professional spheres. Celebrate your achievements and seize new opportunities for growth and well-being. In 'Emotional Resilience Now—A Resilience Action Plan for Leaders,' you will find advanced strategies and insights to support you on your resilience and leadership excellence journey.

Exceptional Emotional Resilience: Masterful Mastery of Resilience

Congratulations on attaining an exceptional level of emotional resilience! Your emotional resilience, which falls within the 173 - 175 range, is truly extraordinary. It stands as a powerful testament to your unparalleled capacity to adapt and thrive amidst life's most challenging trials. Your ability to navigate adversity with both skill and unwavering confidence is a profound and admirable strength. This level of resilience is not just an achievement, but a beacon of inspiration for others seeking to overcome their own challenges. Keep shining!

Here, we present specialized strategies tailored to individuals with an exceptional level of emotional resilience. These approaches are crafted to further amplify and refine your already outstanding capabilities, empowering you to confront even the most demanding situations with unwavering confidence and grace.

Recognize that being in the exceptional range is a tribute to your masterful strength and adaptability. This represents an unparalleled opportunity to continue honing your resilience, ensuring that you're equipped to handle any challenge that comes your way. With unwavering dedication and a forward-looking perspective, you will solidify your position as a leader who not only endures but thrives in the face of adversity. Your exceptional resilience is a beacon of inspiration for others, illuminating the path to triumph over adversity.

Tailored strategies to help you continue to refine and amplify your remarkable emotional resilience:

Mentoring and Coaching   Share your insights and experiences with others to inspire and guide them in building their own resilience.

Champion Collaborative Efforts   Leverage your resilience to foster a collaborative and supportive environment within your team or organization.

Innovative Problem-Solving   Challenge the status quo and seek creative solutions to complex issues.

Crisis Leadership   Excel in leading teams through high-stakes, time-sensitive situations with calm and effectiveness.

Strategic Visionary Thinking   Cultivate long-term strategic thinking and visionary leadership to steer your organization towards success.

Integrate Mindfulness into Leadership   Apply mindfulness practices to enhance focus, decision-making, and overall leadership effectiveness.

Master Change Management   Continue to excel in navigating organizational change, guiding your team through transitions seamlessly.

Embody Empathetic Leadership   Deepen your understanding of others' perspectives, fostering a culture of empathy within your team.

Advance Emotional Intelligence   Further develop your emotional intelligence, honing your ability to understand and influence the emotions of those around you.

Promote Well-Being Initiatives   Champion holistic well-being programs within your organization, emphasizing the importance of physical, emotional, and mental health.

Lead with Ethical Integrity   Uphold the highest ethical standards in decision-making and organizational practices.

Foster a Culture of Trust and Innovation   Build a work environment where trust and innovation flourish, creating a space for bold ideas and experimentation.

Navigate Global Challenges   Leverage your resilience to lead effectively in diverse and cross-cultural environments.

Optimize Time Management and Prioritization   Fine-tune your ability to allocate time efficiently, focusing on high-impact activities.

Strengthen Crisis Communication Skills   Enhance your ability to communicate effectively and provide reassurance during challenging times.

Promote Organizational Learning   Foster a culture of continuous learning and development within your team or organization.

Exercise Self-Care and Boundaries   Continue to prioritize your own well-being, setting clear boundaries and practices for self-care.

Demonstrate Unwavering Optimism   Inspire others with your unwavering positivity and belief in possibilities, even in the face of adversity.

Navigate Complex Stakeholder Relationships   Excel in managing diverse stakeholder relationships, balancing their needs and interests effectively.

Embody Authentic Leadership   Continue to lead authentically, staying true to your values and principles in all interactions.

Remember, with your exceptional level of emotional resilience, you have the potential to inspire and uplift those around you. Your leadership sets a powerful example for others to follow. Keep nurturing your resilience and embracing opportunities for growth and positive change. In 'Emotional Resilience Now—A Resilience Action Plan for Leaders,' you will find advanced strategies and insights to support you on your resilience and leadership excellence journey.

Reassessing Your Emotional Resilience: A Path to Growth

Your emotional resilience is not a fixed trait; it's a dynamic quality that can be cultivated and strengthened over time. Reassessing your emotional resilience can be a pivotal step in your journey towards personal and professional growth.

When to Consider Reassessment

The decision to consider reassessment of your emotional resilience is a powerful testament to your commitment to personal growth and self-awareness. It's a proactive step towards becoming the best version of yourself. That said, the decision to reassess is ultimately a personal one, influenced by various factors.

Here are some scenarios that may prompt you to consider a reassessment:

Significant Life Changes   Major life events, such as career transitions, marriage, divorce, or the birth of a child, can profoundly impact your emotional resilience. If you've recently experienced a substantial change, it may be an opportune time to reassess.

Long-Term Growth Efforts   If you've been actively working on enhancing your emotional resilience through consistent practice and self-improvement strategies, you may want to assess whether these efforts have resulted in noticeable progress.

Post-Adversity Reflection   Following a particularly challenging period, taking time to reflect on how you navigated and coped with the situation can provide valuable insights. It can be illuminating to see if your resilience has evolved as a result.

Self-Perception Misalignment   If you feel that your current emotional state doesn't align with your previous assessment, it may be an indication that a reassessment is in order. Trust your intuition and be open to the possibility of growth.

Desire for Further Growth   Recognizing that emotional resilience is a dynamic quality, you may simply have a strong desire to continue your journey towards even greater levels of resilience and personal excellence.

If you decide to reassess, let these steps guide you through the process:

1. **Reflect on Your Journey.**   Take a moment to acknowledge the experiences, challenges, and triumphs that have shaped your emotional resilience. This reflection provides valuable context for your reassessment.
2. **Choose an Optimal Time.**   Select a moment when you feel calm, centered, and free from immediate stressors. This ensures that your assessment reflects your overall emotional state.
3. **Repeat the Assessment.**   Go through the assessment process again, answering the questions honestly and thoughtfully. This will provide an accurate snapshot of your current emotional resilience.
4. **Consider Your Growth.**   Compare your new score to your previous one. Recognize and celebrate the progress you've made. This newfound level of resilience is a testament to your dedication.
5. **Embrace Tailored Strategies.**   Based on your updated assessment, focus on the strategies designed for your current level of emotional resilience. These specific approaches will support your ongoing growth.

Your emotional resilience is a dynamic quality that can be further cultivated. Use this reassessment as a tool to continue your journey towards even greater levels of resilience and personal excellence.

Achieving a New, Higher Level of Emotional Resilience

Discovering that your emotional resilience has shifted to a different, higher level is a significant milestone on your journey towards personal growth and well-being. Steps to consider when you find yourself at a new level:

1. **Acknowledge Your Progress**   Celebrate your achievement! Recognize the effort and dedication you've invested in developing your emotional resilience. This acknowledgment sets a positive tone for your continued growth.

2. **Embrace the Opportunity**   View this shift as an opportunity for further advancement. Understand that your current level is a reflection of your ongoing efforts, and it signifies your capacity for continuous growth.

3. **Update Your Resilience Toolkit**   With your newfound insights into your emotional resilience, tailor your resilience-building strategies to align with your current level as discussed in "Making the Most from Your Self-Assessment Score." Focus on refining specific characteristics and skills that are most relevant to your current range.

4. **Set New Goals**   Establish fresh, achievable goals that are in harmony with your updated level of emotional resilience. These objectives will guide your ongoing efforts and serve as markers of your progress.

5. **Continue Consistent Practice**   Maintain a regular practice of activities and techniques that support your emotional resilience. Consistency is key in solidifying your progress and adapting to your new level.

6. **Reflect on Your Journey**   Take time to reflect on how far you've come. Consider the challenges you've overcome and the lessons you've learned. This reflection reinforces your sense of accomplishment and resilience.

7. **Seek Support and Guidance**   Engage with mentors, coaches, or a supportive community who can provide encouragement and valuable insights tailored to your new level. Their guidance can be instrumental in your continued growth.

8. **Stay Open to Further Growth**   Recognize that emotional resilience is a dynamic quality. Remain open to the possibility of further evolution and be receptive to new strategies and approaches.

Your ability to adapt and thrive in the face of challenges is a testament to your inner strength and resilience. Embrace your new level with confidence and a forward-looking perspective. Specific guidance related to Step 3, Updating Your Resilience Toolkit follows:

- **Moving from Very Low or Low to Moderate**   If you find yourself transitioning from very low or low to moderate emotional resilience, it's a significant milestone. Celebrate your progress and recognize that you're building a stronger foundation. Focus on the strategies tailored for the moderate range to continue your growth.

- **Gradual Progress from Moderate to Average**   Transitioning from moderate to average indicates steady growth. Acknowledge your achievements and implement the strategies for average emotional resilience. Consistency and a positive mindset will contribute to further improvements.

- **Advancing from Average to Above Average**   Reaching above average reflects your dedication and effectiveness in managing challenges. Continue to refine your strategies, and consider taking on more complex challenges to further strengthen your resilience. Follow the strategies for above average emotional resilience.

- **Excelling from Above Average to High or Exceptional**   If you've reached high or exceptional emotional resilience, you're in an enviable position. Your adaptability and effectiveness in dealing with challenges are commendable. Keep nurturing your resilience and embracing opportunities for growth and positive change by following the strategies in the related section on either high or exceptional emotional resilience as appropriate.

Remember, your emotional resilience is a dynamic quality that can be further cultivated. Use this reassessment as a tool to continue your journey towards even greater levels of resilience and personal excellence.

Responding to a Decline in Emotional Resilience

Experiencing a decline in emotional resilience can be a challenging phase in your journey. It's important to approach this situation with patience, self-compassion, and a proactive mindset.

Steps to consider if you find that your emotional resilience has declined:

1. **Acknowledge Your Experience**   Recognize and acknowledge the shift in your emotional resilience without judgment. Understand that fluctuations in resilience are a natural part of personal growth, and it's okay to go through periods of adjustment.

2. **Identify Triggers and Factors**   Reflect on potential triggers or factors that may have contributed to the decline in your emotional

resilience. This self-awareness is the first step in understanding what areas need attention and improvement.

3. **Seek Support and Guidance**   Reach out to a trusted friend, mentor, coach, or mental health professional who can provide valuable perspective and support during this period. They can offer insights and strategies to help you navigate through the challenges.

4. **Revisit Resilience-Building Techniques**   Review the strategies and techniques you previously employed to develop your emotional resilience. Consider which ones were particularly effective and reintegrate them into your routine.

5. **Explore New Approaches**   In addition to revisiting familiar techniques, be open to exploring new approaches to building emotional resilience. This could include mindfulness practices, stress-reduction techniques, or other strategies tailored to your current needs.

6. **Set Realistic Expectations**   Understand that rebuilding emotional resilience is a gradual process. Set realistic and achievable goals for yourself, and celebrate even small victories along the way.

7. **Practice Self-Compassion**   Be kind and understanding to yourself during this period. Avoid self-blame or negative self-talk. Treat yourself with the same compassion you would offer to a friend facing a similar situation.

8. **Implement Self-Care Routines**   Prioritize self-care activities that nurture your physical, emotional, and mental well-being. Adequate sleep, balanced nutrition, regular exercise, and relaxation techniques play a crucial role in rebuilding resilience.

9. **Engage in Reflection and Journaling**   Take time to reflect on your emotions, experiences, and progress. Journaling can be a powerful tool for gaining clarity, processing feelings, and tracking your journey towards renewed resilience.

10. **Seek Professional Help if Needed**   If you find it challenging to navigate the decline in your emotional resilience on your own, consider consulting a mental health professional. They can provide specialized guidance and support tailored to your specific situation.

Remember, experiencing a decline in emotional resilience is usually a temporary phase, and with dedication and a proactive approach, you should be able to rebuild and strengthen your resilience over time.

Afterword for the Self-Assessment

Congratulations on completing the Emotional Resilience Self-Assessment©. Your dedication to self-improvement and your journey toward greater emotional resilience is commendable. This assessment is a powerful tool designed to help you understand and strengthen your capacity to navigate life's challenges with grace and effectiveness.

As you've seen, emotional resilience encompasses a wide spectrum of traits and skills, ranging from endurance and adaptability to self-compassion and assertiveness. Your unique score reflects where you currently stand on this spectrum, providing valuable insights into areas of strength and areas that may benefit from further development.

To interpret your score, refer back to the scale provided:

- **Very Low Emotional Resilience (35 - 59)** This range suggests an opportunity for significant growth. Focusing on characteristics like endurance, acceptance of failure, and patience can be particularly beneficial.

- **Low Emotional Resilience (60 - 84)** While some level of emotional resilience is present, there is ample room for growth and improvement. Identifying and developing these areas will enhance overall resilience.

- **Moderate Emotional Resilience (85 - 109)** Falling in this range indicates a fair foundation. There are areas where you demonstrate strength but also room for improvement in others.

- **Average Emotional Resilience (110 - 134)** Possessing average emotional resilience means you demonstrate some strength in managing challenges and setbacks. However, there is still considerable room for continued growth.

- **Above Average Emotional Resilience (135 - 159)** This range suggests notable strength in managing challenges and setbacks. While excelling in multiple areas, there is always room for continued growth.

- **High Emotional Resilience (160 - 172)**   Falling within this range indicates a significant degree of adaptability and effectiveness in dealing with challenges. This is a commendable strength.

- **Exceptional Emotional Resilience (173 - 175)**   Achieving this level is a testament to your extraordinary capacity to adapt and excel in the midst of life's trials. Your ability to navigate adversity with skill and confidence is a profound strength.

Following your assessment, you've been provided with tailored plans designed to support your journey toward greater emotional resilience. These plans offer specific strategies and techniques to enhance your unique strengths and address areas for improvement. Remember, building emotional resilience is a gradual process. Be patient with yourself and celebrate your progress along the way.

We understand the importance of a robust scientific foundation in assessments like these. Our methodology is based on a comprehensive analysis of data gathered from extensive surveys, interviews, and research in the field of emotional resilience. The valid range of scores, from 35 to 175, was carefully established through statistical analysis to ensure meaningful categorization. This distribution, with varying categories, was determined to accurately represent the spectrum of emotional resilience in individuals.

The assessment underwent rigorous testing and validation to ensure its reliability and accuracy. Our methodology was reviewed, and feedback from a diverse sample group was incorporated into its final form.

For those in the High and Exceptional ranges, your level of emotional resilience is truly exceptional. You have the potential to inspire and uplift those around you. Your leadership sets a powerful example for others to follow. Keep nurturing your resilience and embracing opportunities for growth and positive change.

In 'Emotional Resilience Now—A Resilience Action Plan for Leaders,' you will find advanced strategies and insights to support you on your journey to even greater heights of resilience and leadership excellence.

As you continue on your path toward greater emotional resilience, remember that setbacks are a natural part of growth. Embrace them as opportunities for learning and development. Your commitment to this journey is a testament to your dedication to personal and professional growth.

Wishing you continued success and growth in your pursuit of emotional resilience.

Warm regards,

William R. Stanek

Closing Reflection

As you reach the closing chapters of this transformative odyssey, take a moment to revisit the photograph that follows. In this serene Hawaiian sunset, where the sun meets the sea, envision not just an end, but a continuation of your leadership journey. Like the rhythmic ebb and flow of waves along the shoreline, your path may have been marked by challenges, yet it's also adorned with moments of beauty and triumph.

Just as the sun dips below the horizon, signaling the close of one chapter and the promise of another, your journey in leadership is a series of endings and beginnings. Embrace them all, for they are the threads that weave the tapestry of your growth and resilience.

The interplay of light and shadow in this Hawaiian sky mirrors the dynamic nature of leadership. Each experience, each decision, shapes your narrative. With each step, you etch your unique story into the sands of time.

As you stand on this shore, you carry with you the wisdom and resilience you've cultivated along this journey. The spirit of the islands infuses your path with vitality and inspiration. Carry it forward, for the leadership narrative you've crafted is a testament to your potential, your purpose, and your impact.

And if ever the winds of uncertainty threaten to steer you off course, return to this photograph. Let the timeless beauty of this moment serve as a beacon, guiding you back to the essence of your leadership journey. Remember, every challenge met, every triumph celebrated, is a testament to your strength and resilience. Carry the lessons learned within these pages, for they are your guideposts in leadership. Embrace the path, for it is uniquely yours to shape, and continue onward, knowing that your journey in leadership is boundless and ever-evolving.

Index

21st century
   rapid changes, 53
21st century leadership
   approach, 51
21st-century world
   interdependencies of, 80
360-degree feedback, 173
8 Pillars of Intelligence
   characteristics, 63
   conceptualization of, 62
   extend beyond, 89
8 Pillars of Leadership
   conceptualization of, 31
   spectrum of, 32
   strengths of, 64
absenteeism
   patterns of, 176
academia
   AQ in, 66
Acceptance and Commitment Therapy, 131
acceptance and letting go, 132
accountability
   enhance, 67
   within organizations, 51
achievements
   recognizing, 138
actionable knowledge
   transforming into, 66
active listening, 124
   in relationships, 72
   practicing, 125
adapt
   to circumstances, 100
adaptability, 103
   critical trait, 53, 138
   foster, 66
   in adversity, 106
   in leadership, 79
   in social situations, 73
   IntraQ,related to, 71
   promoting, 179
adaptive coping, 131

developing, 136
essential, 133
growth mindset, 134
sense of humor, 135
adaptive leaders
   as flexible, 44
   concept of, 44
adaptive leadership
   excel at, 55
   trend, 43, 44
advanced analytics
   leverage, 65
adversity
   as teacher, 55
   handling, 54
   in face of, 55
   thriving in, 107
affirmation
   instructions, 97
agility
   in leadership, 79
Alibaba Group
   case study, 198
ambiguity
   manage, 57
analytical approach
   beyond intuition, 67
analytical intelligence
   for problem-solving, 45
   foundational, 48
   in data-driven business, 45
   premium on, 88
   understanding, capacity to, 77
Analytical intelligence
   what is, 36
Analytical Intelligence
   insights into, 65
   involves, 61
   relevance of, 65
   trainable attribute, 65, 67
analytical mindset
   achieving, 66
analytical prowess

enhance, 68
analytical thinking
   blended, 59
   in crisis, 84
   in organizations, 84
   to achieve, 83
ancient Greece
   leadership, 40
   philosophers, 40
Ant Group
   case study, 198
appreciative inquiry
   for group sharing, 148
AQ
   Analytical intelligence. *See*
Aristotle
   philosopher, 40
artificial intelligence
   leverage, 65
artistic expression
   as outlet, 129
assertive communication
   using, 123
assess information
   in analytical intelligence, 77
assessment
   of emotional resilience, 173
assessment score
   above average, 230
   at higher level, 239
   at lower level, 241
   average, 227
   exceptional, 235
   high, 232
   low, 222
   moderate, 225
   very low, 220
authentic leadership
   role of, 100
authentic self
   values, 70
authenticity
   demonstrate, 114
   lead with, 56
   not weakness, 118
   trait, 84
author
   experiences, 29

foreword, 15
   leadership, forged, 29
   stay in touch, 25
autonomy
   encouraging, 181
balance
   to strike a, 55
balanced leadership
   a linchpin of, 87
   characterized by, 86
   requires, 86
balanced perspective
   maintaining, 57
behavioral observations
   making, 174
Bill Gates
   business acumen, i
Blanchard
   scholar, 41
boardwalk
   as a metaphor, 27
body's stress response, 122
book
   as a compass, 22
   continuous learning, 24
   how to use, 23
boundaries
   establishing, 123
   setting, 135
breakthroughs
   leading to, 63
broader perspectives
   consider, 56
Carlos Ghosn
   case study, 206
Carlyle
   scholar, 41
case studies
   curated, 185
case study
   instructions, 185
celebrating resilience, 182
challenges
   as opportunities, 134
   as teacher, 55
   being open about, 55
   navigating, 53
   overcoming, 54

challenging situations
   fresh perspective, 135
   positive outlook, 53
   reevaluate, 123
   responding to, 128
challenging times
   empowerment from, 55
change
   embracing, 180
changing circumstances
   adaptability in, 57
Christine Lagarde
   case study, 194
clarity
   maintaining, 58
   obtaining, 57
client relations
   crucial in, 74
coaching
   ability to, 73
   providing, 183
cognitive abilities
   evaluating, 60
   snapshot of, 60
cognitive development
   dynamic nature of, 59
cognitive processing
   use of, influence by, 63
cognitive prowess
   hallmark of, limitations of, 59
cognitive reappraisal
   for coping, 131
cohesive teams
   building, 73
collaboration
   conducive atmosphere for, 73
   effective, 73
   excel in, 75
   meaningful, 124
   supporting, 64
collaborative leadership
   trend, 44
collaborative problem-solving
   sessions, group sharing, 147
collective intelligence
   of the whole, 79
collective resilience
   strengthens, 55

commitment
   driven by, 56
committed action
   taking, 133
communicate change
   facilitate, 74
communication
   excel in, 74
   open lines of, 74
compassion
   beyond empathy, 124
   empathetic leadership, 124
   meditation, 97
   showing, 91
competence
   flexibility with, 66
competitive edge
   gaining, 67
   leading to, 63
complex challenges
   guiding leaders in, 76
   leadership in, 76
complex choices
   navigating, 56
complex merger
   scenario, 157
complex problems
   using AQ with, 65
complexity
   navigate, 62
composure
   maintain, 112
   maintaining, 58
concise messages
   becoming adept at, 67
confidence
   flexibility with, 66
conflict
   management of, 54
conflict management
   facilitating, 74
conflict prevention
   excel in, 75
   facilitating, 74
conflict resolution
   excel in, 75
   InnerQ, related to, 72
conflict transformation

facilitate, 74
conflicts
   addressing, 139
connecting
   deeply, 124
connecting actions to values, 132
constructive coping, 103
constructive feedback
   providing, 183
constructive guidance
   provide, 73
constructive mindset
   maintain, 55
contagious effect
   of resilient leaders, 117
contentment
   cultivate, 69
contingency theories
   mid-20th century, 41
continuous growth
   significance of, 52
continuous improvement
   culture of, 67
continuous learning, 138
   culture of, 66
   need for, 178
   spirit of, 80
coping mechanisms, 101
   adaptive, 131
   healthy, 109
coping with change, 110
core values
   identifying, 132
Creative Intelligence
   involves, 61
creative outlet
   journaling, 144
Creativity Intelligence
   what is, 33
crisis management
   pivotal role in, 58
   scenario, 150
crisis response
   scenario, 161
crisis situations
   lead in, 55
critical choices
   under high pressure, 58

critical thinking
   in analytical intelligence, 77
cross-functional collaboration
   encouraging, 183
crossroads
   symbolizes choices, 19
CrQ
   Creativity Intelligence. *See*
cultural competence
   excel in, 75
   InnerQ, related to, 72
cultural dynamics
   heightened awareness of, 79
cultural intelligence
   cultural norms, 44
   diverse cultures, 48
   essential facet, 87
   neglect of, 76
Cultural Intelligence
   what is, 34
cultural norms
   perspectives, practices, 44
   respecting, 64
cultural nuances
   navigating, 76
culture
   cultivate, 55
culture of trust
   fostering, 51
cultures
   understanding, 63
CuQ
   Cultural Intelligence. *See*
data
   transforming, 66
   using, 62
data-driven context
   using, 64
data-driven environments
   navigating, 67
data-driven insights
   use, 66
data-driven strategies
   where crucial, 66
decision
   degree of risk, 57
decision fatigue
   managing, 57

mitigating, 57
decision-making
    accurate, 67
    adaptability in, 57
    evidence-based, 67
    influences, 53
    influences on, 53
    insight into, 55
    insights into, 66
    moral, principled, 76
    under stress, 109
decisions
    based on evidence, 45
deep breathing
    exercises, 122
delegation
    using, 57
determination, 109
dichotomy
    EQ vs IQ, i
diffusing tension, 135
    facilitating, 73
digital age
    rise of, 43
disagreements
    resolving, 72
disruptive technologies
    evaluate, 67
dissent
    managing, 57
diverse cultures
    traversing, 62
diverse fields
    success in, 66
diverse information
    synthesis of, 59
diverse perspectives
    fostering, 76
    InnerQ, related to, 72
diverse stakeholders
    understood by, 67
diverse teams
    foster, 44
    with, 76
diverse work environment
    embracing, 182
diversity
    embracing, 139

modern leadership, 44
drive
    long-term, 56
early 20th century
    trait theories, 41
educational leadership
    scenario, resilience in, 169
effective communication
    becoming adept at, 67
    ensuring, 64
    related to InnerQ, 72
effective decisions
    making, 77
effective leadership, 78
    achieving, 63
    driving force, 118
    nuanced integration, 44
effective responses
    guiding teams towards, 58
effectiveness
    lead with, 56
Either-Or Paradigm
    fallacy of, 52
Elon Musk
    case study, 190
    technological prowess, i
emerging trends
    identify, 67
emotional acumen
    integration of, 80
emotional climate
    assessing, 175
emotional experiences
    honoring, 124
emotional expression
    within team or organization, 118
emotional insight, 108
emotional intelligence
    challenge to wisdom, 46
    critical role, 38
    emergence, 46
    focuses on, 69
    juxtaposed with IQ, 51
    limitations, 51
    synergy with ER, 110
Emotional Intelligence
    Daniel Goleman, 42
emotional regulation, 101

excel at, 75
extends to, 73
in high-stress, 122
profound effects of, 129
techniques, 128
with resilience, 124
emotional resilience
adaptability, 106
as dynamic trait. 99
assessment, 173
complemented by, 83
components of, 101
cultivating, 97
defining, in leadership, 99
differentiating from EQ, 105
dynamic capacity, 58
emotional responses, 107
enhance, 55
group sharing, fostering culture of, 145
impact on culture, 54
in crisis, 84
in decision making, 53
in organizations, 84
inspire a culture of, 118
leaders with, 53
metrics, monitoring, 173
not an absence of, 83
not inherent, 55
problem-solving, 131
reassessing, 238
strengthening, practical exercises for, 141
sustaining, 178
synergy with EQ, 110
transcends EQ, 33
understanding, 53
vs EQ, differentiating, 105
what is, 33
with other intelligences, 107
Emotional resilience
regulating emotions, 122
Emotional Resilience
building blocks of, 120
relevance of, 53
Emotional Resilience Self-Assessment, 215
emotional responses
consistency in, 174
emotional signals

awareness of, 125
emotional strain
managing, 57
emotional well-being
fostering, 69
emotions
being open about, 55
honest expression of, 117
label, 120
processing, 99
recognizing, 121
responses to, 121
understanding of, 77
empathetic leaders
in teams, 124
empathetic leadership
demonstrate, 124
Empathetic Leadership, 124
empathetic listening
in group sharing, 147
empathy, 102
balancing, 118
defining, understanding, 124
demonstrate, 116
empathetic leadership, 124
excel at, 74
improving, 54
InnerQ, related to, 72
lead with, 56
relying on, 57
empirical data
rely on, 67
Employee Assistance Programs
utilization of, 176
employee engagement surveys, 175
employee feedback channels
analysis of, 176
empowered mindset, 129
empowerers
effective leaders, 94
empowerment
encouraging, 181
source of, 55
tool for, 98
encouragement
source of, 55
engagement
mindfulness, 128

entrenchment
  avoiding, 57
EQ
  limitation of, 76
  what is, 32
EQ and IQ
  not mutually exclusive, 86
  synergy between, 51
EQ prominence
  shift to, 47
EQ trumps IQ
  failure of, 47
EQ vs IQ
  framework, 32
EQ VS IQ
  flawed paradigm, 21
EQ vs IQ paradigm
  binary choice, 44
  broken, 44
  challenge to, 90
  limitations, 42
  reduces framework of intelligence, 50
EQ vs IQ Paradigm
  beyond, illustration, 32
  critiques of, 50
EQ VS IQ Paradigm
  limited focus of, 50
ER
  emotional resilience. See
ethical challenges
  navigating, 63
ethical decision-making
  IntraQ,related to, 71
ethical decisions
  making, 64
ethical dilemmas
  addressing, 62
ethical intelligence
  achored in, 87
  applying, 48
  modern leadership, 45
ethical Intelligence
  encompasses, 61
Ethical Intelligence
  what is, 36
ethical lapses
  consequences of, 63
ethical leader

trend, 43
ethical leadership
  concept of, 43
ethical principles
  values, 45
ethical standards
  upholding, 76
EthQ
  Ethical Intelligence. See
European Central Bank
  case study, 194
evaluate data
  critically, 83
evidence-based decisions
  in analytical intelligence, 77
expectations
  clarity in, 138
failure
  handling, 112
failures
  as opportunities, 57
  overcoming, 54
fairness
  promoting, 64
Fiedler
  scholar, 41
flexibility
  instill, 66
  promoting, 179
flexible scheduling, 139
focus groups, 175
Foreword, 15
Frederick Taylor
  early management theory, 41
fresh perspective, 135
fulfillment
  deeper sense of, 135
full potential
  unlocking, 56
Gardner
  model, 50
gather feedback
  tools for, 175
General Motors
  case study, 187
Germany
  Lake Constance, 91
Getting the Most from this Book, 21

global challenges
  adapt to, 64
global pandemic
  scenario, leading through, 153
globalization, 78
goals
  setting, 69
Goleman
  work on EQ, 42
grace
  showing, 91
gratitude journaling, 146
groundedness
  sense of, 127
grounding exercises, 129
group sharing, 145
  and support, 146
  icebreaker, 145
growth
  cycle of, 55
growth mindset
  encouraging, 114
  facilitating, 178
  for coping, 134
  opportunities for, 111
  within a team, 138
growth orientation
  of emotional resilience, 108
guided visualization, 146
hasty decisions
  mitigating, 56
healthy boundaries
  maintaining, 123
heightened emotional states
  responding to, 127
high EQ
  leaders, 46
high-pressure situations
  critical choices in, 58
high-stress environment
  managing, 122
holistic approach
  achieving, 64
  in leadership development, 88
  preparing for, 83
  synergy of, 83
  to leadership, 84
holistic comprehension
  of intelligence, 90
holistic intelligence
  defined, 90
  defining, 88
  view of, 47
Holistic Intelligence
  model of, 89
  transformative potential, 91
holistic leadership, 45
holistic perspective
  blended, 59
holistic view
  of intelligence, 49
honest communication, 137
honesty
  sense of, 76
human intelligence
  model of, 89
  not confined to, 89
human interaction
  broader understanding, 72
identify patterns
  in analytical intelligence, 77
immediate implications
  consider, 65
improvement
  culture of, 66
impulsive reactions
  delay, regulate, 123
  mitigating, 56
inclusion
  modern leadership, 43
inclusive environments
  fostering, 76
inclusive leader
  rise of, 44
inclusive work environment
  embracing, 182
inclusivity
  InnerQ, related to, 72
  promoting, 64
incomplete information
  manage, 57
individual reflection
  for self-awareness, 141
individual strengths
  acknowledge, 142
Industrial Revolution

transformative changes, 41
influence
   excel at, 75
information
   assessing, 66
informed decisions
   enabling, 66
   from resilience, 56
   making, 55, 65, 77
inherent risks
   manage, 57
inner experiences
   deeper understanding, 127
inner fortitude
   source of, 56
inner peace
   cultivate, 69
InnerQ
   Interpersonal Intelligence. See
innovation, 111
   driving, 63
   fostering, 62
   using, 67
insights
   using, 55
inspire
   ability to, 73
inspire others, 70
inspirers
   effective leaders, 94
integrity
   sense of, 76
intellectual abilities
   not static, 59
intellectual intelligence
   cognitive prowess, 46
   limitations, 51
Intellectual Intelligence
   limitations, 59
   measures, 59
intelligence
   diverse manifestations, 38
   holistic view, 49
   in myriad forms, 80
   interplay of, 47
   misconception of, 50
   not one-dimensional, 86
   nuanced understanding of, 48
   paradigm shift, 32
   real world, application of, 61
   traditional assessment of, 50
Intelligence
   dynamic nature of, 29
   transcends, 31
intelligence paradigms
   transcending, 38
intelligences
   interplay of, 62
   synergies between, 52
intense scrutiny
   managing, 58
internal dialogue
   manage, 55, 69
interpersonal intelligence
   in communication, 77
Interpersonal Intelligence
   what is, 35
intrapersonal intelligence
   authenticity, fosters, 70
   insights into, 69
Intrapersonal intelligence
   empowers, 71
   growth mindset in, 70
   in decision-making, 70
   self-confidence, sense of, 70
   time management, contributes to, 70
   transcends EQ, 69
Intrapersonal Intelligence
   relevance of, 69
   what is, 35
IntraQ
   Intrapersonal Intelligence. See
introspection, 69
   framework for, 141
IQ
   intellectual intelligence. See
   limitation of, 76
   overreliance on, 60
   rigid focus on, 46
   what is, 32
IQ assessments
   failure of, 59
   overlook, 59
IQ dominance
   prevalence, 46
   shift from, 47

IQ to EQ
   shift, 46
Jack Ma
   case study, 198
job satisfaction
   prioritized by, 74
journaling, 135
   as outlet, 129
   for reflection, 141
   for self-discovery, 144
journey begins
   your leadership, 27
Julius Caesar
   Roman Empire, 40
knee-jerk responses
   mitigating, 56
lead authentically, 70
leader
   as facilitator, 44
   as servant, 43
   leverage intelligences, 38
leaders
   agile, 66
   as role models, 54
   inspire teams, 54
   not defined by, 79
   not infallible, 79
   testament to, 16
   who thrive, 49
   with resilience, 53
   with resilience are, 103
leadership
   21st century, 51
   a holistic eneavor, 30
   ancient Greece, 40
   being authentic, 114
   call for comprehensive approach, 78
   changing landscape, 39
   consistency, 58
   conventional models of, 78
   historical roots, 40
   multifaceted approach, 76
   multifaceted nature of, 60
   new era of, 93
   not a solitary endeavor, 22
   not confined by, 79
   on behaviors, 41
   oversimplification of, 47

   Roman Empire, 40
   spiritual authority, 40
   transformative phase, 27
Leadership
   8 Pillars of, 31
leadership challenges
   evolving, 52
leadership contexts
   application of, 51
leadership influence
   InnerQ, related to, 73
leadership intelligence
   components of, 77
   exploration of, 31
   facets of, ii
   holistic view of, 45
   in personal life, 91
   nature of, i
   reimagining, 30
leadership journey
   envision, 18
leadership landscape
   dynamic change in, 115
leadership practices
   for long-term success, 181
Leadership Proposition
   Foundational, i
leadership theories
   behavioral, 41
   extremes, 47
   historical progression, 47
   historical roots, 42
   transactional, transformational, 42
learning
   cycle of, 55
learning culture
   cultivatin, 180
learning opportunities
   creating, 182
Lewin
   psychologist, 41
life timeline
   as icebreaker, 146
lifelong learning
   encouraging, 179
   imperative of, 52
Lockheed Martin
   case study, 202

logical reasoning
   in analytical intelligence, 77
long-term consequences
   assessing, 64
   consider, 65
Machiavelli
   pragmatic leadership, 41
magic bullet
   search for, 47
maintaining composure
   extends to, 73
Marillyn Hewson
   case study, 202
market dynamics
   shifting, 79
market trends
   adapt to, 64
Mary Barra
   case study, 187
Mastery Series
   about, 23
meaningful connections
   empathetic leaders, 126
   establish, 73
meaningful contribution, 138
meaningful goals
   setting, 132
meaningful insights
   extracting, 65
mediating conflict
   InnerQ, related to, 72
meditation
   center yourself, 18
   for mindfulness, 127
   on leadership journey, 27
   resilience, 95
mental health awareness
   promoting, 139
mental strain
   managing, 57
mentoring
   ability to, 73
   excel at, 75
mentors
   guidance from, 55
methodology
   for self-assessment, 245
metrics
   for emotional resilience, 173
mid-20th century
   contingency theories, 41
mindful recognition
   of emotions, 132
mindfulness
   engage in, 55
   for deeper self, 127
mindset
   clear and focused, 56
mistakes
   learn from, 57
modeling resilience, 181
   resilient leaders, 118
modern leadership
   emerging trends, 43, 45
   key shift, 43
mood elevation, 129
motivate
   ability to, 73
motivation
   link to, 69
   sustaining, 56
motivations
   understanding of, 77
mountain road
   as a metaphor, 19
multifaceted approach, 78
multifaceted problems
   resolving, 64
multi-intelligence framework
   fosters culture of, 81
   heart of, 80
   invites, 80
   key tenet of, 81
   paradigm shift, 81
multi-intelligences
   domains of, 62
   understanding, 62
multiple intelligences
   support of, 50
   understanding, 50
muscle relaxation
   activate, 128
nation-states
   Renaissance, 41
negotiation skills
   InnerQ, related to, 72

Nelson Mandela
   quote from, xx
networking
   effective, 73
   excel in, 75
new opportunities
   capitalize on, 67
new technologies
   adapt to, 64
Nissan-Renault-Mitsubishi Alliance
   case study, 206
non-judgmental attention, 127
non-verbal cues
   awareness of, 125
objective analysis
   rely on, 67
objectivity
   balancing, 118
   cultivating, 56
obstacles
   overcoming, 54, 69
open-hearted willingness, 124
operational efficiency
   enhance, 63
optimism
   transformative journey, 94
optimism and hope, 102
optimistic
   more, 129
organization
   best interest of, 56
   leadership consistency in, 58
   resilience in, 55
organizational change
   managing, 74
organizational culture
   influences on, 74
   learning-oriented. 66, 67
   shaping, 58
   synergies, 84
organizational hierarchy
   beyond, 79
organizational objectives
   communicating, ensuring, 67
organizational relevance
   achieving, 64
organizational silos
   transcend, 81

organizational success
   enabling, 66
organizational sustainability
   achieving, 64
organizational values
   aliging with, 63
organizations
   inspire, 56
organized religion
   ethical conduct, 40
paradigm shift
   essential, 21
   visualizing, 32
path
   embrace and shape, 18
peace-building
   facilitate, 74
peer relationships
   for support, 138
peer support circles
   in group sharing, 147
peer support systems
   encouraging, 138
perceived threat
   handling, 122
performance reviews
   analysis of, 176
perpetual growth
   attitude of, 66
perseverance, 109
   exhibit, 115
perseverence
   source of, 56
persistence and determination, 101
personal achievements
   celebrate, 142
personal aspirations
   awareness of, 69
personal life
   AQ in, 66
perspective
   gaining, 133
   reframe, 131
perspectives
   different, achieving, 66
perspective-taking, 124
   empathetic leaders, 125
persuasion

InnerQ, related to, 73
philosophers
   ancient Greece, 40
photo sharing
   as icebreaker, 145
pivot
   leaders must, 79
   when necessary, 57
pivoting
   when necessary, 66
Plato
   philosopher, 40
policies and practices
   perception of, 176
policy-making
   AQ in, 66
political dynamics
   heightened awareness of, 79
political leadership
   rise of, 41
positive affirmations
   as outlet, 129
positive change
   innovate, 66
positive emotional climate, 117
   facilitating, 73
positive outlook, 101
   maintain, 103
positive relationships
   maintaining, 74
potential outcomes
   consider, 56
potential risks
   evaluate, 67
PQ
   Practical Intelligence. *See*
practical intelligence
   as street smarts, 44
   encompasses, 76
   for translating knowledge, 48
   pivotal role, 51
   role of, 87
Practical Intelligence
   focuses on, 61
   what is, 34
practical problems
   innovative solutions to, 64
practical wisdom
   role of, 60
practices
   mindfulness, 127
presenteeism
   patterns of, 176
principled decision-making
   ethical intelligence, 51
prioritization
   using, 57
proactive problem-solving
   encouraging, 183
problem-solving
   in analytical intelligence, 77
   multifaceted approach to, 65
problem-solving skills, 101
   refining, 66, 67
processes
   streamline, 63
productivity
   prioritized by, 74
professional networks
   building, 73
promoting positivity
   facilitating, 73
psychological safety
   for resilience, 137
   fostering, 181
purpose
   sense of, 56
rapid technological advancements, 78
rapport
   building, 183
rational decisions
   making, 56
real world
   applicability, 24
realistic assessment
   making, 116
realistic expectations
   in practice, 134
   setting, 133, 180
real-world scenarios
   curated, 149
recalibrate strategies
   leaders must, 79
reflection
   closing, 247
   cultivate gratitude, 142

    end of journey, 211
    for self-compassion, 143
    on aspirations, 27
reflection journaling
    why use, 143
reflective practices, 135
    engaging in, 179
reframe
    capacity to, 123
reframing
    perception, 131
regulate emotions
    empathetic leaders, 125
reimagine leadership
    our journey, ii
Reimagining Leadership
    library, 17
Relational Intelligence, 36
relationship-building
    effective, 73
relationships
    broader understanding, 72
    managing, 63
relaxation response
    activate, 128
relevant patterns
    discerning, 65
Religious figures
    Moses, Buddha, Confucius, 40
remarkable human beings
    capacity to become, 91
Renaissance
    nation-states, 41
renewal
    tool for, 98
ReQ
    Relational Intelligence. See
research
    AQ in, 66
resilience
    embracing, reflection on, 95
    ensure, 67
    foster, 66
    harnessing, 56
    high degree of, 53
    IntraQ,related to, 71
    meditation on, 95
    not static, 56

    reflection, meditation on, 97
    significance of in leadership, 56
    vs EQ, 105
resilience in leadership
    case studies, 185
resilience leaders
    setbacks temporary, 113
resilience-building, 178
resilient leaders
    adversities,navigating, 116
    drive innovation, 117
    harness energy, 117
    innovation, 115
    lessons from, 112
    leverage emotions, 113
    mindset, 112
resilient organizational climate
    cultivating, 175
Resilient Soul
    guiding affirmation, 97
resistance
    managing, 57
resource allocation
    optimize, 63
resources
    allocating judiciously, 123
response strategies
    enhancing, 149
retention
    prioritized by, 74
retention rates
    monitoring, 176
risk management
    AQ role in, 67
risk scenarios
    navigate, 67
road not taken
    meditation, reflection, 19
role reversal
    for group sharing, 147
roles
    clarity in, 138
Roman Empire
    leadership, 40
scenario analysis, 149
sea of data
    discern relevant in, 66
seizing opportunities

leaders must, 79
self-assessment, 211
   instructions, 216
   power of, 213
   scientific methodology, 245
self-assessment score
   assessment score. *See*
   interpreting, 219
self-assessment tools, 173
self-awareness, 102, 108
   critical dimension, 77
   developing, 120
   empowers, 83
   individual reflection, 141
   IntraQ,related to, 71
   narratives, 121
   not static, 121
   sense of, 120
self-care
   critical role of, 84
   develop, 54
   IntraQ,related to, 71
   prioritizing, 179
   using, 57
self-care practices
   engaging in, 103
   for coping, 134
self-compassion, 134
   practicing, 135
self-drive
   link to, 69
self-improvement, 69
self-knowledge, 69
self-reflection, 69, 101, 135
   engage in, 55
   promoting, 139
   tool for, 98
self-reflection practices
   engaging in, 103
self-regulation
   critical dimension, 77
self-soothing, 123
self-talk
   manage, 55
sense of purpose
   fostering, 182
Servant leader
   trend, 43

servant leadership
   concept of, 43
setbacks
   as learning opportunities, 115
   as opportunities, 57
   handling, 53
   overcoming, 69
short-term gains
   vs broad impact, 64
skill development, 138
   facilitating, 179
   opportunities for, 183
Skinner
   psychologist, 41
small wins
   celebrating, 114
   importance of, 114
SMART goals, 133
social contexts
   reading, 73
social cues
   read, 73
social dynamics
   heightened awareness of, 79
   mastering, 77
   navigating, 60
social support
   for coping, 133
societal norms
   aliging with, 63
solution-oriented mindset, 131
   having, 103
source of distress
   handling, 122
SpaceX
   case study, 190
spiritual authority
   intertwined, 40
stability
   sense of, 55
stakeholder relations
   crucial in, 74
Steve Jobs
   analytical acumen, i
Stogdill
   scholar, 41
strategic perspective
   enable, 65

strategies
    adjusting, 66
street smarts
    role of, 87
strength
    source of, 55
strengths
    understanding of, 77
stress
    handling, 53
    manage, 54
    reduction of, 54
stress management
    engage in, 55
strong emotions
    objectivity, 56
strong support network
    having, 103
structured approach
    analytical intelligence, 48
success
    achieving, 64
sunset
    as a metaphor, 18
support network
    building, 137
    emphasis on, 55
supportive community
    fostering, 179
sustainability
    ensure, 67
synergistic effect
    creating, 80
systematic mindset
    achieving, 66
team
    best interest of, 56
    leveraging strengths, 73
team achievements
    recognizing, 138
team dynamics
    assessing, 176
    healthy, 139
team member
    concerns, managing, 74
team members
    connect work to purpose, 139
    connecting with, 54

feedback, 139
teams
    inspire, 56
    resilience in, 55
teamwork
    effective, 73
technological disruptions
    response to, 79
technological tools
    use, 65
technologies
    adapt to, 64
technology
    leverage, 65
    power of, 43
technology sector
    scenario, innovating in, 165
tenacity
    exhibit, 115
Tesla
    case study, 190
thoughtful leader
    designed for, 21
time constraints
    managing, 58
time management, 134
    contributes to productivity, 70
timely decisions
    making, 65
toolbox
    as a metaphor, 21
traditional IQ
    extend beyond, 67
trait theories
    early 20th century, 41
transactional
    leadership theory, 42
transform knowledge
    into action, 66
transformational
    leadership theory, 42
transformative journey
    navigate, 93
transition process
    facilitate, 74
transparency
    enhance, 67
    relying on, 57

transparent communicatio
  promoting, 181
transparent communication, 137
  empathetic leaders, 126
trust
  building, 183
  deeply, 124
  foster, 55
trusted advisors
  guidance from, 55
turnover rates
  indicative of, 176
Two truths and a lie game
  as icebreaker, 145
uncertainty
  coping with, 110
  manage, 57
  navigate, 66
unconscious biases
  mitigate, 64
understanding
  demonstrate, 116
unexpected developments
  adaptability in, 57

unforeseen challenges
  response to, 79
unprecedented connectivity, 78
unpredictable variables
  manage, 57
vulnerability
  balance, 55
  demonstrate, 114
  not weakness, 118
weaknesses
  understanding of, 77
well-being
  prioritize, 54
  prioritized by, 74
well-designed workspaces
  benefits of, 137
work effectively
  in teams, 73
work environment
  constructive, 64
  high-performing, 64
work-life balance
  importance of, 138
  promoting, 183

About the Author: William R. Stanek

An esteemed author, globally recognized bestseller, and trusted consultant to Fortune's elite for over three decades.

Biography

Across a distinguished career spanning more than three decades, our esteemed author has emerged as a preeminent figure in the realm of leadership and intelligence. His journey through the echelons of technology, business and leadership has been marked by extraordinary achievements, often amidst the most challenging and pivotal moments in history.

A significant portion of his professional odyssey unfolded against the backdrop of some of the most transformative periods in modern history.

From navigating the complexities of the Cold War to grappling with the intricacies of the Iraq War and beyond, William demonstrated an uncanny ability to not only weather the storm but to thrive amidst it. This exceptional capacity to excel in high-pressure environments propelled him into leadership positions far beyond his rank, a testament to his keen judgment and exceptional leadership acumen.

His foray into the military and various other arenas revealed a fundamental truth: that genuine leadership transcends titles and tenure. It hinges on the capacity to inspire, influence, and adeptly guide teams through even the most formidable challenges. In his role as a technology consultant, he became known as the "fixer," the individual called upon when situations appeared dire. Surprisingly, more often than not, he discovered that the heart of many seemingly insurmountable problems lay not in technological failings, but rather in the nuanced dynamics of leadership and intelligence.

Over the years, William garnered a reputation that is nothing short of legendary among top management. His work became synonymous with excellence, as he navigated the halls of corporate power, leaving behind not footprints, but echoes of wisdom forged through attentive listening, astute evaluation, and triumphant achievement. Those in the know recognized his exceptional expertise, spoken of in hushed tones and safeguarded against competitors eager to tap into his unparalleled insights.

He operated with a finesse that matched his ability to guide top management. While he discreetly orchestrated transformative shifts behind the scenes, the impact of his counsel resonated throughout boardrooms and executive suites. His influence was pervasive, leaving an indelible mark on the path to success for countless organizations.

In this book, William emerges from the shadows, generously sharing his formidable insights with a wider audience. His journey, marked by humility, wisdom, and an unwavering commitment to the art of leadership, serves as an invaluable guide for leaders at every level and in every industry. It is a testament to the power of leadership intelligence, a holistic approach that encompasses emotional resilience, practical intelligence, and ethical intelligence, among other intelligences.

William is on LinkedIn at https://www.linkedin.com/in/williamstanek/

Find William on Twitter at http://www.twitter.com/WilliamStanek and on Facebook at http://www.facebook.com/William.Stanek.Author.

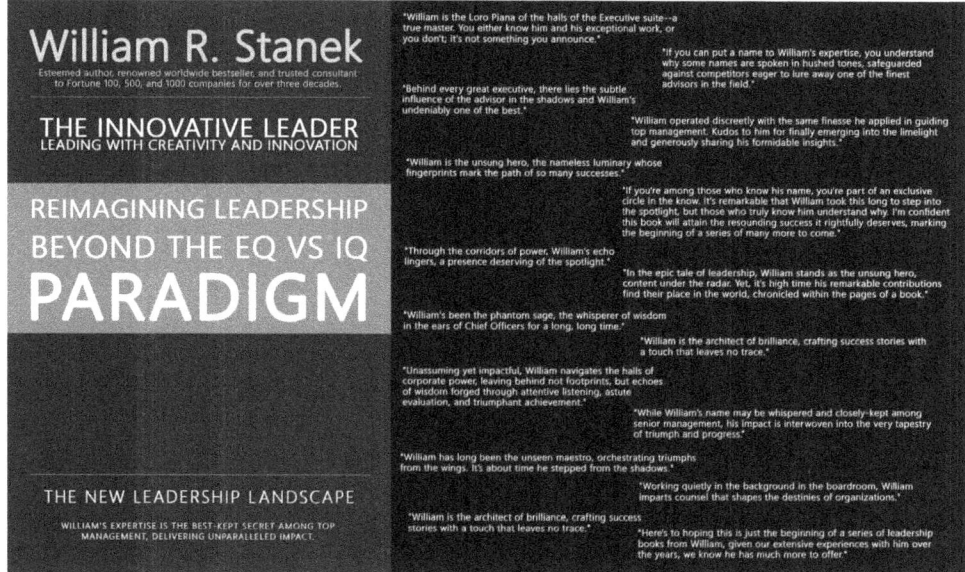

William R. Stanek (http://www.williamrstanek.com)

Thank you for purchasing this book. If you found this book to be useful, helpful or informative, raise your voice and support William's work by sharing about this book online.

Unsure how to share? Here are some tips:

- Blog about the book

- Write a review at your favorite online store

- Post about the book on Facebook or elsewhere

- Tweet about the book

Stay in touch with William on Linkedin, Facebook and Twitter!

Beyond his contributions to the world of business and leadership, William is also an avid artist and photographer. His creative pursuits provide a unique perspective that enriches his writing. To explore William's artistic endeavors and discover the world through his lens, visit his online art and photography portfolio at

https://360studios.pictorem.com

The Day Ends at the Seashore Limited Rare Print - The Sunset Collection in Canvas Print with Floating Frame

The 8 Pillars of Leadership

Dynamic Nature of Intelligence: The prevailing notion that cognitive abilities and emotional tendencies remain static throughout our lives is a limited perspective. We view the mind not as an unchanging entity, but as a dynamic vessel capable of adopting new strategies and approaches to learning. While the core capacity for processing information may have a baseline, the methods and depths of this processing can be refined and expanded upon.

Leadership Prowess through Intelligence: True leadership prowess, as we see it, transcends mere data processing. It encompasses a profound understanding, application, and integration of information. Through structured exercises, critical reflection, and practical application, our book serves as a compass for those committed to an ongoing journey of intellectual growth and development.

1. Emotional Resilience as a Dynamic Skill: Emotional resilience, often perceived as an inherent disposition, is, in fact, a dynamic skill that can be fortified through dedicated effort. Engaging in exercises designed to foster emotional strength and endurance empowers individuals to navigate through challenging situations with grace and proficiency.

2. Nurturing Creative Thinking: In a world marked by constant innovation and change, nurturing creative intelligence is imperative. Leaders must be adept at generating, combining, and transforming ideas into innovative solutions. This dynamic skill set is crucial for fostering a culture of innovation within organizations.

3. Practical Intelligence - Street Smarts in Action: Often referred to as "street smarts," practical intelligence is a learned behavior, not a fixed attribute. It encompasses adaptability, common sense, and the ability to apply knowledge in practical contexts. This form of intelligence is cultivated through experience, reflection, and intentional practice.

4. Embracing Cultural Intelligence – Bridging Borders: In our increasingly globalized world, the ability to understand and engage effectively with individuals from diverse cultural backgrounds holds immense significance.

This intelligence equips leaders with the invaluable skills of cultural awareness, knowledge, and adaptability, enabling them to deftly navigate the intricacies of an interconnected world.

5. Intrapersonal Intelligence for Clarity and Purpose: Individuals with high intrapersonal intelligence possess a profound self-awareness. This understanding of one's own emotions, strengths, weaknesses, and motivations enables them to navigate their professional and personal lives with clarity and purpose.

6. Developing Interpersonal Intelligence: Extending beyond emotional intelligence, interpersonal intelligence encompasses the ability to understand and navigate social dynamics. It involves building and maintaining relationships, effective communication, negotiation, and conflict resolution. This dynamic skill can be developed through intentional practice and reflection.

7. Cultivating Ethical Intelligence: Ethical intelligence is not a fixed trait, but a learned behavior cultivated through experiences, values, and self-reflection. Engaging in exercises that challenge moral judgment and ethical reasoning elevates ethical intelligence, contributing to a culture of integrity and accountability.

8. Refining Analytical Intelligence: Critical thinking, logical reasoning, and problem-solving abilities comprise analytical intelligence, a dynamic skill set that can be honed and refined over time. Through structured exercises and practical application, individuals can enhance their capacity to assess information, identify patterns, and make sound decisions based on evidence.

Unlocking Full Potential: The 8 Pillars of Leadership stand as a testament to the belief that intelligence, in all its diverse manifestations, is not a fixed trait but a malleable skill set, ripe for development and refinement. By immersing themselves in the content and exercises presented, readers embark on a transformative journey towards heightened self-awareness, refined decision-making, and more impactful leadership. This, we assert, embodies the true essence of intelligence—an ever-evolving capacity with the potential to shape not only individuals, but entire organizations and communities.

More Great Resources for Business Leaders from Stanek & Associates

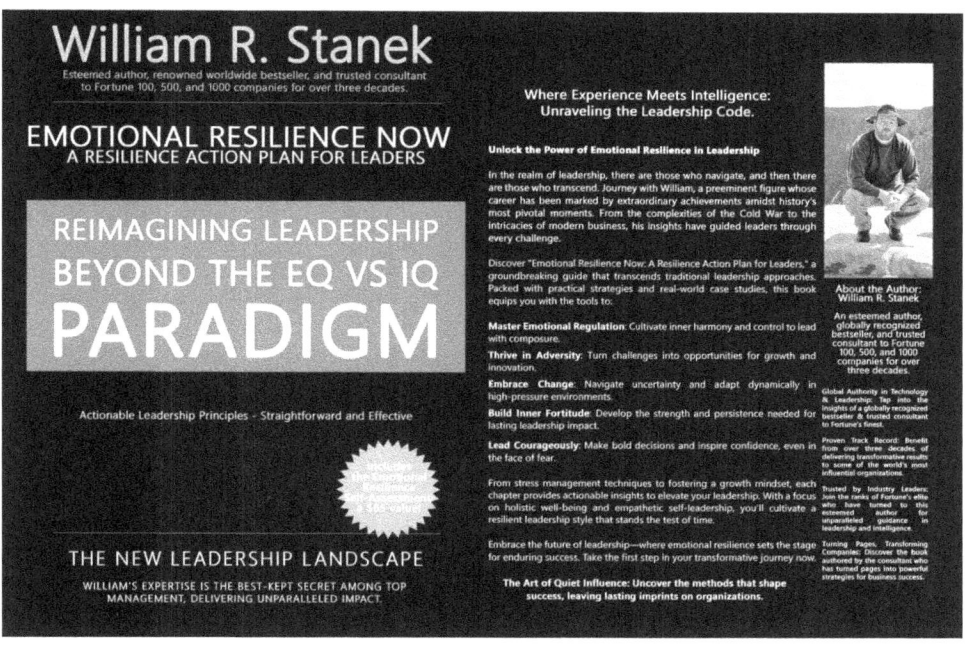

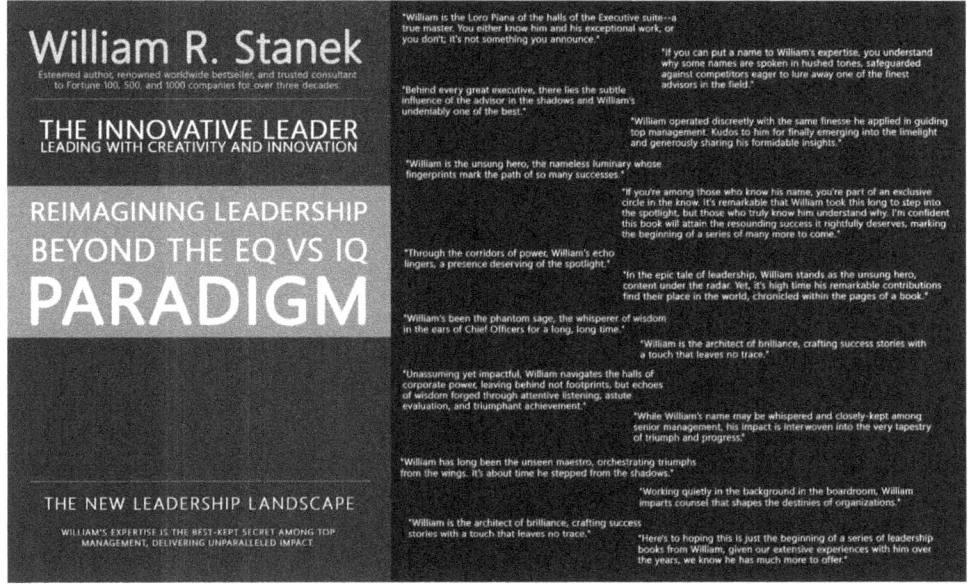

www.ingramcontent.com/pod-product-compliance
Lightning Source LLC
Chambersburg PA
CBHW080607170426
43209CB00007B/1353